Amerikastudien
American Studies   A Quarterly

Edited for
the German Association
for American Studies by

GENERAL EDITOR

Oliver Scheiding

EDITORS

Christa Buschendorf
Andreas Falke
Hans-Jürgen Grabbe
Alfred Hornung
Sabine Sielke

ASSISTANT EDITORS

Tanja Budde
Ashley Rae McNeil

Volume 59 · 2 (2014)

Universitätsverlag
WINTER
Heidelberg

EDITORIAL OFFICE

Professor Dr. Oliver Scheiding,
Amerikanistik / American Studies,
Department of English and Linguistics,
Johannes Gutenberg-Universität Mainz,
Jakob Welder Weg 18,
D-55128 Mainz
Telefon ++49-6131-39-22357
Telefax ++49-6131-39-20356
E-Mail: amst@uni-mainz.de
Website: http://dgfa.de

Subscriptions
Amerikastudien ★ *American Studies (Amst)* is published quarterly. The subscription price is € 79,70 plus postage. The subscription is renewed automatically for the following year, if notice of cancellation is not received by December 1 of the current year.

Universitätsverlag WINTER GmbH, Heidelberg
Postfach 10 61 40, D-69051 Heidelberg

Typesetting:
OLD-Media, D-69126 Heidelberg
Printing and bookbinding:
Memminger MedienCentrum GmbH, D-87700 Memmingen

Contents

Religion and the Marketplace

JAN STIEVERMANN, ANTHONY SANTORO, and DANIEL SILLIMAN (Guest Editors)

ARTICLES

DANIEL SILLIMAN, JAN STIEVERMANN, and ANTHONY SANTORO	Introduction: Religion and the Marketplace 121
UTA BALBIER	'Selling Soap and Salvation': Billy Graham's Consumer Rhetoric in Germany and the United States in the 1950s" 137
HANS KRABBENDAM	Opening a Market for Missions: American Evangelicals and the Re-Christianization of Europe, 1945-1985 153
GEOFFREY PLANK	Quaker Reform and Evangelization in the Eighteenth Century 177
INKEN PROHL	California 'Zen': Buddhist Spirituality Made in America 193
BARRY HANKINS	Evangelicals and Catholics Together: How it Should Have Been in the Roaring Twenties Marketplace of Ideas 207

FORUM

HANS-JÜRGEN GRABBE	Amerikastudien als "kooperatives Experiment": 60 Jahre Deutsche Gesellschaft für Amerikastudien 221
UDO J. HEBEL, CARMEN BIRKLE, and PHILIPP GASSERT, introd. and comp.	Usable Pasts, Possible Futures: The German Association for American Studies at Sixty 241

REVIEWS 257

(The following reviews are freely available at www.dgfa.de and www.winter-verlag.de/de/programm/zeitschriften/amerikastudien/)

KLAUS SCHMIDT	Review Essay: Edward Watts and David J. Carlson, eds., *John Neal and Nineteenth-Century American Literature and Culture* (2012)

TIBOR FABINY	Reiner Smolinski and Jan Stievermann, eds., *Cotton Mather and Biblia Americana – America's First Bible Commentary: Essays in Reappraisal* (2010)
PHILIPP SCHWEIGHAUSER	Philip F. Gura, *Truth's Ragged Edge: The Rise of the American Novel* (2013)
JOHANNES VOELZ	François Specq, Laura Dassow Walls, and Michel Granger, eds., *Thoreauvian Modernities: Transatlantic Conversations on an American Icon* (2013)
MARTIN KLEPPER	Susanne Rohr and Miriam Strube, eds., *Revisiting Pragmatism: William James in the New Millennium* (2012)
NICOLE J. CAMASTRA	Miriam B. Mandel, ed., *Hemingway and Africa* (2011)
BIRGIT DÄWES	Kathryn Hume, *Aggressive Fiction: Reading the Contemporary American Novel* (2012)
MICHAEL BUTTER	Sebastian M. Herrmann, Carolin Alice Hofmann, Katja Kanzler, and Frank Usbeck, eds., *Participating Audiences, Imagined Public Spheres: The Cultural Work of Contemporary American(ized) Narratives* (2012)
SIGRUN MEINIG	Ulfried Reichardt, *Globalisierung: Literaturen und Kulturen des Globalen* (2010)
MICHAEL BASSELER	Christof Mauch and Sylvia Mayer, eds., *American Environments: Climate—Cultures—Catastrophes* (2012)

BIBLIOGRAPHY

LAURA CAPRIOARA and DAMIEN SCHLARB	Publications in American Studies from German-Speaking Countries, 2013 259

CONTRIBUTORS 315

Introduction: Religion and the Marketplace

Daniel Silliman, Jan Stievermann, and Anthony Santoro

While popular accounts of the 'American difference' may overstate the point, there can be no doubt that religion is more vital in the United States than in other Western nations.[1] European visitors to the United States—from Alexis de Tocqueville to G. K. Chesterton to generations of university exchange students—have regularly noted the peculiar vibrancy and multiplicity of religious beliefs and practices in America. So too contemporary scholars from various disciplines have long found that any number of important aspects of American culture, politics, and public life can be better understood if religion is taken into account. To cite just a few recent examples, serious examinations of religious beliefs and practices have yielded deeper and more nuanced understandings of American foreign policy, free market labor practices, labor movements, and the history of immigration. Such subjects as Bob Dylan's corpus, postmodern literature, and the commercial and cultural juggernaut that is Oprah Winfrey have all been illuminated recently via a turn to the religious. Indeed, there has been a much-noted 'religious turn' in academia more generally, but this turn has been perhaps nowhere as pronounced or as profitable as among scholars of American history and culture.[2] Although German Americanists have made valuable contributions to this development, the scholarly community on this side of the Atlantic would do well to give even more attention to the ways in which religious ideas and traditions shape and influence American culture.[3]

---

[1] For recent, reliable data on American religiosity and balanced assessments, see Chaves, Wuthnow's *After the Baby Boomers*, and Putnam and Campbell. The *Pew Forum on American on Religion & Public Life* also is a very valuable and trusted source of sociological data on American religion (http://www.pewforum.org/).

[2] For recent compendia and handbooks that provide access to the current state of the field, see Goff; Goff and Harvey; Laderman and Leon; Lippy and Williams; and Stein. For up-to-date textbook introductions, see Lippy; Butler; Wacker; Balmer; Gaustad and Schmidt; Albanese; and Noll. For an extensive bibliography and very helpful survey of the main trends in the 'New Religious History' scholarship, see Hochgeschwender. Good points of entry into current debates are still Stout and Hart; and Tweed.

[3] For excellent examples of German scholarship on religious influences on American culture, see Hochgeschwender. A special field of interest among German scholars working on America is the interplay of politics and religion, especially those of the Religious Right, in the United States. See Schäfer; Prätorius; Riesebrodt; and Brocker. German scholars have made particularly noteworthy contributions to the study of American religious history from a transatlantic perspective that takes into view the many reciprocities with Continental Europe: see Grabbe; Häberlein; Hahn-Bruckhardt; Lehmann and Wellenreuther; Mettele; Smolinski and Stievermann; and Waldschmidt-Nelson. Over the past decade or so, German scholars of American history and culture have also edited several valuable collections on other themes of American religion. See Brocker; Cortiel; Gebhardt; Herget and Hornung; Hertlein and Schnackertz;

Scholars studying the religious dimensions of American culture, indeed, American Studies generally, have benefitted specifically from considerations of the many intersections of American religions and marketplaces. 'Religion and the marketplace' is currently one of, if not *the*, conceptual framework within which American religiosity is understood. It can be an immensely useful conceptual framework, albeit somewhat paradoxical in how it is deployed. To be clear, referring to religion and the marketplace as a conceptual framework implies that 'religion and the marketplace' does not denote one theoretical approach or apparatus, any more than gender or ethnic studies do. It rather refers to a field of research interests that explain various aspects of America's religions by looking at how they interact with different kinds of marketplaces. The conceptualizations of the marketplace used by scholars working within this general framework have been quite diverse, ranging from mostly metaphorical or analogous explanations of American religions in economic terms to quite literal examinations of business practices in the religious sphere. Equally varied are the phenomena and questions on which these different concepts have been brought to bear.

Three Avenues for Religion and the Marketplace Studies

Generally speaking, one can distinguish three main avenues within religion and marketplace studies. First, scholars have conceived of the nation's shifting religious landscapes as analogous to capitalist economies—driven by the dynamics of supply and demand—in order to understand American religious vitality, diversity, the changing demographics of denominations, and the transformations of religious practices or behaviors. The *locus classicus* of this variety is Roger Finke and Rodney Stark's *The Churching of America, 1776-2005*, which explicitly makes the case that the mechanism of marketplace competition accounts for the growth and decline of various religious groups.[4] The authors take a supply-side approach, arguing that disestablishment and the constitutional guarantee of religious freedom in the new republic broke up the monopolies of state-sponsored churches and created a new environment in which innovative 'upstart' organizations, notably the various Methodist and Baptist groups, thrived because they were more apt at developing strategies for actively winning the souls and purses of Americans than other churches. The radical pluralization of America's religious landscape since the 1950s has also been explained by Robert S. Ellwood and Wade Clark Roof via reference to an increasingly diversified marketplace that continues to fine-tune its products to different target groups. In another recent example, Robert D. Putnam and David E. Campbell's *American Grace* uses the same idea of a 'religious marketplace' to explain the startlingly high rates at which Americans change religions. As they note, "America is increasingly a domain of choice, churn, and surprisingly low brand loyalty. That is the demand side of the religious marketplace. On the supply side, we would expect

---

Kremp; and Nagler and Haspel. On religion and the marketplace, in particular, see Hochgeschwender and Löffler.

[4] See also Whitham; and Young.

successful 'firms' (denominations and congregations) in such a fickle market to be especially entrepreneurial in 'marketing' their product" (148). By analyzing what has elsewhere been described as America's "quest culture" of "religious seekers" within the conceptual framework of markets (see Wuthnow, *After Heaven*), Putnam and Campbell are able to make use of a variety of economic ideas—including supply and demand, consumers and brands—and thus make religious practices legible by noting how they exhibit characteristics of market practices. These works align with other studies explicitly engaging with religious branding, such as Mara Einstein's *Brands of Faith*.

The second broad category of research conducted within the marketplace framework comprises investigations of the tangible intersections between business or consumer practices and religious beliefs and practices. Here, R. Lawrence Moore's *Selling God* stands out as a widely influential work on religious forms of entrepreneurship and the use of marketing strategies for denominational growth, which have evolved since the early colonial commodification of religious products through the comprehensive economization of society during the Jacksonian period and that are today most prominently embodied by America's televangelists.[5] Historians have examined various kinds of religious products in their respective historical and cultural contexts, including the religious book market of the nineteenth century, contemporary media culture, and music.[6] Studies of the commodification of religious beliefs or practices, such as Leigh Eric Schmidt's *Consumer Rites*, and of ways these beliefs and practices are consumed, such as Vincent J. Miller's *Consuming Religion* or Heather Hendershot's *Shaking the World for Jesus*, also fall in this category.[7]

Third, scholars have looked at the relationship between religion and the marketplace in the United States by studying the interdependencies between the development of religious beliefs or rhetoric and the evolution of capitalist mentalities or economic theories. Mark Valeri, for instance, examines how changing ideas of piety in Puritan New England informed the business practices of Boston merchants, shaping early American commerce. Bethany Moreton, in her widely praised *To Serve God and Wal-Mart* (2010), investigates how the business practices and marketing language of Wal-Mart are deeply imbued with a kind of evangelical theology that, in turn, has been shaped by late twentieth-century consumer capitalism.[8]

---

[5] On the colonial and early national periods, see Engel, Hackett, Innes, Noll, and Valeri. On the Jacksonian market revolution and its impact on antebellum religion, see Davenport; Sellers; Schantz; Startup; Sutton; Ratner; and Wallace. On televangelists, see Lee and Sinitiere; and Walton.

[6] On the mass media generally, including book markets, radio, television, and the internet, see Abrams; Badaracco; Borden; Brown; Clark; Chidester; Farrell; Frykholm; Gribben; Hagen; Hart; Hedstrom; Hoover and Clark; Kintz and Lesage; Lynch; John S. McClure; Nord; Oberdeck; and Wosh. On music specifically, see Bivins; Ersoz; Gimlour; and Gooch.

[7] For the scholarly debate on the commodification of Native American spirituality, see Jocks; and Jenkins. Other important works on the subject of religious consumption include Lofton; Lynch; Lyon; Kaufman; Miller; Moore; and Schmidt.

[8] See also Connoly; and Douchuk.

While these second and third categories of scholarship are flourishing, and while the marketplace framework is gradually being made to live up to its interpretive promise by scholars who keep refining and augmenting it, it is not without its critics. Important concerns about this interpretive framework have been raised. First, scholars such as Robert Wuthnow have noted that some interpretations of the religious marketplace have been little more than a new iteration of the classic 'master narrative' interpretation, which claims to explain everything about religion in America. It has been noted that an overemphasis on competition can obscure other facets of American religious experience, such as cooperative and ecumenical efforts. These criticisms have been directed especially at Finke and Stark, who have been questioned in regards to their embrace of a moneterian worldview and its underlying anthropological assumptions about *homo economicus*, as well as their questionable prioritization of the supply-side of religious competition. Concerns have also been raised about the dangers of complicity, particularly where scholars explain religion through the marketplace using a national, neoliberal ideology. There is always a danger of uncritically adopting the evaluative framework, for instance accepting at face value the designation of 'winners' and 'losers.' Finally, such explanations have been suspected of reifying notions of America's exceptionalism in a new guise.[9]

These are important criticisms, and they should be taken seriously. However, there is no other extant framework of comparable explanatory power capable of elucidating so many different dimensions of America's religious cultures. 'Markets' continue to be the main way in which American religion, religions, and religiosity are understood.[10] Even those who have voiced serious skepticism about potential totalizing tendencies of the conceptual framework have acknowledged its heuristic potential, if employed with circumspection. Wuthnow, for example, notes that while we should not make the mistake of constructing yet another master narrative, attending to the many specific reciprocities between religious and economic spheres is helpful "in drawing attention to the fact that Americans are so thoroughly socialized to shop, buy, sell, and otherwise behave as consumers that their religious behavior is influenced accordingly"; the marketplace framework, he notes, is a good "reminder that American religion is big business" ("Religion" 281).

Sean McCloud, author of *Divine Hierarchies: Class in American Religion and Religious Studies*, makes the case that however critical we might wish to be of the marketplace framework and its underlying assumptions, thinking of the interdependencies between religious activities and economic practices is an unavoidable reality for scholars of American religion. After all, in this present historical moment there is no dimension of American culture and society that has not been af-

---

[9] The clearest and most concise articulation of these criticisms can be found in Wuthnow, "Religion." These arguments have also importantly been made by Hochgeschwender; Bruce; Sharot; and others.

[10] Metaphors of 'markets' and 'brands' have been regularly used, for example, by commentators looking to explain that the recent demographic shift in the United States involved a significant increase in the religiously unaffiliated and a sharp decline in Protestant mainline churches. See Glenn; Grossman; Kosmin and Keysar; and Rudnick.

fected by the logic of the market. Analogously, scholars critical of the nationalist narratives in their discipline and who have propagated new transnational paradigms for American Studies likewise cannot afford to ignore the powerful ways in which the nation state and nationalism have shaped the realities of U.S. culture and society on every level. In the same way, as McCloud argues,

> those studying contemporary American religion cannot study it WITHOUT attending to the market. Specifically, the turn from industrial to consumer capitalism after World War II, the rise of neoliberal economic policies, and the growth of transnational markets and global cultures means that Americans (and others) increasingly practice their religions (or spiritualities or whatever such imaginaries might be called) through the mediation of consumer goods and practices. Simply put, religion does not exist outside the market in the 21st century and those who wish to study religion academically (versus theologically and journalistically) have no choice but to find ways to describe how the fields of 'religion' and 'market/economy' interact, blend, and ultimately in practice dissolve into each other. (Personal correspondence)

The question, then, is not whether scholarly examinations of American religion and culture will take the mediations of ideations and practices of markets into consideration, but how careful and thoughtful such considerations will be.

Critical Advocacy of a Conceptual Framework

This special issue of *Amerikastudien* has been undertaken in the spirit of a critical advocacy of the marketplace framework, one that is aware of its potential pitfalls and yet maintains its demonstrable usefulness. We are convinced that, when done judiciously, examinations of the relationships between religions and markets are productive for American Studies. We also believe that paying attention to the interactions, interpenetrations, and inter-relations of markets and religions need not imply complicity with either specific beliefs held by any of America's denominations, or the belief in the nation's competition-driven religious vitality as an essential feature of American exceptionality, or the quasi-religious belief in the market as the universal determinant of human life. No doubt, complicity is a concern that should be taken seriously. It seems to us the crucial remedy is critical self-awareness, close attention to details, and insistence on nuances and complications. In line with much recent scholarship, we hold absolutist and transhistorical definitions of either religion or the marketplace to be questionable at best and proceed on what might be called the 'complexity assumption': diverse religious beliefs and practices have always coexisted and interacted with equally diverse forms of economic ideologies and activities, and the two spheres cannot be neatly separated either by the people in whose lives these spheres intersect or on the observational or explanatory level by the scholar. We thus share Mark Noll's sentiment that "[s]ingle-cause explanations—whether from the Bible, Max Weber, Karl Marx, E. P. Thompson, or any other authority—simply do not work as a satisfying explanation for religious-economic connections" (*God and Mammon* 8). To avoid complicity in the ideology being studied, we must, of course, abstain from duplicating the ideological valuations of the examined discourses.

The task of explicating how those valuations function in the beliefs and practices of religious people, however, remains important. In doing so, we need to resist the temptation to offer any absolutist interpretations of American religion and culture. The complexity assumption emphasizes that economic and religious forms have always been changing; both religion and economics are capacious terms that historically encompass a great variety of ideas, practices, and cultural and social formations. Indeed, business practices and people's understandings of what constitutes the marketplace have changed and varied at least as dramatically as their faith practices and their understandings of true religion.

For this very reason, most scholars currently working on questions of religions and markets are self-consciously limiting themselves to time- and place-specific phenomena. These scholars scrutinize the influence of market dynamics on the development of particular religious traditions or groups at particular moments in time. They examine concrete instances of religious practices shaped by economic models or assumptions and are attentive to how markets, both literal and conceptual, provide the contexts for the religious ideas and behaviors of specific groups. By and large, the desire for overarching religion and marketplace theories a là Finke and Stark seems to have faded in favor of micro-studies. These new micro-studies are increasingly attentive to the great diversity of American religious traditions beyond Protestant evangelicalism, which were at the center of Finke and Stark and Moore's studies. This is also the route taken by this collection, which makes no attempt to offer a new grand theory of how religion and economics worked together in the making of American culture. Rather, the essays gathered here foreground the multifarious meanings and historical instantiations of the marketplace in the United States, just as they emphasize the plurality of American religions by including traditions such as Quakerism and American Zen Buddhism. These studies are united by a common understanding of the importance of how religious and spiritual beliefs and practices are situated in, conditioned by, and explained through markets, as both continue to change in dynamic interrelations. Yale's Kathryn Lofton articulated this understanding in her address to scholars at the 2011 Biennial Conference of Religion and American Culture. She said, "What I am asking is whether we believe markets provide contexts not only for religious decision-making, but also for religious domains, systems, or fields of valuation. To that, I say: yes" ("Neoliberalism" 53). The contributors to this collection likewise offer emphatic affirmations.

Diverse Scholarship

Each of the following five essays begins with an understanding of the usefulness of the market framework in explaining American religions and demonstrates this utility in their considerations of particular aspects of American culture, both past and present, by looking at them through various facets of the marketplace lens. They are, as it were, dispatches from the outer edges of this field of inquiry and as such are quite diverse. Where one essay looks at a religion imported and exported across the Pacific Ocean, another investigates transatlantic movements of religion, while yet another concerns itself with conflicting movements within the continental United States. One essay examines religious activity in the eighteenth century, several focus on the period immediately after World War II, and others take up inquiries of religions and markets at the turn of the twentieth century. Our contributors also explore different paths and cross-sections among the three basic varieties within the religion and marketplace framework: where one inquires how a particular religion has been commodified, another looks at how two religious traditions' relative positions have changed in the denominational landscape and how that can be explained by conceiving of the field in which they were positioned as a market. Where two essays investigate co-extensive movements of a single religious tradition—the postwar neo-evangelical movement—they differ in what they examine: one shows how a culture of consumerism explains that movement; the other demonstrates that a commitment to the concept of 'free' markets, both literal and metaphoric, shaped an important aspect of that same movement. This diversity represents the breadth of the current inquiry into religion and the marketplace. From five rising and established American Studies scholars in the United States and Europe, these essays are part of the latest push in this tradition of scholarship and together offer specific examples that represent and advance the current state of the field, while at the same time showing where more work needs to be done. It is not entirely coincidental that the majority of our essays are ultimately more interested in religiously inflected ideas of the market than concrete instances of religious practices defined by economic models or assumptions. This is the area that certainly needs most attention from researchers and where many exciting projects will be undertaken in the future.

In the first essay, "'Selling Soap and Salvation': Billy Graham's Consumer Rhetoric in Germany and the United States in the 1950s," Uta Balbier looks at how Graham's evangelical message was intertwined with capitalism and the promise of a middle-class lifestyle. Balbier contends that the style of Graham's crusades, the content of his message, and its attractiveness in the postwar period are all related to explicit and implicit invocations of conceptions of markets. The famed evangelist's style, Balbier writes, "drew comparisons to sales and marketing," which provided and that comparison was the grounds on which Graham was opposed by some and welcomed by others. Further, Graham presented conversion in terms of a business transaction and described heaven as a consumerist paradise, complete with big American cars. Graham's message thus resonated with those who thought of themselves as consumers while he taught others to think of themselves in that way. "He spoke," Balbier writes, "directly to the dreams and aspirations of the middle class." Balbier reveals how Graham consciously and unconsciously used market rhetoric and stylings as he attended to his followers various aspirations. She further shows how this confluence of aspiration and market presentation clarifies postwar evangelicalism's relationship to contemporary American consumer ideology and helps explain the variety of American and European responses to Graham in the 1950s.

Hans Krabbendam's "Opening a Market for Missions: American Evangelicals and the Re-Christianization of Europe, 1945-1985," looks at the same neo-evangelical movement but examines a different aspect of that tradition's relationship to conceptions of markets. Krabbendam shows how the capitalist values of competition and free markets operated in internal discourses justifying and motivating proselytizing efforts. Postwar missionaries regularly spoke of Europe as a newly opened market and described the dominant organizations as threatening monopolies that needed to be broken up. There were, Krabbendam writes, many reasons for the burst of evangelical missionary activity in Europe from the 1940s through the 1980s, but the shape and tone of those efforts can best be explained by considering the ideas of markets at work within evangelical missionaries' own discourse.

Another outreach-oriented group that can be helpfully understood within the framework of religion and the marketplace is the subject of the third essay, "Quaker Reform and Evangelization in the Eighteenth Century." Geoffrey Plank examines proselytizing efforts in a very different time period, long before the ascendancy of postindustrial consumer capitalism, and demonstrates how the Quaker's efforts at winning converts seems counter-intuitive. It was, he says, as if this group were disregarding the rules of competition one would expect with a religious marketplace or dissenting from the idea that more adherents is necessarily better. Through a number of bold reforms, in fact, this group made it significantly harder to be a Quaker; rather than broadening their message to make it more appealing, they pushed instead for what they called a "severity of righteousness." Plank argues that we can see this as a rejection of the market imperative of growth, and yet the strategy was undertaken with the idea that it would make the group more competitive against other religious groups by creating a high-demand profile for potential converts, where the group was defined as a spiritual elite in which membership was desirable and to be earned, not simply obtained. Rather than representing an exception to market-based motivations for religious behavior, eighteenth century Quakers' actions make more sense if one considers them within the framework of market valuations.

The fourth essay, Inken Prohl's "California 'Zen': Buddhist Spirituality Made in America," argues that contemporary Zen Buddhism cannot be understood without examining how it was commodified and how Zen as a commodity was both imported into and exported from the United States. Prohl makes the case that Zen Buddhism has been globally refashioned by the export of 'California Zen.' The practices and theology of Buddhism that were brought to the United States by D.T. Suzuki were, Prohl writes, re-made in the American context of markets and consumption. This re-fashioned Buddhism was then exported back to Buddhist countries, such as Japan. Thinking about Buddhism in terms of this transpacific religious market allows for a nuanced understanding of contemporary Buddhist practices and orientations, as well as explaining why so many other products, practices, and orientations seek to align themselves with Buddhism through branding or other appropriations of aesthetics, language, or practice.

In the final essay, "Evangelicals and Catholics Together: How it Should Have Been in the Roaring Twenties Marketplace of Ideas," Barry Hankins argues that historical animosities between conservative Protestants and Catholics in American culture can be helpfully understood with reference to the marketplace of ideas. Hankins compares contemporary alliances between Catholics and evangelicals on prominent cultural conflicts, such as abortion, to the conflicts visible in the 1928 presidential campaign, when a Catholic secured his party's nomination for president for the first time. Hankins persuasively argues that markets, rather than theology or other issues, is the most useful framework for understanding why these two groups' relationships dramatically shifted in the twentieth century.

The Heuristic Utility of Religion and the Marketplace

The essays collected here demonstrate the heuristic utility of the marketplace framework in a number of ways. These authors reveal how a variety of religious phenomena are at some level defined by the logic of market competition or concrete economic practices, which helps explain the specific forms of religious phenomena, how certain religious movements developed, and why religious groups undertook the activities they did. As evinced by Balbier's, Hankins's, and Prohl's studies, that which might otherwise appear to be *sui generis* or incomprehensible can be explained using the religion and marketplace framework. Whether markets are understood primarily in analogical or in literal terms, these scholars show how helpful it is to think of religious movements in these ways. Further, these essays—particularly Plank's—examine how the framework of religion and marketplace is applicable even counter-intuitively. That is, they investigate instances where it would seem that market explanations should not work, where the religious phenomenon in question is exactly the opposite of how it should be if market conceptions functioned as they are thought to function. Certain religious groups, traditions, and activities have been understood as anti-market, or as irrational, in the sense that they cannot be adequately explained in the terms normally used to explain economic behavior. These essays show that the religion and marketplace framework is useful in these cases as well. Finally, these essays also explore how language and concepts of markets were at work in historic religious discourses, providing motivations and justifications for religious people's activities. In doing this, the essays—especially Balbier, Krabbendam, and Plank's—show that market conceptions are not only external to religious groups, applied by scholars seeking to explain religion in American culture, but are also internal, used by the groups themselves. These conceptions are neither static nor merely descriptive, but dynamic, in the sense that economic rhetoric is an internal force shaping and directing these religious traditions and movements. In these ways, with regards to their specific, concrete subjects, these essays serve to demonstrate the continued usefulness of considering religion and the marketplace in the United States.

Ultimately, we believe that the strength of this special issue rests on a three-part foundation. First, the essays collected here use the religion and marketplace framework and avail themselves of the findings and methodological developments of prior scholarship in all three distinct categories of research on religion and the marketplace while also adding new insights to those categories and to the framework more broadly. Second, the case studies themselves extend the concept of the marketplace: geographically, in terms of agency and power relations within marketplace exchanges, within and between organizational structures; and in terms of seeing how supply- and demand-side phenomena interact with each other, rather than focusing on one at the expense of the other. Third, and perhaps most importantly, the authors collected here are historians and religious studies scholars with widely divergent temporal and thematic specializations. The fact that they can be brought together as they speak both to the inherently interdisciplinary nature of this issue and of its primary concern—religion and the marketplace—and to the vitality and utility of the marketplace metaphor. It also, we believe, imposes an imperative that scholars must continue to refine and test the various marketplace constructs in order to understand religion not just in the United States, but globally.

Works Cited

Abrams, Douglas Carl. *Selling the Old-Time Religion: Fundamentalists and Mass Culture, 1920-1940*. Athens: U of Georgia P, 2001. Print.

Albanese, Catherine L. *America, Religions, and Religion*. 4th ed. Boston: Wadsworth, 2007. Print.

Badaracco, Claire H., ed. *Quoting God: How Media Shape Ideas about Religion and Culture*. Waco, TX: Baylor UP, 2005. Print.

Bivins, Jason C. *Religion of Fear: The Politics of Horror in Conservative Evangelicalism*. New York: Oxford UP, 2008. Print.

Borden, Anne L. "Making Money, Saving Souls: Christian Bookstores and the Commodification of Christianity." *Religion, Media, and the Marketplace*. Ed. Lynn Schofield Clark. New Brunswick: Rutgers UP, 2007. 67-89. Print.

Boyer, Paul S. "Biblical Prophecy and Foreign Policy." *Quoting God: How Media Shape Ideas about Religion and Culture*. Ed. Claire H. Badaracco. Waco, TX: Baylor UP, 2005. 107-22. Print.

Brocker, Manfred. *Protest-Anpassung-Etablierung: Die Christliche Rechte im politischen System der USA*. Frankfurt/M./New York: Campus, 2004. Print.

---, ed. *God Bless America: Politik und Religion in den USA*. Darmstadt: Primus, 2005. Print.

Brown, Candy Gunther. *The Word and the World: Evangelical Writing, Publishing, and Reading in America, 1789-1880*. Chapel Hill: U of North Carolina P, 2004. Print.

Bruce, Steve. *Religion and Choice: A Critique of Rational Choice*. New York: Oxford UP, 2000. Print.

Butler, Jon, Grant Wacker, and Randall Balmer. *Religion in American Life: A Short History*. 2nd ed. New York: Oxford UP, 2011. Print.

Callahan, Richard J., Jr. *Work and Faith in the Kentucky Coal Fields: Subject to Dust*. Bloomington: Indiana UP, 2009. Print.

Chaplin, Jonathan, and Robert Joustra, eds. *God and Global Order: The Power of Religion in American Foreign Policy*. Waco, TX: Baylor UP, 2010. Print.

Chaves, Mark. *American Religion: Contemporary Trends*. Princeton: Princeton UP, 2011. Print.

Chidester, David. *Authentic Fakes: Religion and American Popular Culture*: Berkeley: U of California P, 2005. Print.

Clark, Lynn Schofield, ed. *Religion, Media, and the Marketplace*. New Brunswick: Rutgers UP, 2007. Print.
Connolly, William E. *Capitalism and Christianity, American Style*. Durham: Duke UP, 2008. Print.
Cortiel, Jeanne, Kornelia Freitag, Christine Gerhardt, and Michael Wala, eds. *Religion in the United States*. Heidelberg: Winter, 2011. Print.
Davenport, Stewart. *Friends of Unrighteous Mammon: Northern Christians and Market Capitalism, 1815-1860*. Chicago: U of Chicago P, 2008. Print.
Dochuck, Darren. *From Bible Belt to Sunbelt: Plain-Folk Religion, Grassroots Politics, and the Rise of Evangelical Conservatism*. New York: Norton, 2012. Print.
Einstein, Mara. *Brands of Faith: Marketing Religion in a Commercial Age*. London: Routledge, 2008. Print.
Ellwood, Robert S. *The Fifties Spiritual Marketplace: American Religion in a Decade of Conflict*. New Brunswick: Rutgers UP, 1997. Print.
Engel, Catharine Carte. *Religion and Profit: Moravians in Early America*. Philadelphia: U of Pennsylvania P, 2011. Print.
Ersoz, Meryem. "Gimme that Old-Time Religion in a Postmodern Age: Semiotics of Christian Radio." *Media, Culture, and the Religious Right*. Ed. Linda Kintz and Julia Lesage. Minneapolis: U of Minnesota P, 1998. 211-25. Print.
Ferrell, Lori Anne. *The Bible and the People*. New Haven: Yale UP, 2008. Print.
Finke, Roger. "The Illusion of Shifting Demands: Supply-Side Interpretations of American Religious History." *Retelling U.S. Religious History*. Ed. Thomas A. Tweed. Berkeley: U of California, 1997. 108-24. Print.
Finke, Roger, and Rodney Stark. *The Churching of America, 1776-2005: Winners and Losers in Our Religious Economy*. New Brunswick: Rutgers UP, 2005. Print.
Frykholm, Amy Johnson. *Rapture Culture: Left Behind in Evangelical America*. Oxford: Oxford UP, 2004. Print.
Gebhardt, Jürgen, ed. *Religious Cultures—Communities of Belief*. Heidelberg: Winter, 2009. Print.
Gellman, Erik S., and Jarod Roll. *The Gospel of the Working Class: Labor's Southern Prophets in New Deal America*. Champaign: U of Illinois P, 2011. Print.
Gilmour, Michael J. *Gods and Guitars: Seeking the Sacred in Post-1960s Popular Music*. Waco, TX: Baylor UP, 2009. Print.
Glenn, Heidi. "Losing Our Religion: The Growth of the 'Nones.'" *Morning Edition*. National Public Radio. 13 Jan. 2013. Web. 7 Apr. 2013.
Goff, Philip, ed. *The Blackwell Companion to Religion in America*. London: Blackwell-Wiley, 2010. Print.
Goff, Philip, and Paul Harvey. *Themes in Religion and American Culture*. Chapel Hill: U of North Carolina P, 2004. Print.
Gooch, Cheryl Renee. "Rappin' for the Lord: The Uses of Gospel Rap and Contemporary Music in Black Religious Communities." *Religion and Mass Media: Audiences and Adaptations*. Ed. Daniel A. Stout and Judith M. Buddenbaum. London: Sage, 1996. 228-42. Print.

Grabbe, Hans-Jürgen, ed., *Halle Pietism, Colonial North America, and the Young United States*. Stuttgart: Steiner, 2008. Print.
Gribben, Crawford. *Writing the Rapture: Prophecy Fiction in Evangelical America*. New York: Oxford UP, 2009. Print.
Grossman, Candy Lynn. "As Protestants decline, those with no religion gain." *USA Today*. Gannett Company. 8 Oct. 2012. Web. 7 Apr. 2013.
Hackett, David G. *The Rude Hand of Innovation: Religion and Social Order in Albany, New York, 1652-1836*. New York: Oxford UP, 1991. Print.
Häberlein, Mark. *The Practice of Pluralism: Congregational Life and Religious Diversity in Lancaster, Pennsylvania, 1730-1820*. University Park: Pennsylvania State UP, 2009. Print.
Hagen, Tonja J. *Redeeming the Dial: Radio, Religion and Popular Culture in America*. Chapel Hill: U of North Carolina P, 2001. Print.
Hahn-Bruckart, Thomas. *Friedrich von Schlümbach: Erweckungsprediger zwischen Deutschland und Amerika*. Göttingen: Vandenhoeck & Ruprecht, 2011. Print.
Hart, D.G. *That Old-Time Religion in Modern America: Evangelical Protestantism in the Twentieth Century*. Chicago: Dee, 2002. Print.
Hedstrom, Matthew. *The Rise of Liberal Religion: Book Culture and American Spirituality in the Twentieth Century*. New York: Oxford UP, 2012. Print.
Hendershot, Heather. *Shaking the World for Jesus: Media and Conservative Evangelical Culture*. Chicago: U of Chicago P, 2004. Print.
Herget, Winfried, and Alfred Hornung, eds. *Religion in African American Culture*. Heidelberg: Winter, 2006. Print.
Hertlein, Saskia, and Hermann Josef Schnackertz, eds. *The Culture of Catholicism in the United States*. Heidelberg: Winter, 2012. Print.
Hochgeschwender, Michael. "Religion, Nationale Mythologie und Nationale Identität: Zu den Methodischen und Inhaltlichen Debatten in der Amerikanischen 'New Religious History.'" *Historisches Jahrbuch* 124 (2004): 435-520. Print.
---. *Amerikanische Religion: Evangelikalismus, Pfingstlertum und Fundamentalismus*. Frankfurt/M.: Verlag der Weltreligionen, 2007. Print.
Hochgeschwender, Michael, and Bernhard Löffler. *Religion, Moral und liberaler Markt: Politische Ökonomie und Ethikdebatten vom 18. Jahrhundert bis zur Gegenwart*. Bielefeld: Transcript, 2011. Print.
Hoover, Dennis R., and Douglas M. Johnston, eds. *Religion and Foreign Affairs: Essential Readings*. Waco, TX: Baylor UP, 2012. Print.
Hoover, Stewart M., and Lynn Schofield Clark, eds. *Practicing Religion in the Age of the Media: Explorations in Media, Religion, and Culture*. New York: Columbia UP, 2002. Print.
Hudnut-Beumler, James. *In Pursuit of the Almighty's Dollar: A History of Money and American Protestantism*. Chapel Hill: U of North Carolina P, 2007. Print.
Innes, Stephen. *Creating the Commonwealth: The Economic Culture of Puritan New England*. New York: Norton, 1995. Print.
Jama, Lazerow. *Religion and the Working Class in Antebellum America*. Washington, DC: Smithsonian, 1995. Print.

Jenkins, Philip. *Dream Catchers: How Mainstream America Discovered Native Spirituality*. New York: Oxford UP, 2004. Print.
Kaufman, Suzanne K. *Consuming Visions: Mass Culture and the Lourdes Shrine*. Ithaca: Cornell UP, 2008. Print.
Kintz, Linda, and Julia Lesage, eds. *Media, Culture, and the Religious Right*. Minneapolis: U of Minnesota P, 1998. Print.
Kosmin, Barry A., and Areila Keysar. *Religion in a Free Market: Religious and Non-Religious Americans: Who, What, Why, Where*. Ithaca: Paramount, 2006. Print.
Lee, Shayne, and Phillip Luke Sinitiere. *Holy Mavericks: Evangelical Innovators and the Spiritual Marketplace*. New York: New York UP, 2009. Print.
Lehmann, Hartmut, ed. *Alte und Neue Welt in wechselseitiger Sicht: Studien zu den transatlantischen Beziehungen im 19. und 20. Jahrhundert*. Göttingen: Wallstein 1995. Print.
---. *Transatlantische Religionsgeschichte 18. bis 20. Jahrhundert*. Göttingen: Wallstein, 2006. Print.
Lippy, Charles H. *Introducing American Religions*. London: Routledge, 2009. Print.
---, ed. *Faith in America: Changes, Challenges, New Directions*. Westport, CT: Praeger, 2006. Print. 3 vols.
Lippy, Charles H., and Peter Williams, eds. *Encyclopedia of Religion in America*. Washington, DC: CQ, 2010. Print. 4 vols.
Lofton, Kathryn. *Oprah: The Gospel of an Icon*. Berkeley: U of California, 2011. Print.
---. "Neoliberalism and American Religion." *Proceedings: Second Biennial Conference on Religion and American Culture*. Ed. Philip Goff and Rebecca Vasko. Indianapolis: Center for the Study of Religion and American Culture, 2011. Web. 7 Apr. 2013.
Lynch, Christopher Owen. *Selling Catholicism: Bishop Sheen and the Power of Television*. Lexington: UP of Kentucky, 1998. Print.
Lyon, David. *Jesus in Disneyland: Religion in Postmodern Times*. Cambridge: Polity, 2000. Print.
McCloud, Sean. *Divine Hierarchies: Class in American Religion and Religious Studies*. Chapel Hill: U of North Carolina P, 2007. Print.
---. Personal correspondence with the authors. 25 Nov. 2011. E-mail.
McClure, John A. *Partial Faiths: Postsecular Fiction in the Age of Pynchon and Morrison*. Athens: U of Georgia P, 2007. Print.
McClure, John S. *Mashup Religion: Pop Music and Theological Invention*. Waco, TX: Baylor UP, 2011. Print.
McLeod, Hugh. *Piety and Poverty: Working-Class Religion in Berlin, London and New York, 1870-1914*. Boulder, CO: Holmes, 1996. Print.
Mettele, Gisela. *Weltbürgertum oder Gottesreich: Die Herrnhuter Brüdergemeine als globale Gemeinschaft 1727-1857*. Göttingen: Vandenhoeck & Ruprecht, 2008. Print.
Miller, Vincent J. *Consuming Religion: Christian Faith and Practice in a Consumer Culture*. New York: Continuum, 2004. Print.

Moore, R. Laurence. *Selling God: American Religion in the Marketplace of Culture.* New York: Oxford UP, 1995. Print.

Moreton, Bethany. *To Serve God and Wal-Mart: The Making of Christian Free Enterprise.* Cambridge, MA: Harvard UP, 2010. Print.

Nagler, Jörg, and Michael Haspel, eds. *Abraham Lincoln und die Religion: Das Konzept der Nation unter Gott.* Weimar: Wartburg Verlag, 2012. Print.

Noll, Mark. *The Old Religion in a New World: The History of North American Christianity.* Grand Rapids, MI: Eerdmans, 2001. Print.

---, ed. *God and Mammon: Protestants, Money and the Market, 1780-1860.* New York: Oxford UP, 2001. Print.

Nord, David. *Faith in Reading: Religious Publishing and the Birth of Mass Media in America.* New York: Oxford UP, 2004. Print.

---. "Free Grace, Free Books, Free Riders: The Economics of Religious Publishing in Early Nineteenth-Century America." *Religion, Media, and the Marketplace.* Ed. Lynn Schofield Clark. New Brunswick: Rutgers UP, 2007. 37-66. Print.

Oberdeck, Kathryn J. *The Evangelist and the Impresario: Religion, Entertainment, and Cultural Politics in America, 1884-1914.* Baltimore: Johns Hopkins UP, 1999. Print.

Prätorius, Rainer. *In God We Trust: Religion und Politik in den USA.* München: Beck, 2003. Print.

Preston, Andrew. *Sword of the Spirit, Sheild of Faith: Religion in American War and Diplomacy.* New York: Knopf, 2012. Print.

Putnam, Robert D., and David E. Campbell. *American Grace: How Religion Divides and Unites Us.* New York: Simon, 2010. Print.

Queen, Edward L. II, Stephen R. Prothero, and Gardiner H. Shattuck Jr., eds. *Encyclopedia of American Religious History.* 3rd ed. New York: Facts on File, 2009. Print.

Ratner, Lorman A., Paula T. Kaufman, and Dwight L. Teeter, Jr. *The Paradoxes of Prosperity: Wealth-Seeking Versus Christian Values in Pre-Civil War America.* Champaign: U of Illinois P, 2009. Print.

Riesebrodt, Martin. *Die Rückkehr der Religionen: Fundamentalismus und der "Kampf der Kulturen."* München: Beck, 2000. Print.

Roll, Jarod. *Spirit of Rebellion: Labor and Religion in the New Cotton South.* Champaign: U of Illinois, 2010. Print.

Ronwanièn:te Jocks, Christopher. "Spirituality for Sale: Sacred Knowledge in the Consumer Age." *Religion and American Culture.* Ed. David G. Hackett. 2nd ed. New York: Routledge, 2003. 481-95. Print.

Roof, Wade Clark. *Spiritual Marketplace: Baby Boomers and the Remaking of American Religion.* Princeton; J: Princeton UP, 2001. Print.

Rudnick, Alan. "Why the 'nones' are leaving church, but not God." *AlanRudnick.org* 10 Oct. 2012. Web. 7 Apr. 2013.

Schäfer, Axel R. *Piety and Public Funding: Evangelicals and the State in Modern America.* Philadelphia: U of Pennsylvania P, 2012. Print.

---. *Counterculture Conservatives: American Evangelicalism from the Postwar Revival to the New Christian Right.* Madison: U of Wisconsin P, 2011. Print.

Schantz, Mark S. *Piety in Providence: Class Dimensions of Religious Experience in Antebellum Rhode Island*. Ithaca: Cornell, 2000. Print.

Schmidt, Leigh Eric. *Consumer Rites: The Buying and Selling of American Holidays*. Princeton: Princeton UP, 1997. Print.

Schuck, Peter H., and James Q. Wilson, eds. *Understanding America: The Anatomy of an Exceptional Nation*. New York: PublicAffairs, 2008. Print.

Sellers, Charles Grier. *The Market Revolution: Jacksonian America, 1815-1846*. New York: Oxford UP, 1991. Print.

Sharot, Stephen. "Beyond Christianity: A Critique of Rational Choice Theory of Religion from a Weberian and Comparative Religion Perspective." *Sociology of Religion* 63.4 (2002): 427-54. Print.

Smolinski, Reiner, and Jan Stievermann, eds., *Cotton Mather and Biblia Americana—America's First Bible Commentary*. Tübingen: Mohr Siebeck, 2010. Print.

Stark, Rodney. *A Theory of Religion*. New Brunswick: Rutgers UP, 1996. Print.

Startup, Kenneth Moore. *The Root of All Evil: The Protestant Clergy and the Economic Mind of the Old South*. Athens: U of Georgia P, 1997. Print.

Stein, Stephen J., ed. *The Cambridge History of Religions in America*. 3 vols. Cambridge: Cambridge UP, 2012. Print.

Stout, Daniel A., and Judith M. Buddenbaum, eds. *Religion and Mass Media: Audiences and Adaptations*. London: Sage, 1996. Print.

Stout, Harry S., and D.G. Hart, eds. *New Directions in American Religious History*. New York: Oxford UP, 1997. Print.

Sutton, William R. *Journeymen for Jesus: Evangelical Artisans Confront Capitalism in Jacksonian Baltimore*. University Park: Pennsylvania State UP, 1998. Print.

Tweed, Thomas A., ed. *Retelling U.S. Religious History*. Berkeley: U of California, 1997. Print.

Valeri, Mark. *Heavenly Merchandise: How Religion Shaped Commerce in Puritan America*. Princeton: Princeton UP, 2010. Print.

Waldschmidt-Nelson, Britta. *Christian Science im Lande Luthers: Eine amerikanische Religionsgemeinschaft in Deutschland, 1894-2009*. Stuttgart: Steiner, 2009. Print.

Wallace, Anthony F.C. *Rockdale: The Growth of an American Village in the Early Industrial Revolution*. Lincoln: U of Nebraska, 2005. Print.

Walton, Jonathan. *Watch This: The Ethics and Aesthetics of Black Televangelism*. New York: New York UP, 2009. Print.

Wellenreuther, Hermann. *Niedergang und Aufstieg: Die Geschichte Nordamerikas vom Beginn der Besiedlung bis zum Ausgang des 17. Jahrhunderts*. Trier: WVT, 2000. Print.

---. *Ausbildung und Neubildung: Die Geschichte Nordamerikas vom Ausgang des 17. Jahrhunderts bis zum Ausbruch der Amerikanischen Revolution 1775*. Trier: WVT, 2001. Print.

---. *Von Chaos und Krieg zu Ordnung und Frieden: Die Amerikanische Revolution erster Teil, 1775-1783*. Trier: WVT, 2006. Print.

Whitham, Larry. *Marketplace of the Gods: How Economics Explains Religion*. New York: Oxford UP, 2010. Print.

Wosh, Peter J. *Spreading the Word: The Bible Business in Nineteenth Century America*. Ithaca: Cornell UP, 1994. Print.
Wuthnow. Robert. *After Heaven: Spirituality in America Since the 1950s*. Berkley: U of California P, 1998. Print.
---. *After the Baby Boomers: How Twenty- and Thirty-Somethings Are Shaping the Future of American Religion*. Princeton: Princeton UP, 2007. Print.
---. "Religion." *Understanding America: The Anatomy of an Exceptional Nation*. Ed. Peter H. Schuck and James Q. Wilson. New York: PublicAffairs, 2008. 275-309. Print.
Young, Lawrence A., ed. *Rational Choice Theory and Religion: Summary and Assessment*. New York: Routledge, 1996. Print.

'Selling Soap and Salvation': Billy Graham's Consumer Rhetoric in Germany and the United States in the 1950s

UTA BALBIER

ABSTRACT

In the 1950s and 1960, the American evangelist Billy Graham held his first large revival meetings in Germany. This article explores how the German evangelical organizers and German Christians more generally related to Graham's particular campaign style that blended mission and marketing. It uses Graham's revival meetings in Germany to explore the multi-layered interplay between religion and consumption in West Germany in the 1950s and 60s and shows how rapidly changing economic circumstances in post-War Germany and emerging new consumption patterns also had an impact on how Germans discussed, experienced, and practiced religion. This article argues that the impact that Billy Graham had on the German religious landscape cannot be assessed solely on the basis of church membership (which only showed marginal if any increase after the revival meetings), but argues that Graham brought a significant cultural change to the German religious landscape which slowly embraced the American concept of selling and consuming faith.

"I am selling the greatest product on earth, why shouldn't it be promoted as well as soap?" (8). With this now-famous quote, given in a 1954 interview with *Time* magazine, evangelist Billy Graham set new standards even in the traditionally market-oriented rhetoric of American evangelicalism. Graham also set new standards in German Protestant discourse when he used the same line during a press conference in Düsseldorf that same summer shortly before the opening of his first German crusade, a revival meeting that would attract several thousand German Christians, non-Christians, and Christians-to-be.

In his first address to German audiences, Graham noted that he had worked as a door-to-door brush salesman before becoming an evangelist. Joking about how he used to set his foot on the threshold to prevent doors from being closed in his face, he explained that the modern evangelist had to make use of the marketing methods normally employed by salesmen. After all, he explained that he and his team are just salesmen of the most important treasure existing on earth ("Dies ist die Stunde Gottes"). The same talk saw Graham using various metaphors to relate his evangelism to business and industrial production. For instance, he described his fellow twenty-five evangelists as his team and praised the team's functional division of labor during the London crusade that had run for twelve weeks between March and May 1954.

Graham's market-oriented rhetoric, introduced during his 1950s and 1960s revival campaigns, did not provoke an uproar in German Protestant circles. On the contrary, after some initial resistance, the German press, many Protestant church officials, and German pietist circles displayed their openness to Graham's way of discussing religion in terms of marketing, trade, and lifestyle. In the context of the rapidly evolving consumer capitalism in mid-twentieth century Germany, consumerism also increasingly influenced religious life.

In recent years the histories of consumer capitalism and consumer culture have received growing scholarly attention in Germany.[1] We are also seeing a fresh interest in the contemporary history of religion in Germany that is ambitiously pushing the boundaries of the traditional field of church history.[2] In the study of contemporary religion in the United States, the relationship between consumer capitalism, with its deep impact on social and cultural practices, and the development of religious life has been widely explored and theorized. By contrast, neither the historiography of German consumer capitalism nor German post-war religion has given adequate attention to the complex interplay between religious practices and identities and the changing realities of consumer societies.

In the United States, scholars such as Bethany Moreton, Vincent Miller, and Kathryn Lofton have explored how cultural commercialization and consumption-oriented lifestyles have changed the way people express and experience their faith as well as the ways that they search for spiritual fulfillment. These scholars have also traced the impact of consumerism on the formation of new religious identities.[3] The swift rise of German consumerism in times of the *Wirtschaftswunder* confronted German Christians with challenges and questions similar to those facing their American brethren. Although urban mass revivalism had been part of German religious life since the late nineteenth century, Graham's revival campaigns provided the first occasions for many German Christians and observers of the religious scene to engage with a new form of openly and programmatically market- and consumption-oriented religiosity (Moore). This essay aims to contribute to a better understanding of the impact of German economic prosperity, the clear commitment to a capitalistic social order in the Western part of the country, and the proliferation of consumer practices on the German religious landscape. It also seeks to contribute to the transnationalization of U.S. religious history and American Studies more generally. Considering Graham's efforts in Germany separately from his U.S. efforts will enable us to gain deeper insights into the global attractiveness of his mission.[4]

A particular concern this paper will address is how Graham's style contributed to the transformation of a German pietist milieux. German Protestantism, of course, has a long native tradition of pietist and revivalist movements within the various regional churches, which after World War II became the *Landeskirchen* of the newly formed states.[5] Alongside these *Landeskirchen* existed the 'free churches,' such as the German Baptist, Methodist, and Pen-

---

[1] See Berghoff and Spiekermann; Haupt and Torp; and Siegrist, Kaelble, and Kocka.

[2] See Grossbölting; Bösch and Hölscher.

[3] The adaptability of this concept in the European context is discussed and broadly dismissed in Boeve.

[4] Graham's success has often been explored in the context of his particular attractiveness in the realm of U.S. culture, as done in Wacker, but this approach falls short in explaining Graham's attractiveness abroad.

[5] See Gäbler; Geldbach; and Voigt.

tecostal. These were all conversion-centered, shared the biblical and missionary orientation of the Lutheran and Reformed pietists, and frequently collaborated with their pietist brethren in ecumenical endeavors. The most important of these ecumenical efforts was the *Deutsche Evangelische Allianz*, which emerged from the international *Evangelical Alliance*, founded in 1846.[6] Beginning with the *Erweckungsbewegungen* (revival movements) of the nineteenth century, these German pietist and free churches entertained close relationships with the world of Anglo-American evangelicalism and were influenced by the developments of new types of revivalism and evangelization methods (e. g. tent evangelization, holiness camps) in the Atlantic world. In fact, the German holiness movement (*Gemeinschaftsbewegung*), which re-energized German pietism in the late nineteenth century, started as a religious import from Britain and the United States. In general, however, the wholesale 'Anglicization' of these pietist milieux was always resisted. Instead German churches maintained and fostered their own confessional identities. This resistance turned to nationalistic isolationism during the world wars, and only in the post-war period did these groups open up again to international influence. Especially American evangelicalism, like American culture as a whole, seemed to promise liberation from problematic traditions and the possibility of reinventing oneself through what Winfried Fluck terms "self-Americanization." For German pietists and free church groups, this transformation involved a redefinition from pious *evangelische Christen*—in the older, more comprehensive sense of the word meaning Protestant Christians—to *evangelikale Christen* as an adaption of the American concept of *evangelical Christian*. 'Evangelical Christian' as a concept implied a continuing commitment to a conservative, bibliocentric theology and conversionism, and it also connoted a self-confident, open-minded attitude toward the modern world and middle-class culture. As I will argue, this shift to an evangelical identity was intimately connected to an endorsement of Graham's market- and consumer-oriented interpretation of the Protestant faith.[7]

In what follows, I first introduce Graham's particular liaison with the rise of consumerism and then discuss the first encounters between German audiences, press, and church officials and Graham's campaigns and their distinctive style in the 1950s. In the final part, I outline how German evangelicals' self-conception changed due to their interactions with Graham and his team after Graham's three-week 1960s campaigns in Berlin, Hamburg, and Essen.

---

[6] For the history of the Alliance, see Beyreuther; Schirrmacher and Jung.

[7] Graham's importance role in the formation of a German 'evangelical movement' has been acknowledged, but so far the specific appeal of his market- and consumer-oriented style has been largely overlooked. See Schirrmacher and Jung, 38-39; and especially the detailed account of Graham's visit to Germany in Bauer, 201-221.

Billy Graham and the Business of Evangelicalism

Billy Graham held his first revival meeting in Los Angeles in the fall of 1949.[8] The Southern Baptist preacher was thirty-one years old, held a degree from Wheaton College, was an ordained minister, had travelled the world for the evangelical organization Youth for Christ, and he was about to claim center stage in what would become a national revival.[9] Between 1949 and 1954, Graham preached to twelve million people. In the summer of 1957, he conducted a sixteen-week long Crusade, as he and his team called the revival meetings, at New York's Madison Square Garden, regularly selling out its 20,000 seats. Graham's crusades always followed the same structure: choirs sang, a sermon was given, and finally Graham called his audience to step forward to accept Christ as their savior. The crusades took place in urban surroundings and ran for several weeks.

From the earliest days of his ministry, an important part of Graham's success derived from his strategic interplay with the media and use of modern forms of marketing, such as billboards and radio announcements. These particular marketing tools not only advertised the evangelical revival campaigns, they also seamlessly blended 1950s advertisement culture with modern mass evangelism. Graham's ever-bigger revival campaigns posed an organizational and financial challenge that Graham and his team met by constantly working to improve their planning and business structures.

By 1950 Graham and his key associates had founded the Billy Graham Evangelistic Association (BGEA), headquartered in Minneapolis, Minnesota. Led first by George Wilson from a one-room office with one secretary, the association symbolized these young evangelists' financial and organizational ambitions. The expanding reach of Graham's citywide campaigns necessitated major structural and organizational changes during this time. Following the successful revival campaigns in Los Angeles and Boston in 1949, Graham's next crusade took place in Columbia, South Carolina, and saw an important personnel change when Graham hired Willis Haymaker as the campaign's central manager. Haymaker, a former associate of Billy Sunday and Gipsy Smith, further professionalized Graham's campaign business, while the crusades moved on to campaigns in Portland, Atlanta, Memphis, and Washington, DC (Martin 129).

The BGEA faced its biggest organizational challenge on the other side of the Atlantic, however, while preparing for the Greater London Crusade. Running from March 1 through May 22, 1954, and attracting around two million people, the London crusade was carried out by several local campaign teams responsible for everything from communication to prayer, music, finances, children's missions, and church collaboration. This proved to be an especially efficient setup, and the organizational structure established in London set the standards for the

---

[8] For biographies, see Aikman; Martin; McLoughlin, *Billy Graham*; and Wacker, *America's Pastor*.

[9] For a history of American evangelicalism see Balmer; Noll; and McLoughlin, *Modern Revivalism*. For the re-emergence in the 1940s and 1950s, see Carpenter.

organization of the New York campaign in 1957 as well as the first major German threeweek revival tour in 1960.

By the time of the London crusade, the Minneapolis office had grown as well. Staff numbers increased to eighty and Graham's growing presence through his newspaper column, his "Hour of Decision" broadcast, and his World Wide Pictures movie company generated new revenue streams. Graham's rising publicity also guaranteed increased income through donations (Martin 138, 236). Graham's missionary work had turned into a major, albeit strictly non-profit, business operation.

The resemblances between Graham's work and the business and consumerist world went beyond the business-like structures of the campaigns and included meticulously kept and analyzed attendance records as well as other statistical information gleaned from the crusades. As Graham biographer William Martin observes, when comparing Graham to one of his best-known nineteenth century predecessors, "D. L. Moody refused to keep statistics lest he be drawn into exaggeration or boasting. Billy Graham and his team were too wed to the modern ethos to adopt that approach, but they did begin to use a consistent procedure" (108). Initially Graham's teams relied on police statistics or on numbers provided by venue managers for attendance figures, but they quickly devised additional statistical metrics for their own analysis. One of their innovations was a revival of a practice pioneered by Billy Sunday during his evangelist tours: distributing and collecting 'decision cards' at the end of each service. These cards allowed them Graham to keep more precise records of potential converts.

The business-like organization of the revival campaigns was also reflected in the staging of events. Admirers and critics on both sides of the Atlantic noted how much the young evangelist resembled the typical 1950s salesman in dress, gesture, and rhetoric. His trademark grey business suit positioned him clearly in the secular sales and marketing workforce. His revival meetings, culminating in the call to the individual to make a decision to accept Christ as his or her Savior, were often compared to sales events. In this case, the events focused on a preacher who emphasized the importance of a personal, individualized decision to purchase a particular product and framed the individual's decision in the language of consumption and business transactions (Balbier, "'God's Own Consumers'").

Graham's constant use of metaphors derived from consumer capitalism enabled him to communicate efficiently with his middle-class followers, yet also attracted significant criticism. German journalist Barbara Klie wrote a particularly harsh description of Graham's campaign style in 1955. Klie complained that Graham's preaching transformed the relationship between God and the human being into a simple business relationship: "The doctrine of grace is turned into a business transaction: God says: I gave my son for you, now give up your sins and you'll be forgiven" (Klie 35; my translation).

Press portrayals of Graham contributed to the ways he was perceived on stage and went beyond commenting on the style of the services and the content of his sermons and zeroed in on Graham's own lifestyle. Articles published around the world turned Graham, his wife, and his family into a billboard advertisement for the white, middle-class American family and way of life in the 1950s. The articles profiling Graham's wife Ruth were particularly loaded with all of the major markers of the 1950s suburban lifestyle, from discussions of modern kitchen appliances to air travel. Even those publications critical of the preacher, such as an article published in the German magazine *Der Spiegel* in 1954 under the headline "Religion for Mass Consumption" ("Zwölf Ernten" 21-26), published photographs of Graham playing golf and driving a nice car.

This staging of Graham as a jet-set traveler, making appearances all over the world, had a particular impact on the culture of 1950s evangelicalism. The international press that covered his 1954 crusades celebrated modern mobility by publishing an enormous number of pictures showing Graham stepping off a plane or walking down the gangways of transatlantic cruise liners. The 1950s had produced a new Western image of the traditional itinerant preacher that appealed to Christian consumers in the United States, United Kingdom, and Germany. This image would inspire them to find their own ways of combining their newfound mobility and consumer practices with their commitment to faith and mission.

Billy Graham in Germany: Business as Usual

When Graham brought his style of campaigning and self-styling over to Germany, he stirred up a lively discussion in the national press and official church and evangelical circles about the relationships between faith and consumption and between marketing and mission.[10] While urban mass evangelization was by no means new in Germany, revival meetings had never before been promoted with such a massive advertising campaign and creativity. For Graham's one-day appearance in Mannheim in 1955, for example, the local organizing committees distributed 100,000 flyers and 6,000 posters and used advertisements in cinemas as well as on trams (Protokoll).

Picking up on what Graham said at his first press conference in Düsseldorf, the German press immediately began describing Graham's religious mission in terms of production, marketing, and sales—and it did so with clear admiration. Terms usually related to the industrial realm, such as 'assembly line' or 'production,' as well as terms related to business and trade, such as 'marketing' and 'statistics,' figured prominently in the headlines describing Graham's first campaigns in Germany in Berlin and Düsseldorf in 1954 and in five other German cities in 1955 ("40.000 Menschen"). Further, many articles pointed out that Graham's mission revolved around the production and categorization of believers, describing in detail the division of labor within his team and his practice of recording and keeping accurate crusade statistics. Observers also noted Graham's modern mode of travel and the high-tech setting of his crusade stage; indeed, Graham's portable microphone was turned into an icon of modern evangelicalism. The conservative press in particular approved of Graham's methods, its coverage replete with positive images of mobility, modernity, and technical progress ("Mit Bibel"). The

---

[10] For the broader context of the first German crusades, see Balbier, "Billy Graham in West Germany."

preacher was portrayed as the consummate 'modern apostle': good-looking, tall, slender, and well dressed. Fashion, style, and religion blended together in the German press coverage of the crusades.

These passages and catchwords clearly show that with the spread of the American consumer empire across the Atlantic, Germans went beyond simply developing an "intimate familiarity with the American way of life" (de Grazia 3). This familiarity manifested in the way Germans perceived Graham as one of their own, or, rather, as someone they wanted to become. The press portrayal of Graham shows that beyond familiarity, Germans had learned to understand and speak what Victoria de Grazia terms the new consumer "empire's vernacular" (4). Even leading German Protestant bishops as, for example, Otto Dibelius of Berlin Brandenburg adapted the new discourse of faith, industrial labor, and technology. A remark Dibelius made in 1966 captures what he and many Germans saw in the young American preacher:

> He is an American through and through and uses with confidence all of the technological achievements of our time. [...] He is familiar with the globe and all its continents. He doesn't work alone, but in the best American manner, he has teams everywhere who prepare his missionary work. [...] He uses all of the modern modes of work and travel. In sum: he is a modern being, for that everything modern is absolutely natural. (3; my translation)

For Dibelius, Graham's campaigns symbolized the compatibility of modernity and traditional faith, of consumer life-styles and old beliefs. In short, for Dibelius, Graham's melding of Christianity with the modern marketplace represented the future of religious life.[11] Nevertheless, what many members of the official Protestant Church saw as a glimmer of hope in a period marked by rising fears of secularization was initially rejected by the more traditionalist segments of German pietists.

Graham's open support for sales and marketing techniques, in particular his team's attitude toward organizing Christian missions as promotional tours, created pronounced tensions between the American team and the German hosts and organizers of the first revivals in West Germany. Significantly, in 1954, Walther Zilz, head of the *Deutsche Evangelische Allianz* (German Evangelical Alliance [GEA]), openly dismissed Graham's mission and its impact during the Greater London Crusade. Zilz directed particularly caustic criticism toward a German evangelical publication about the Greater London Crusade entitled *Eine Weltstadt horcht auf.* Paul Deitenbeck—a leading critic of liberal theologian Rudolf Bultmann as well as a proponent of modernization and strong Graham supporter—had published the short booklet pamphlet that attracted Zilz's venom. Zilz denigrated the booklet's pamphlet style as 'American' and disapproved of Deitenbeck's focus on conversion statistics as well as the latter's obvious admiration for Graham. Both of these, Zilz fulminated, were inconsistent with the Bible and

---

[11] There is no room in this essay to discuss the full range of critical voices that were raised against Graham's mission, but such criticisms came from theologians, ministers, and left-wing intellectuals, with a wide array of different arguments reaching from a general consumer critique and anti-Americanism to particular concern against a mixing of faith and entertainment and the German history of propaganda and mass persuasion.

represented an unacceptable modern, secular and propagandistic interference with Christian mission (Zilz an Deitenbeck). On several occasions, however, Zilz declared that the GEA's animosity toward Graham stemmed from his marketing methods, not from his message, with which they had little quarrel. Indeed, during the long discussions between members of the German Evangelical Conference, the GEA, and the Billy Graham Team, Graham's marketing style was consistently among the most contested points of discussion.

Despite claims to the contrary, however, the real conflict between the American salesmen of faith and the German missionaries ran much deeper than disputes over style and marketing, as became obvious during a short episode that took place during the preparation for Graham's second German tour in 1955. For a variety of reasons, the relationship between German evangelicals and Robert Evans, Graham's representative in Europe, reached an all-time low in 1955. Superficially, the conflict appeared to center on a purely organizational matter, namely the question of which city Graham should visit for the final revival meeting of the 1955 tour. Evans proposed Essen, explaining that the city's proximity to the greater Ruhr area would furnish the largest prospective audiences on the revival tour and would thus give Graham the ability to close the crusade before his largest audience. This strictly administrative argument appeared to one of the German evangelicals as *"allzumenschlich"* ("all-too-human")—that is, secular (Müller 2). Evans's push for attendence did not stop there; in the logistical discussions about the Frankfurt event—whether it should be held in the 10,000-seat festival hall or the 20,000-seat stadium—Evans pushed for the latter. Making an argument of congruence, Evans stressed that every other city on the tour was hosting the events in venues accommodating more than twice as many participants as the Frankfurt festival hall. To hold the event in such a large city in such a conspicuously small venue, he argued, would hurt the campaign's image. When one of the Germans declared that every single sinner converted would be of joy to the Lord, and hence balked at the American's attempt to organize by the numbers, Evans shot back: "That might be the case in heaven, but not on earth!" (Zilz an die Mitglieder; my translation).

This example highlights the question at the root of the conflict between the American and German organizers: were evangelical Christians nowadays, as the Germans feared, on a secular sales mission that had to be organized, financed, and advertized, or on a religious mission whose rules should be defined by spiritual concerns, not secular market analysis? Many members of the GEA continued to reject the American rationalization and technicalization, which they saw as the secularization of Christian missionary work. What church officials such as Dibelius saw as the future of German Protestantism is what key figures of the GEA considered a selling out of Christian principles and a blind obedience to modernization and secularization processes. The GEA thus refrained from providing Graham's 1954 and 1955 revival campaigns with any administrative or financial support. Affiliates working within the GEA's broader ambit, such as Deitenbeck, still played important roles in making these first German crusades happen, but they did so without any official institutional support.

The Business of Mission

Five years later, however, when Graham returned to Germany for a three-week crusade in Essen, Berlin, and Hamburg, the German organizing committee had changed its mind about the use of marketing and organizational structures, as the central organizing committee's minutes indicate. The minutes show a heavy use of business language, a clear new focus on organization and marketing and on raw numbers. The progressive self-modernization as self-Americanization of German pietists was not only apparent in an increasing amount of advertisement and marketing materials, but also in the brand new business identity assumed by the German organizing committee. Along with German society generally, German pietists' lives were caught up in enhanced rationalization and planning processes. As a result, they now openly embraced what had appeared secular and foreign in the early and mid-1950s. This time around, the GEA was the leading force behind Graham's German campaigns. As Gisa Bauer points out, the German word *"evangelikal"* as a term of self-reference was most likely first used in the context of Graham's 1959-60 campaign (29). One evening in 1960, Peter Schneider, a member of the Berlin *Stadtmission* who served as Graham's interpreter for this crusade, decided to translate Graham's appeal to join the "evangelical community" not as *"evangelische Gemeinde,"* but as *"evangelikale Gemeinde"* (29). With this distinction he intended to mark the difference between the crusade audience and the established *Landeskirchen*, which evangelicals perceived as too theologically liberal and disinterested in missionary work. Over the following decade, the term gained increasing currency and came to serve as an important point of reference in the gradual self-redefinition of German pietist communities (29).

On November 6, 1959, the central organizing committee for the Essen, Hamburg, and Berlin crusades met for the first time in Hamburg. Paul Schmidt, head of the GEA, presided, with Wilhelm Brauer, Friedrich Heitmüller, and Paul Deitenbeck (who had become a member of the GEA's executive committee)—all supporters of Graham's 1954 and 1955 crusades—also in attendance. Other well-known names in the 'field of mission among the people' (*Volksmission*) appeared as well, such as Fritz Bachmann, superintendent of the evangelical church of the Rhineland, and Gerhard Bergmann, a representative of the German tent mission (Protokoll). Deitenbeck began the meeting with a meditation on Joshua and the battle of Jericho and then announced that the organizers, sponsors, and supporters were ready for something entirely new—something that would not fail for financial reasons. The committee expressed its sincere wish to host Billy Graham for a full week in three different cities. The committee settled on the idea of renting 20,000-seat-capacity tent for each city at a total cost of 300,000 DM. Both the costs and the anticipated audiences were unprecedented numbers for German missionaries. Once the committee estimated that each evening's collection could net 100,000 DM, they unanimously decided to take the risk.

The fact that evangelical mission had indeed turned into a business-like operation had a significant impact on the way the organizers planned the upcoming crusade meetings. A central organizing committee was established to supervise the actions of the three separate local committees. Each local committee was composed of seven task forces specialized in aspects of management and organization, marketing and public relations, fire marshals and transport, music, finances, prayer groups organization, and the education of spiritual guides. This structure was clearly modeled on the planning process that went into the London crusade. In fact, the German organizers telegraphed their intentions to emulate that crusade when they invited English ministers to come to Germany in 1959 to share the experiences they had gained during the Greater London Crusade (Protokoll).

German evangelicals had professionalized the process of organizing the crusades. Following the examples of their American and English brethren, they adopted new business structures and practices and a new self-understanding. This international influence on the modernization of the German evangelicalism milieu affected not only the upper echelons of the organizations but also ordinary German Christians. The extent to which the laity was open to these foreign missionary practices became clear with the implementation of the 'Andreas Plan' (also known as Operation Andrew) in 1960. Operation Andrew was a shorthand title for a complex operation whereby the churches would charter buses to take their members—and, most importantly, guests of their members—to the crusade events. It was the brainchild of the British evangelicals who organized the London crusade in 1954. Before the crusade began, a prayer-partner newsletter introduced Operation Andrew to the British audience. The newsletter opened with three biblical citations referring to Andrew and how he brought his brother to Jesus, and the flyer emphasized not only the biblical precedent and missionary considerations underlying the operation, but also the fact that modern urbanization was a significant prod toward the development of this new missionary tool: "The immensity of the task in reaching the population of the largest city in the world is indeed tremendous. Under the title of 'Operation Andrew' we submit to you a scheme which is at once scriptural, practical and effectual" (Prayer Partner News-Letter).

The newsletter contained strict orders as to how Operation Andrew should work: only church members who would bring one unchurched acquaintance to the crusade were permitted to travel on the chartered buses. The journey to and from the crusade was to be used for praying, singing, and discussions about questions of faith. At the crusades, the travel companions would sit together in reserved seating sections. The London organizers defined Operation Andrew as the perfect space for individual evangelism. Operation Andrew was exported as a concept to the United States, where it was particularly useful during the 1957 New York crusade. By 1960, the model had been exported to Germany.

In early December 1959, Paul Schmidt, Wilhelm Brauer, and Peter Schneider—the driving forces behind the German organizational efforts—met with Jerry Beavan and Charlie Riggs, two representatives from Graham's team. At this meeting, the Germans explained some of the important findings they had gleaned from their experiences with the Operation Andrew concept. They found that face-to-face evangelism added a personal element to an otherwise massive event (Besprechung). By late June 1960, in a circular passed around the central organizing committee, the "Andreas Plan" as it was called in German, was mentioned for the first time under the section marketing. The circular discussed the missionary scheme among other organizational questions concerning the tents, advertisements, special events, and the music. Attached to the letter was a brochure that explained the goals and methods of the new missionary tool; this brochure was circulated among all of the congregations participating in the 1960s crusades (An die Mitglieder). The brochure touted the Andreas Plan not only as a solid logistical tool, but also as a promising missionary tool: "*Er bietet verkehrstechnisch und missionarisch viele Vorteile*" (Großstadt-Evangelisation).

As in the United States and in Sydney where roughly 20,000 people had used the Andrew buses during the 1959 campaign, thousands of German Christians used the organized bus transport. Seven hundred congregations near Hamburg were invited to join the Andreas Plan, and most accepted (Timmermann 36). In Berlin each evening fifty chartered buses brought 4,000 people to the crusade (Goltz). More than a logistical expedience, Operation Andrew became the icon of the modern pilgrimage—an icon devised and provided by Billy Graham's team. During the 1950s crusades many German newspapers had dedicated a significant part of their coverage to the description of the transport to the crusades, as if the media attempted to capture the new mobility in faith in the images of the thousands of cars, buses, and trains that were used to bring people to and take them from the crusades. Against this background, the *Westfälische Allgemeine Zeitung* dedicated one of its crusade articles to Operation Andrew under the headline "Evangelisation beginnt im Bus" ("The Evangelical mission begins on the bus"), and many other stories at least mentioned the program (13).

The church papers payed even more attention to the phenomenon, discussing the operation in the terms of mission, communication of faith, and the search for moments of community in an otherwise unfamiliar mass revivalism. Hanns Lilje's *Sonntagsblatt* published an article on Operation Andrew in preparation for the Hamburg Crusade. The article did not naively predict the success of the program, but still expressed the deep belief that the plan could actually bring people who had not set foot inside a church for years in contact with Christianity. It also addressed the fact that the plan provided an important link between individual evangelism and mass experience (36). Many contemporary organizers and supporters of the Billy Graham campaigns were wondering how to establish a firm connection between local church life, the individual seeker, and the more anonymous mass experience at the revival meetings held in large sports stadia. Operation Andrew seemed to be a rather practical answer to their prayers. The GEA concurred, viewing the program as one of the strongest and most vibrant connections between the revival event and the local churches (Billy Graham Information für die Gemeindeblätter).

Indeed, the operation made a lasting impression. Berlin's central church paper covered Operation Andrew after the closing of the crusade and discussed it in the context of the need for more everyday missionary efforts. Wilhelm Timmermann asked if Christians should transform Operation Andrew into a daily task by communicating their faith to coworkers and neighbors and leading them to church (36). In this context, Operation Andrew became a symbol for a more communicable faith and remained a constant feature of the crusades practice and experience in Germany. It was practiced again in Berlin in 1966, and during Graham's 'Euro

'70 Campaign,' ten buses were chartered to bring audiences to each German city in which the Crusade was held and televised. In each city, at least 500 people arrived via one of the Operation Andrew buses.

Conclusion

The multiple ways that American evangelicalism interacts with the world of business and consumption indicates religious culture's compatibility with modern life and identity. Billy Graham's campaigns provide a unique lens to study the way consumerism affected evangelical revivalism, such as pilgrimages and the crusades. Metaphors of consumption marked Graham's unique rhetoric and his salesmanesque vocabulary shaped the staging of his crusades services, which culminated in his highly individualized altar call. Graham spoke directly to the quotidian needs and dreams of consumers as he validated their lifestyle.

The historiography of German Protestantism has so far missed opportunities to discuss how the German religious landscape reacted to the rapidly expanding consumer culture that marked the 1950s and the following decades. I have chosen to focus on the transformation of the German pietist milieu and on how it reacted to and was influenced by Graham's campaign style. We have seen a dramatic change between the 1950s and 1960s: though rejecting Graham's mission as too secular in the 1950s, German pietists adapted to the changing social circumstances of the late 1950s and, by 1960, were actively organizing Graham's campaigns in Essen, Hamburg, and Berlin. Not only were they organizing the events, they also adapted Graham's language, organizational approach, and focus on financial and audience statistics. This stunning reversal shows how much the culture of consumption and the increasing commercialization of everyday life changed the self-conception of those groups who had begun to call themselves German evangelicals.

It is important to note that this identity change was inspired, not dictated, by interaction with the Anglo-American campaign style. German evangelicals rose to the new challenge in their unique way, which differs in many ways from the paths chosen by their British and American brethren. This is revealed for example in the different ways Operation Andrew was discussed and practiced in London, Berlin, and New York. We witness here the full complexity of what Fluck terms "self-Americanization."

The fact that these changes, produced by the interplay of Protestantism and the rise of a modern consumer society in Germany, extended beyond the transformation of the evangelical milieu becomes obvious in the changing rhetoric of leading voices in mainline Protestantism. Public statements by Bishop Otto Dibelius about Billy Graham clearly show that the Bishop was not just aware of the challenges that the rise of consumerism posed to the Protestant Church in Germany, but that, from his point of view, embracing this emergent consumerism could be pivotal to the future of the German Protestantism. By 1970 German Protestant rhetoric sounded strikingly similar to Graham's remarkable comment made at a 1954 press conference in Düsseldorf. In 1970 Hans-Otto Wölber, bishop of the evangelical Lutheran church of Hamburg, declared in an interview regarding Graham's unique campaign style during the Euro '70 that "If I want to know if a detergent is really good, then I have to accept that commercials are persuading me, and I have to buy it and I have to use it. That means that I have to make a decision" (Euro-Tele-Evangelisation 4; my translation). With this rhetoric, the bishop did not just embrace and endorse the use of marketing the realm of faith, he also mirrored the emphasis on choice and decision that had embedded Graham's preaching so clearly into the consumer culture of the 1950s United States.

This rhetorical shift in the official Protestant Church suggest that Graham's campaign had an impact on the culture of Protestantism in Germany beyond the emerging evangelical movement. German Christians were living as consumers and were increasingly in search of a religious life that blurred the boundaries between their identities as Christians and as consumers. These subtle transformations regarding the expression and experience of faith mirrored developments taking place in the United States, albeit under different circumstances, and invites further research in the often neglected transnational dimensions of U.S. and European religious history. They also point toward the lasting impact of Graham's campaigns on both sides of the Atlantic. Graham might not have been able to increase membership in mainline Protestant or in the Free Churches, but he was well able to change the way German Christians expressed, chose, and lived their faith.

Works Cited

"40.000 Menschen hören Billy Graham im Stadion." *Frankfurter Allgemeine Zeitung* 23 June 1955: 5. Print.

An die Mitglieder des Zentralkomitees für die Großstadt-Evangelisation mit Billy Graham, Berlin, 30 Juni 1960. Circular. Archive of the German Evangelical Alliance, Bad Blankenburg.

Aikman, David. *Billy Graham: His Life and Influence*. Nashville: Nelson, 2010. Print.

Balbier, Uta Andrea. "'God's Own Consumers': Billy Graham, Mass Evangelism, and Consumption in the United States in the 1950s." *Decoding Consumer Societies*. Eds. Berghoff and Spiekermann. New York: Palgrave McMillian, 2012. 195-209. Print.

---. "Billy Graham in West Germany: German Protestantism between Americanization and Rechristianization, 1954-70." *ZeithistorischeForschungen / Studies in Contemporary History* 7:3 (2010): n. pag. Web 3 Feb. 2015.

Balmer, Randall. *Blessed Assurance: A History of Evangelicalism in America*. Boston: Beacon, 1999. Print.

Bauer, Gisa. *Evangelikale Bewegung und evangelische Kirche in der Bundesrepublik Deutschland. Geschicthe eines Grundsatzkonflicts (1945 bis 1989)*. Göttingen: Vandenhoeck & Ruprecht, 2012. Print.

Berger, Peter, Grace Davie, and Effie Fokas. *Religious America, Secular Europe: A Theme and Variations*. London: Ashgate, 2008. Print.

Berghoff, Hertmut, and Uwe Spiekermann, eds. *Decoding Consumer Societies*. New York: Palgrave McMillian, 2012. Print.

Besprechung mit Jerry Beavan und Charlie Riggs in Berlin, Hamburg, und Essen. Memorandum. 3-5 Dec. 1959. Archives of the German Evangelical Alliance, Bad Blankenburg.

Beyreuther, Erich. *Der Weg der Evangelishen Allianz in Deutchland*. Wuppertal: SCM R. Brockhaus, 1969. Print.

Billy Graham Information für die Gemeindeblätter. N. d. Archives of the German Evangelical Alliance, Bad Blankenburg.

Boeve, Lieven, ed. *Consuming Religion in Europe? Christian Faith Challenged by Consumer Culture*. Special edition of Bulletin of the European Society for Catholic Theology 17 (2006). Print.

Bösch, Frank, and Lucian Hölscher, eds. *Kirchen – Medien – Öffentlichkeit: Transformationen kirchlicher Selbst- und Fremddeutungen seit 1945*. Göttingen: Wallstein, 2009.

Carpenter, Joel. *Revive Us Again: The Reawakening of American Fundamentalism*. New York: Oxford, 1999. Print.

de Grazia, Victoria. *Irresistible Empire: America's Advance through Twentieth-Century Europe*. Cambridge, MA: Harvard, 2006. Print.

Dibelius, Otto. "Billy Graham: Seine Lebensarbeit gehört der modernen Welt." *Berliner Sonntagsblatt* 12 June 1966: 3. Print.

"Dies ist die Stunde Gottes." Vortrag des Evangelisten Dr. Billy Graham am 24. Juni 1954 im Appollo-Theater in Düsseldorf. Archive of the German Evangelical Alliance, Bad Blankenburg.

Euro-Tele-Evangelisation. "Euro 70" mit Dr. Billy Graham im Spiegel der Presse, herausgegeben von der Grosstadtevangelisation der Deutschen Evangelischen Allianz. Evangelisches Landesarchiv Berlin, Graham 191.

"Evangelisation beginnt im Bus." *Westfälische Allgemeine Zeitung*. 9 September 1960. 13. Print.

Fluck, Winfried. "California Blue: Americanization as Self-Americanization." *Americanization and Anti-Americanism: The German Encounter with American Culture After 1945*. Ed. Alexander Stephan. New York: Berhahn, 2005. 221-37. Print.

Gäbler, Ulrich, Martin Sallman, Martin Brecht, eds. *Der Pietismus im neunzehnten und zwangzigsten Jahrnhundert*. Vol. 3 of *Geschichte des Pietismus*. Göttingen: Vandenhoeck & Ruprecht, 2000. Print.

Geldbach, Erich. *Freikirchen: Erbe, Gestalt and Wirkung*. Göttingen: Vandenhoeck & Ruprecht, 1989. Print. Bensheimer Hefte 70.

Goltz, Walter. Billy Graham in Berlin. Archives of the German Evangelical Alliance, Bad Blankenburg.

Graham, Billy. Interview. *Time* 25 Oct. 1954: 8. Print.

Grossbölting, Thomas. *Der verlorene Himmel: Glaube in Deutschland seit 1945*. Göttingen: Vandenhoeck & Ruprecht, 2013. Print.

Großstadt Evangelisation mit Billy Graham, verfasst vom Deutsche Zentralkomitee, Mai 1960. Circular. Evangelisches Zentralarchiv 71/1827.

Haupt, Heinz-Gerhard, and Claudius Torp, eds. *Die Konsumgesellschaft in Deutschland 1890-1990*. Frankfurt/M.: Campus, 2009.

Klie, Barbara. "Der Prediger auf dem Fußballplatz." *Süddeutsche Zeitung* 4 June 1955: 35 Print.

Lofton, Kathryn. *Oprah: The Gospel of an Icon*. Berkeley: U of California P, 2011. Print.

Martin, William C. *A Prophet with Honor: The Billy Graham Story*. New York: Morrow, 1991. Print.

McLoughlin, William Gerald. *Billy Graham: Revivalist in a Secular Age*. New York: Ronald, 1960. Print.

---. *Modern Revivalism: Charles Grandison Finney to Billy Graham*. New York: Ronald, 1959. Print.

---. *Revival Awakenings and Reform: An Essay on Religion and Social Change in America, 1607-1977*. Chicago: U of Chicago P, 1979. Print.

Miller, Vincent J. *Consuming Religion: Christian Faith and Practice in a Consumer Culture*. New York: Bloomsbury, 2004. Print.

"Mit Bibel, Mikrophon und Cowboyhut." *Frankfurter Allgemeine Zeitung*. 3 Apr. 1954: 2. Print.

Moore, R. Laurence. *Selling God: American Religion in the Marketplace of Culture*. New York: Oxford UP, 1995. Print.

Moreton, Bethany. *To Serve God and Wal-Mart: The Making of Christian Free Enterprise*. Boston: Harvard, 2009. Print.

Müller, Erich. Briefabschrift. 10 May 1954. Archive of the German Evangelical Alliance, Bad Blankenburg.

Noll, Mark. *American Evangelical Christianity: An Introduction*. Oxford: Wiley-Blackwell, 2000. Print.

Prayer Partner News-Letter No. 7. Attachment: Operation Andrew. Billy Graham Center London Crusade. Billy Graham Center Archives 9/B5-2.

Protokoll der ersten Sitzung des Zentralausschusses fuer die geplante Gross-Evangelisation mit Billy Graham. November 6, 1959 in Hamburg. Private Archive of the German Evangelical Alliance, Bad Blankenburg.

Schirrmacher, Thomas, and Friedhelm Jung. *Die deutsche evangelikale Bewegung. Grundlinien ihrer Geschichte und Theologie*. Bonn: Verlag für Kultur und Wissenschaft, 2004. Print.

Siegrist, Hannes, Hartmut Kaelble, and Jürgen Kocka, eds. *Europäische Konsumgeschichte: Zur Gesellschafts- und Kulturgeschichte des Konsums (18. bis 19. Jahrhundert)*. Göttingen: Campus, 1997. Print.

Stephan, Alexander, ed. *Americanization and Anti-Americanism: The German Encounter with American Culture After 1945*. New York: Berghahn, 2005. Print.

Timmermann, Wilhelm. "Billy Graham und der Andreas-Plan." *Berliner Sonntagsblatt* 16 Oct. 1960: 36. Print.

Voigt, Karl Heinz. *Freikirchen in Deutschland (19. und 20 Jahrhundert)*. Leipzig: Evangelische Verlagsanstalt, 2004. Print.

Wacker, Grant. *America's Pastor: Billy Graham and the Shaping of a Nation*. Cambridge, MA: Harvard UP, 2014.

---. "Billy Graham's America." *Church History* 78.3 (2009): 489-511. Print.

Zilz, Walther. Zilz an Deitenbeck, 16 Mai 1954. Letter. Archive of the German Evangelical Alliance, Bad Blankenburg.

---. Zilz an die Mitglieder des Vorstandes de Deutschen Evangelischen Allianz, 9 Mai, 1955. Letter. Archive of the German Evangelical Alliance, Bad Blankenburg.

"Zwölf Ernten im Jahr." *Spiegel* 23 June 1954: 21-26. Print.

Opening a Market for Missions: American Evangelicals and the Re-Christianization of Europe, 1945-1985

HANS KRABBENDAM

ABSTRACT

In the mid-1940s the newly revitalized evangelicals in the United States fostered great plans to evangelize the world. They felt that their efforts were thwarted by two monopolistic arrangements. The first monopoly was the result of the official position of the more liberal World Council of Churches. Because this global organization had strong backing from the established churches in the United States and presented itself as the official spokesperson for global Protestantism, evangelicals felt locked out of prospective missionary opportunities in Europe and its colonies. In order to open these religious markets, the evangelical leadership launched an alternative organization, the World Evangelical Fellowship, and simultaneously embarked on a re-Christianization campaign. The second monopoly became visible once American missionaries landed in Europe. They encountered restrictions caused by nation states and established churches. Their efforts to overcome both obstacles moved through five stages. In the late 1940s, they defined Europe as a mission field. In the next decade they launched a great number of mission programs. This resulted in the formation of an alternative evangelical subculture in Europe in the 1960s, which diversified in the 1970s, and fragmented in the 1980s, with the new media revolution in TV and satellite. Halfway through this process, in the 1960s, evangelicals had found viable ways to displace monopolistic exclusion by religious pluralism. This not only led to the incorporation of Europe in global evangelicalism, but also opened opportunities for new and surprising joint ventures with competitors.

In 1946 a Dutch Reformed minister expressed his admiration for a new wave of American youth ministers who came to the Netherlands to stage a series of religious rallies: "The Youth for Christ team has done more in six weeks than our Dutch Reformed church has done in all of its history" (*Youth for Christ* 55). This reaction echoed the enthusiasm for a new type of ministry rather than being an evaluation of historical developments. This same sense of excitement was felt in North America. Two years later Oswald J. Smith, pastor of the Peoples Church in Toronto, returned from a six-week European trip and said, "Let us pray and let us work that Europe, one of the greatest of all mission fields, may be evangelized before it is forever too late" (21). Both ministers' statements illustrate the shift in the American-European religious balance that took place after World War II, but the second also expresses doubt about the possibility of realizing the plan to re-Christianize Europe.

The direction of religious influence from Europe to the United States had slowly begun to shift in the course of the nineteenth century. At the beginning of that century, the European ministers who accompanied or followed the millions of immigrants to America still greatly outnumbered the occasional American missionary traveling to Europe. American ministers in Europe were most commonly sent over to support Protestant denominational missions in Catholic or Eastern Orthodox countries. There were also those seeking to establish churches in the Holiness tradition. These activities had been small-scale until the last quarter of the century when evangelists such as Dwight Moody and holiness preachers such as Robert and Hannah Pearsall Smith had successfully awed European audiences. They were succeeded by evangelists such as Oswald Smith and Frank Buchman (of the Moral Rearmament Movement) in the early twentieth century.

After the Great War, mission-minded Americans flocked to Africa and Asia and surpassed the number of European missionaries. In 1911 almost 8,000 Americans were involved in Protestant missions beyond their own continent, compared to 12,000 Europeans. Only sixty years later, the numbers swelled to 34,000 Americans among 52,500 Protestant missionaries in the world, or almost two-thirds of the total number (Noll 80). After World War I the majority of Protestant missionaries came from North America and marked a quantitative shift among Western Protestants, but the post-World War II period also witnessed a second, qualitative shift. Europe's Protestant position changed from being an equal to a junior partner in the evangelical enterprise in the interwar years, and after World War II it became a sending—rather than a receiving—region.

After World War II the balance in finances and activism among Protestants in the West shifted from Europe to the United States. Millions of dollars in church relief flowed from prosperous America to war-torn Europe. Americans rebuilt churches, established care centers for refugees, and assisted families below the poverty line. The numbers of American Protestant missionaries in Europe grew from a few score in 1948 to more than 3,700 in 1985 (in addition to thousands of Mormons and Jehovah's Witnesses). These Protestants stayed much longer than other missionaries and were succeeded by fresh recruits (Beaver, "Distribution"; Wilson 1-3).

When historians mention the presence of American religion in postwar Europe, it is usually in the context of the Cold War (which itself was an instrument to combat Communism), or to assess the performance of American cults such as the Mormons or Jehovah's Witnesses in the Old World. Though Cold War concerns occupied the minds of religious leaders in the West, they were not the key motive for evangelical activity in Europe. Billy Graham's frequent anti-Communist statements might have led to this conclusion, but it was concern for a 'market,' rather than Communism that best explains American evangelists drive to go global (Kirby; Crouse; Preston; Herzog, 191-211).

This essay argues that concerns about monopolistic trends compelled American evangelicals to embark on missions in Europe as part of their program to secure missions worldwide. Though these evangelicals used theological concepts to describe their situation, their interpretation of the missionary market matched the economic concept of monopoly. In economics, a monopoly is a market situation in which a single company (or a few working in a cartel) renders all the services or products to the exclusion of competition by others. Often the anti-monopolist campaigners hope to break the existing monopoly and then replace it with their own (Postel 146-47). American evangelicals approached Europe in exactly this way. They feared they were being driven from the religious marketplace by liberal

Christians who had joined together nationally in the Federal (after 1950 known as National) Council of Churches and internationally in the World Council of Churches (WCC). This motive was especially strong among evangelicals in the first two decades after World War II.

While far from claiming that this anti-monopolistic impulse was the only interior motive for American evangelicals in taking the gospel to Europe, this essay argues that it does explain the timing and the format of this enterprise. One of the first aims of the new evangelical leadership was the prevention of a global liberal monopoly. A second major concern about monopolies arose once American evangelicals landed in European nations where either the state, the established church, or a combination of both restricted their activities. These two factors explain why American evangelicals invested their energy and meager finances in the creation of an organizational alternative to the WCC, and why they were reluctant to seek cooperation with established churches in Europe.

At the end of the 1960s, this fear of monopolistic exclusion subsided due to evangelicals' own quantitative expansion and the changing position of their opponents. This led to the European recognition of evangelicalism as a third force in Christendom—next to Roman Catholicism and mainstream Protestantism. This new situation changed evangelical strategy from opposition to cooperation, eventually resulting in cordial contacts with co-religionists in the twenty-first century.

To register these shifts, it is first necessary to examine American evangelicals' attitudes towards Europe with regard to practical matters, as Europe was the keeper of the keys to the colonies. Secondly, Europe was on a more theoretical level the prime example of what had gone wrong in history and how the abandonment of religion had facilitated this process. It is convenient to divide this narrative in five periods: the discovery of Europe as a mission field in the late 1940s; the launch of mission programs in the 1950s; the creation of an alternative force in the 1960s; diversification in the 1970s; and diffusion in the 1980s, when the arrival of televangelists and increasing media competition significantly changed communications and perceptions.[1]

The Discovery of Europe as a Mission Field in the 1940s

Evangelical missionaries came to Europe within a year after the end of World War II. In March 1946 a commercial aircraft brought six American evangelists to Preswick airport, close to Glasgow. From there, Billy Graham and five associates took the American postwar revival beyond American borders. As fear of monopoly was not yet one of their concerns, this international outreach had an improvised character. It was originally intended to reach men and women serving

---

[1] This paper will not deal with the differences between evangelicals and fundamentalists in their use of business methods in their missions, nor will it focus on prosperity gospel, Pentecostals and Charismatics, or include televangelists. These groups have received sufficient treatment, because they were most explicit in their messages and distinctive in their economic concerns. Neither will this article cover the activities of new religious movements from American soil, though these were certainly seen as serious competitors to fill Europe's spiritual vacuum.

in the military overseas, an extension of the religious revival of the period, which had been triggered by Youth for Christ. When the news of this burst of religious fervor spread in the media, Youth for Christ received invitations from believers worldwide to stir revivals in their areas, and civilian locations took priority. Theologically, a new sense of urgency inspired by the apocalyptic mood of global war made traditional believers hasten to take the gospel to the ends of the earth, to usher in the end times, and to add Europe as a target area (Shufelt).

The novelty of Graham's first campaign inaugurated an enduring American interest and investment in Europe, different from the occasional visit by American revivalists before the war. Thanks to monthly updates in the Youth for Christ magazines, news of the international revival's scope reached evangelicals at home. This was in line with the Protestant missionary goal, in John R. Mott's terminology, "to evangelize the world in this generation" (Mott). Depression and war stalled this endeavor, but victory and prosperity revived it.

The Youth for Christ revival of the 1940s resonated with the experiences of evangelical chaplains and missionary-minded service men who had witnessed the devastation of Europe first hand. They had concluded that this disaster was spiritual in origin and Europe needed their help to solve its problems (Carpenter 178-84). One of them, Samuel Faircloth, was a 1943 graduate from Wheaton College and a classmate of Billy and Ruth Graham. He took a degree from Eastern Baptist Theological Seminary in Philadelphia and enlisted as a chaplain serving the U.S. Fifth Army in Italy as a member of the Conservative Baptist Foreign Mission Society (CBFMS). This group deemed the American Baptist Convention too liberal because it accepted missionary work candidates who denied some cardinal doctrines of the Christian faith, such as the reliability of the scriptures, the necessity of atonement, and the bodily return of Christ. Since the Northern Baptist denomination did not allow the organization of a separate mission society, the CBFMS split off.

Faircloth was of the opinion that the destruction of Europe and the cruelty of its dictators was a result of secular humanism, which had started "from the inside" in Germany well before the war. He saw the Nazi terror as a logical consequence of decades of anti-Christian philosophy and the tradition of higher criticism of the Bible in German universities. This tradition had disarmed the countervailing powers of the German clergy, and left their flocks unprotected against Nazism. Other American soldiers shared his historical interpretation. After their demobilization, these evangelicals laid plans to return to the continent with gospel tracts instead of bombs. Faircloth and other U.S. chaplains helped Protestant ministers reunite with their scattered congregations in southern Europe. Faircloth became a missionary in Portugal in 1949, and would stay there until 1985 (Faircloth, Interview).[2] From his isolated position, he sought contact with the World Council

---

[2] After serving as a missionary to Portugal between 1949 and 1985, Samuel Faircloth became academic dean and Vice President for Academic Affairs of the evangelical Tyndale Theological Seminary in Badhoevedorp, Netherlands, from 1985 through 1990. See also Smith 19: "As I see it, it all started with higher criticism. Modernism came from Germany and when the Bible went, morals went. It is always so. Then comes judgment, and that has been the history of

of Churches. Upon his meeting with WCC secretary Willem A. Visser 't Hooft, however, he concluded that the unity the WCC attempted to achieve was driven too much by organizational doctrine that was "fabricated" and not "a sovereign work of the Holy Spirit" (Interview).[3]

Growing out of the postwar revival and the first-hand experience of soldiers, these activities were given greater organizational structure through the National Association of Evangelicals (NAE). This organization of traditional Christians in America had little confidence in the mainline American Protestant denominations that they saw as embodying a growing liberalism, the same liberalism they considered to be the cause of the war. The global ambition of the World Council especially filled the evangelicals with concern.

James DeForest Murch, the editor of *United Evangelical Action*, house organ of the NAE, warned American Protestants that the WCC would very likely develop into a super-church. He envisioned "one church for one world" as the goal of the new global organization and drew a parallel to the monopoly of the Roman Catholic Church in the middle ages. Murch saw too many ominous mechanisms at work in the WCC to be at ease. The potential result of one super-church would be to allow all kinds of theological aberrations and leftist social policies and would disrupt effective evangelism and missions. Murch found a monopolistic agenda in the WCC—an agenda that would threaten to oust those who brought the traditional evangelical message ("Amsterdam" 46).

Despite the fact that the WCC denied the charges of being a super-church and emphasized that it was only a council, the goal of global unity made many evangelicals uncomfortable and alert. Some gave the WCC the benefit of the doubt and hoped that its evangelical contingent in the established churches would move the organization in their direction. Still, most remained suspicious.[4] The German-American industrialist and evangelical philanthropist John Bolten even used the biblical parable of the mustard seed as a metaphor for the power of the Kingdom of God and the WCC to warn of the threat of the overgrown tree of apostate Christendom in which nations might take refuge. This unusual interpretation led him to believe that the "Monster Church" would "drive us soon underground and kill us."[5] While not all evangelicals endorsed this aggressive image of the WCC, many shared Bolten's concern about the risk of being marginalized. Urged by his call to mobilize and organize evangelical Christians globally against the WCC threat, the officers of the NAE set out to expand internationally. To strengthen their own position, they sought conservative and free churches with whom they could design an alternative organization.

Germany." Germans feel theologically superior, the only hope is with the next generation. For evangelical commitment to the armed forces, see Loveland 1-33.

[3] CBFMS missionaries also had contact with the ICCC, but affiliated with EFMA.

[4] Murch warned against exclusion of evangelicals by liberals and condemned the criticism of capitalism.

[5] Bolten was treasurer of the World Evangelical Fellowship from 1951-61. Almost all commentators apply this parable in Matthew 13: 31-32 to the potential of the Kingdom of God, not of God's enemy.

Ambitions and fears culminated in 1948. Amsterdam hosted the formal launch of the World Council of Churches and a number of American evangelical organizations crossed the Atlantic to find partners in Europe, specifically in the strategic Netherlands and prosperous Switzerland. NAE representatives met in Beatenberg, Switzerland, where they tried to launch an international evangelical network, while Youth for Christ organized its first international meeting in St. Clarens, also in Switzerland. Members of the American Council of Christian Churches (ACCC)—the stalwart fundamentalists who regarded the World Council of Churches as the Antichrist, the opponent of the church in the end times—also met. They challenged the WCC directly by organizing a conference at the doorstep of the WCC's founding assembly in Amsterdam. Most evangelicals shared many of the ACCC's arguments against the WCC, but disagreed with its separatist strategy, seeing it as a force to divide rather than unify evangelicals. The ACCC actively sought international partners for its mission and tried to present the NAE as a weak, predominantly Pentecostal group, while promoting itself as a powerful organization (Wright, Letter to Kok). However, the ACCC's head-on confrontation with the monopolistic threat failed because its separatist strategy kept it at the margins. These concerns about a monopolistic threat thus encouraged competition rather than unity between the two clusters in the creation of new European religious network (Zeilstra 207-74).

Most American evangelicals did not seek the destruction of the WCC, but wanted to stay connected to it without getting officially involved. Billy Graham, for instance, was a frequent visitor to the WCC assemblies and kept an open dialogue with them. Still, the leaders of the NAE rejected the formal institution of the Council, its binding concepts, its concentration of power, and its exclusion of groups who were not represented in national church bodies. They feared they would be locked out of the international market since the WCC presented itself as the official liaison between national governments and religious organizations. Instead, they preferred a loose organization structured like the NAE. Their solution was not only an alternative to the alleged monopolistic agenda of the World Council, but also an organization that offered shelter to para-church organizations that did not fit into the denominational structure.

Historian Michael S. Hamilton notes the importance of this alternative model of organization. He argues that the strength of a denomination, and also a council of denominations such as the National Council of Churches and WCC, is centralized power, which grants privileges to members and exclusion to non-members, similar to the operation of the United Nations. The para-church organizations might have entered the World Council as a kind of NGO, but that solution was not as yet in sight and still would not have made them full members. So these fell outside of the official organization. Consequently, they set up their own umbrella organizations that included denominations.

A second incentive for the NAE to expand internationally was their bond with two missionary councils: the Interdenominational Foreign Mission Association (IFMA), the 25 year-old association of mission agencies supported by various churches; and the newly founded Evangelical Foreign Missions Association (EFMA), which welcomed both ecclesiastical and para-church organizations.

Without formally delegated power, these associations operated like corporations. Paradoxically, the theological pluralists of the WCC were organizational centralizers and in that respect exclusive, while the theological traditionalists were exclusive in doctrine but organizationally pluralist. Internationally, evangelicals had to create an alternative network as well. Clyde Taylor, the NAE representative in Washington, D.C., traveled to Britain to secure EFMA access for mission work in the British colonies in Africa from the British government. He received this approval thanks to his contacts within the established missionary board, but he strove for direct access to the colonies. Taylor found the existing British organization, such as the century-old Evangelical Alliance, ineffective because it only organized annual prayer meetings with non-evangelicals. He expected that the organization would soon be overrun by the WCC.

The NAE felt squeezed in between the powerful WCC and the divisive International Council of Christian Churches (the international extension of the ACCC). In his search for partners in Holland, Taylor encountered competition from both sides. Denominations affiliated with the WCC held many trump cards. Taylor found out, for instance, that the largest Protestant church in the Netherlands had as its contact person for the World Church Service (the international organization for humanitarian aid) the same person who was the liaison to the government. This individual had the authority to issue permits for rebuilding, transfering money abroad, and importing tracts free of charge. Meanwhile, the ICCC actively solicited support among the smaller protestant churches in Europe, but had to overcome considerable antipathy for its explicit Americanism. National boards of evangelical organizations in Europe were cautious and did not immediately jump on the NAE bandwagon. American evangelicals had to first persuade their European partners that they were not monopolistic themselves. They had to tone down their American features, such as their adamant activism and proud patriotism (Taylor, "Confidential" 3).[6]

Consequently, the NAE-organizers emphasized the informal character of the first meeting in Clarens and prepared the sessions in close consultation with European partners who would meet as equals and remain autonomous. Financed by travel allowances, more than one hundred delegates from fourteen countries met in accommodations of St. George's School, a Church of England boarding school at Lake Geneva. Essentially, the strategy was to pretend there was no strategy. The Europeans accepted the NAE-declaration of faith, agreed to open up their own national associations to churches, societies, and individuals, and promised financial aid to those countries with organized evangelicals. *United Evangelical Action* would serve as the medium for publishing news about Europe. However, some British evangelicals did not support the founding of an International Coordinating Committee to form an International Association of Evangelicals (Wright, "Minutes" 1). The British leadership of the World's Evangelical Alliance, founded in 1846, was not persuaded by the current call for cooperation, since it had already been functioning for a century. It was also more optimistic than the Americans about the World Council of Churches and advised the evangelicals not to aban-

---

[6] Americans dominated the ICCC, which scared a number of European groups away.

don the WCC and leave it in the hands of the 'Modernists,' which could result in a pact with Rome. Traditionally, the World's Evangelical Alliance agreed on a more inclusive foundation than the NAE. The Americans were not satisfied with this slow vehicle, though they tried to accommodate it as much as possible (Randall, "American").

The American delegation traveled to Italy, returned to Switzerland for the European Youth for Christ conference at Beatenburg (an evangelical Bible school founded in 1934 that hosted a number of international conferences on world evangelization), and subsequently visited other evangelical assemblies in Europe. The delegation linked up with others such as the International Fellowship of Evangelical Students (IFES) and Youth for Christ. While the American delegation noticed a variety of approaches—the IFES was more European and was student-led, while YFC had a large American contingent and was adult-led—both groups practiced what the evangelical leaders called "storming the gates of the enemy in Europe" ("Youth for Christ World Conference"; Wright, "Minutes" 7). Elwin Wright, the NAE secretary for international cooperation, traveled to meet German evangelicals and led the delegation at the founding conference of the WCC in Amsterdam.

NAE executive secretary Rutherford L. Decker, pastor of the Baptist Temple in Kansas City and a future (1960) presidential candidate for the Prohibition Party, concluded, "I came away from Europe more profoundly convinced that united evangelical action is the need of the hour all over the world" ("Confidential Resume" 9). To this mission of positive action, the WCC and the ICCC presented organizational obstacles. Decker observed that Protestant Europe was divided between historically established churches that were unfamiliar with evangelism, and small missionary-minded free churches that depended on strong personalities and distrusted others. He saw a movement towards cooperation as the churches felt the pressures of the aftermath of the war and its resulting poverty and the threat of communism, yet he saw that they lacked a plan and the means. Americans, however, could provide both. Decker recommended making the existing activities more efficient before launching new initiatives. In practical terms, this meant that evangelicals would concentrate on translating and distributing evangelical literature and tracts while closely cooperating with the World's Evangelical Alliance.

Political and economic tensions due to the Berlin Blockade and the formation of NATO postponed the follow-up meeting for a time. But 1950 ushered the sense that times were urgent, as reflected by the United States and European venues of the conferences. "We are rapidly approaching the time when it may become more difficult for evangelicals to continue their worldwide propagation of the gospel," Wright contended, "unless they are able to join their hands effectively in defense of their Christian liberties" ("Movement"). Decker cited the political power of the WCC along with the Communist and Catholic threats. The 'Evangelical International's' main task was to protect freedom of religion. The Americans, however, believed that the Europeans acted too slowly (Taylor, "Implementing" 27).

Several European countries with small evangelical minorities responded positively to this American courting. The majority of denominations in the Netherlands, a country more pluralistic than most, joined the WCC. A few smaller denominations stayed aloof and considered the NAE proposal a safe middle ground. The NAE appeared confessionally reliable and action driven because it welcomed associations as well as churches. Twenty-one people from eight different denominations founded the Netherlands Evangelical Alliance in 1949 (Dresselhuis and Oussoren; Murch, Letter; Wright, Letter to G. E. Hoek March, and Letter to G. E. Hoek November).[7] The Dutch were happy to host the next conference in Woudschoten in August 1951, which led to the foundation of the World Evangelical Fellowship. This should have tied the movement closer to Europe, but only evangelicals in Spain and Britain showed real commitment to the project. The other continental European representatives found the infallibility clause in the WEF constitution too legalistic and restrictive. These skeptics met a year later in Siegen, Germany, and decided to stay in contact though not seek full cooperation since they found the Americans too aggressive in their rejection of everyone who did not adhere to their understanding of the inspired status of the Bible, too separate from their church communities, and too self-assured in their presentation. They did not want to submit themselves to an American litmus test of reliability. In September 1952, they founded the European Evangelical Alliance in Hamburg, which would remain a separate organization until 1968. The British did not want to choose between their American and European friends and decided to join both organizations.[8]

The American push to create a network of national evangelical associations in Europe to support American missions worked as an alternative to the centralized WCC and was expected to bolster failing local churches. They furnished Europeans with a working American "business plan" that they could emulate. In October 1949, J. Elwin Wright wrote home triumphantly about the Dutch efforts at coordination: "They are proceeding with care and great expectations to develop a very worthwhile organization here. In every respect they are following our pattern" (Wright, Letter to home). Thus, the first period found the NAE operating between two competitors, both of which claimed to offer the best model for global religious cooperation. Though the NAE rejected both models, they also found common ground with their opponents. They rejected the liberalism and exclusivist monopoly-character of the WCC, but appreciated its organizational force. While they approved of the search for doctrinal cohesion that the ICCC promised (though applied too strictly), they rejected its lack of cooperation. Because they felt an urgent need for action, the evangelicals focused as much of their forces as they could on their tradition and maintained a flexible structure. It seemed the best strategy to counter the threat of an ecumenical dominance.

---

[7] Interestingly, it was the Evangelical Broadcasting Association, EO, that took on this central role in the late 1960s.

[8] For the battle for the Bible, see Hankins 136-59; Howard; Hinkelmann 4-6; and Kessler 97. The EEA joined the WEF in 1968. The Dutch became observers of the Alliance.

American Evangelical Pioneers in Europe in the 1950s

American evangelicals' antithetical rhetoric and alternative organization should not obscure the fact that they ran on a number of parallel tracks with ecumenicals. Both sent relief, assisted refugees, protested against discrimination of Protestants in Southern Europe, and were united in their rejection of the state church as an organizing principle. Yet their relative power was very uneven. The ecumenical organizations had official connections with the major European denominations. The evangelicals had a few contacts with individual pastors and evangelists, mostly from free-church denominations and para-church organizations. However, their small size and limited means were compensated for by evangelist Billy Graham. The media attention Graham received showed that it was possible to get things done, even internationally, without the formal structure of the WCC; and his rising visibility lifted him above the walls that separated kindred souls in European churches, providing a spiritual fellowship and organizational continuity.

In the 1950s Graham became a brand name for evangelicalism after he established his ministry in America and had run successful rallies in Los Angeles. His crusades in 1954 and 1955 acquainted the citizens in London, Amsterdam, Berlin, Copenhagen, Paris, Geneva, Oslo and a score of other cities with his American-style outreach. The Greater London campaign, held in the Harringay Arena in March and April 1954, drew hundreds of spectators from all over Europe, many of whom were convinced that something similar could be arranged in their own countries. These campaigns activated European evangelical Christians to reach out, not only to the unchurched, but also to each other (Randall, "Conservative").

Graham's campaign drew headlines in the press, but when he left Europe, the fieldwork had to be done by others. Youth for Christ had been building a string of national independent boards all over Europe and functioned in the network that had grown up around the 1948 meetings in Switzerland and the Netherlands. These bridgeheads in all European countries linked up with a number of other American missionary organizations.

In 1952 missionary reports began to include Europe as a separate category for the first time. The 250 American missionaries in Europe comprised only one percent of the total American missionary enterprise. Some of them were fraternal workers sent by American denominations, mostly Presbyterians and Baptists, to assist sister churches in Europe, but most were members of mission organizations. The largest concentration of these new missions were found in Italy, Belgium, France, Portugal, Spain, and Austria, with minor ones in Britain, Holland, and Norway (Beaver "Distribution," "Expansion"). American mission agencies soon divided labor between northern and southern Europe. The ministries of American evangelicals in northern European countries targeted youth and mobilized Christians for evangelism, while in the south they distributed literature and tried to start new churches.[9]

---

[9] For the seven main activities—church planting, personal evangelism, mass evangelism, literature distribution, broadcasting, theological education, support of national churches—see Wagner 41-50.

Experiences in evangelical missions in Portugal and France illustrate how evangelicals entered a new market. In the summer of 1949, the Faircloth family (Sam, his wife Arlie, and baby daughter Becky) left for Portugal with fifty-three pieces of luggage, including three church organs, three bicycles, and four large boxes of second-hand clothing (Faircloth, Field Letter, 1 June 1949). The tiny Portuguese Baptist Convention had asked the Americans to open a seminary to educate nationals as pastors for their churches. Portugal, then ruled by dictator Antonio Salazar, was the poorest country in western Europe. Foreigners were followed constantly by secret police trained by the Nazi Gestapo and struggled to obtain and retain their visas.

Faircloth counted 5,000 born-again Portuguese in a population of seven million. He found willing audiences but few able preachers and therefore founded the Baptist Theological Seminary of Leiria in 1950. This institution graduated over sixty percent of the Baptist ministers during the years 1950-65, when it was replaced by another seminary supported by the Southern Baptist Foreign Mission Society. Faircloth reported a monthly score of ten to thirty converts in various parts of Portugal, as he cruised the country in a "mechanical missionary" (a Dodge vehicle). A growing number of people attended services in early 1950, which provoked angry responses from Catholics and Communists. But thanks to international evangelical cooperation, the young mission was able to organize a twenty-day Youth for Christ rally in the summer of 1950 (Field Letters, 1949-50). At the beginning of Faircloth's second term five years later, the seminary had grown from three to twenty-seven students, the first Portuguese ministers had been ordained, and new churches were in the planning stages. Support from America helped to buy a new car, lawn mowers, tool chests, and photographic supplies for publicity purposes. American diplomatic pressure helped Faircloth overcome visa restrictions. In late 1956, the church body counted thirty-one churches in addition to twenty-five missionary posts, with 2,215 regular attendees at its services. Twenty-one ordained pastors, fifty-eight preaching laymen, and twelve women workers were involved in leadership, but they were still a long way from their target of one hundred churches (Field Letters, 1955-1956).

These and similar initiatives caused Europe to appear on the radar of the broader evangelical constituency in the early 1950s. In 1951 the Belgian Gospel Mission joined the Interdenominational Foreign Mission Association. The *IFMA News Bulletin* published in December that year listed Europe as a separate category for the first time, announcing that The Evangelical Alliance Mission (TEAM) had sent four missionaries to France, Wycliffe Bible Translators planned to set up a Linguistic Institute in Britain, and Genoa, Italy, had hosted a conference for thirty-five missionaries.

In the *Bulletin* the reputation of Europe grew darker every year: "One cannot help but think of Communism as almost synonymous with Europe, as this Godless religion seems to grip more and more of the peoples of Europe in an ironclad grasp." Evangelical reports from Spain in July 1954 confirmed that the Catholic hierarchy feared Protestants more than Communists. The mid-1950s appeared to be the darkest hour. Yet the Italian legal decision to grant legitimacy to the Assemblies of God raised positive expectations for other Protestant groups (*IFMA News*).

The newly designed *IFMA News* brought more positive news in 1957 about radio stations available for purchase, newly founded literature organizations, and new elections that would increase civil liberties. In April 1959, *IFMA News* rejoiced: "The Summit Meeting in May, the solidarity of NATO, and other political issues, and the increasing economic stability all add up to important and strategic days that could mean much for the future of Europe. It is a day of opportunity for the gospel."

The entry into the new market was strongest in the countries that were culturally farthest removed from the United States: Catholic-dominated, dictator-led, Communist-threatened, and often poor. This was one aspect of presenting Europe to evangelicals at home. The other growing awareness was that Europe lacked religious zeal and, even worse, prevented the spreading of the gospel. This discovery pointed to specific needs for which candidates were recruited.

Competition and Growth to Maturity in the 1960s

While the Faircloths stand as an example of denominational missions that sought to establish a presence in Europe, Robert P. Evans (1918-2011) was a vital link in the evangelical network in Europe. The son of Baptist missionaries in French-speaking Africa, Evans shared a number of entries on Faircloth's vita. He was a graduate of Wheaton College and the Eastern Baptist Theological Seminary in Philadelphia, and he served as a Chaplain in the United States Navy and Marine Corps between 1943-46. These experiences positioned Evans to be a perfect executive secretary for Youth for Christ, the organization that engaged him in setting up activities all over Europe. In 1949 he founded the European Bible Institute in Paris and remained the key evangelical contact in Europe as coordinator of the Greater Europe Mission (GEM) that grew out of this operation in 1952. Four years later, the GEM had fifty-one workers, mostly in France and Germany, who were mainly involved in teaching evangelical theology and evangelism (Evans, Newsletter; Letter). In a later reflection on Graham's first appearances in Germany in the early 1950s, Evans noted that the Lutheran leadership resisted the evangelism campaign because it broke the monopoly of the Lutheran Church in bringing the next generation to faith. The promotion of an evangelical alternative was one of Evans's objectives, and he recruited hundreds of Americans and trained hundreds of Europeans to participate in this endeavor (Evans, Interview).

Evans offered the most complete argument for Europe as a mission field. His 1962 book *Let Europe Hear* sought to correct the American perception that Europe was still a Christian continent. Evans argued it was in fact over-civilized, pagan, and de-Christianized. Each country had its specific cultural problem which explained its resistance to traditional Christianity: France was materialistic and therefore indulgent; Germany sought its salvation in cults and seemed bewitched; Denmark and most of Scandinavia had lost hope in the future; and nations with strong Christian traditions such as Holland had become ossified. No change for the better was in sight since the next generation seemed to have lost all interest in Christianity and the existing churches remained passive. Evans attributed this situation to the Protestant Reformation that, he said, failed to bring the full gospel when it tied churches to territories. Christianity had lost authority through internal quarrels, was corrupted by nationalism, limited in scope, and most of all, had become too rational. The Reformation's legacy had led to intellectual change, but not a change of heart (47-89).[10]

Europe's freedom was at stake because of threats from Romanism, Communism, traditional Protestantism, secular existentialism, and militant cults. The first three threats were matters of monopoly, the second two were direct competitors for the minds and hearts of Europeans. In terms of foreign investment strategies, evangelicals had to choose 'greenfield operations,' in other words, launching new businesses. A 'take-over' was not possible, and a 'joint venture' was undesirable because it would only sustain the monopoly.[11]

Evans and others succeeded in attracting thousands of Americans to religious work in Europe. His Greater Europe Mission was the largest missionary enterprise in Europe with one hundred workers, thanks to its three Bible schools in France, Italy, and Germany. In 1964 the home office in Wheaton circulated more than one hundred thousand missionary prayer letters and sent out 30,000 quarterly newsletters. In the same year an aggregate of 120 evangelical organizations in Europe offered a great variety of programs focused on distributing Bibles and literature, reaching children and youth, trying to establish evangelical churches, and educating evangelists (Frank, "Director's Report" 7; *North American* 66).

In February 1961, *IFMA News* began to impress upon its readers that Europe as a mission field was the "Ignored Continent." A spokesperson for evangelicals in Europe called for ten thousand missionaries in the next decade. The subsequent issues laid bare the drama of the European church. Bob Evans pointed to the invasion of new religious movements that had invested millions of dollars in sending thousands of missionaries into Europe. In comparison with the Mormons, who had 3,500 missionaries working in Europe, evangelicals lagged far behind. Thus the concern shifted from fighting an alleged monopoly to confronting new competition in which the historic European church, with less than three per cent of the population attending church services, was part of the problem, not the solution. Negative ideas about Europe accumulated without differentiating the particular situation in each nation. James H. Kane, mission instructor at Barrington College, Rhode Island and Lancaster Bible College, reported in 1963 that all Christian visitors to Europe after World War II came home shaking their heads: "Europe is the neediest of all mission fields today" ("Where are we").[12]

It was one thing to reject the monopoly of the WCC and to enter new territories and flood them with gospel literature. But it was another thing altogether to replace or change the traditional churches. To accomplish a change of mentality in

---

[10] For a secular view of Europe at that time, see Calleo.

[11] Similar arguments were repeated in numerous contributions Evans made to evangelical publications. See "Can Europeans" 17, 26-27.

[12] A few years later, Kane lamented the decline in mission interest, which was noticeable in the drop of students in Missions in American Christian Colleges and Bible schools. He attributed this to increased competition from the Peace Corps and the growing popularity of short-term missionary trips ("Major Concerns").

Europe the agencies had to recruit more missionaries, raise more funds, and better cooperate with other missionary partners. This effort was made in the 1960s when the evangelical movement gained strength. In this decade the number of missionaries in Europe increased from 250 to 1,500, which was about five per cent of all missionaries active in American Protestant agencies. Even though budgets increased ten-fold during this decade, in absolute numbers American evangelicals spent only a few million dollars in Europe annually. Despite this growth, re-Christianization of the old continent was a far cry from what the missionaries envisioned. Most of these American missionaries continued to work in isolation with a handful of small congregations (Dayton).[13]

In the 1960s the various evangelical agencies adopted each other's specialties when sending a new mission group into the field. For instance, Portuguese Baptists trained for mass evangelism at the Billy Graham campaigns in London, and a Youth for Christ music team came to play at Portuguese outreach meetings. This combination of national growth and international support stimulated the missionaries in Portugal to prepare for a national campaign. In France the Conservative Baptist missionaries hosted cooperative campaigns with Operation Mobilization, the youth camp of Young Life, and with students from the Greater Europe Mission's Bible School in Lamorlaye, Paris ("Missions Situation Europe").

As the fear of being cut off from the market proved unwarranted, the American evangelicals had to reconsider their relationship to the ecumenical network. After all, Billy Graham's campaigns met considerable support from traditional Protestants and various evangelical mission agencies established themselves in many countries. The greatest difference between these adversaries was their relationship to the main European churches. To the ecumenical organizations, churches in Europe were partners; to the evangelicals, European churches were obstacles. The 1960s was a period of evangelical positioning, both in Europe and in the United States. Youth for Christ moved between established churches and independent groups. European staff discussed the relationship with the churches and concluded a bit self-assuredly, "Brethren with whom we find it difficult to agree may be longing for what we have to give them—namely, our testimony to the saving and keeping power of the Lord Jesus Christ. But we must have a humble spirit in our approaches to them" ("Report of European Youth for Christ"). Moreover, they thought that they could compensate for a reception in a 'cold' church on Sunday with 'warm' fellowship during the week. In the meantime they tried to involve ministers from mostly free churches in their follow-up training of new converts.

---

[13] Only fragmental financial documentation about the budgets is available. The Greater Europe Mission's budget grew from $134,444.84 in 1954 to $504,810.50 in 1964 to $828,567.25 in 1968 to $1,964,003.69 in 1973. ("Auditor's Reports Greater Europe Mission"). The EEC had a 1969 budget of $220,047.52 ("Auditor's Reports European Evangelical Crusade"). The Evangelical Alliance Mission spent about $120,000 of its $3 million budget on Europe in 1964, and in 1973, spent $500,000 of its $6 million budget in Europe ("Evangelical Alliance Mission Finances"). The Worldwide European Fellowship, Inc. spent $67,535.56 on missionaries in the fiscal year 1963-1964 and $98,275.35 in 1966 ("Worldwide European Fellowship Finances").

Evangelicals began to realize they could live neither with, nor without, the mainstream churches in the United States and Europe. As long as they were the underdog they could be critical, but now that they had built a strong base, they could add partnership to their strategies. A sense of a new evangelical self-worth was noticeable in the draft declaration written for the conclusion of the 1966 Congress on the Church's Worldwide Mission, in Wheaton, Illinois. It boldly stated that evangelicals were responsible for two-thirds of the Protestant missionaries in North America and Europe, even as it self-consciously rejected isolation, inefficiency, over-organization, and neglect of social evils ("Tentative Preliminary Draft," "The Wheaton Declaration").[14] This statement expressed an awareness of the force of renewal within the Catholic church (without abandoning its caution since the changes could be cosmetic) while at the same time being alert to competition by cults and non-Christian religions. Though the draft still sternly warned against liberal Protestantism, which "ha[d] created an ecclesiastical organization aimed at achieving a religious monopoly," the final statement changed the wording into "moving in the direction of a worldwide religious monopoly." This small nuance revealed a change in the evangelical perception away from the WCC as a principled monopoly that needed to be attacked, to a perception of the WCC as a practical monopoly that evoked a practical response.

Representatives from the WCC observed both the strength and the ambition of the international evangelical network and were shocked by the hostility that they encountered at the 1966 Wheaton conference. Evangelical leaders took up the WCC's invitation to meet on an informal, personal basis to present positions to each other. The result was channels of communication remained open and common ground was found (Taylor, Letter to Pitts; Shuster, Interview).[15]

The 1966 Wheaton Conference had been Graham's idea since the early 1960s, but it had taken the evangelical leadership more time to agree on the proper people to invite. Graham changed his course by adding to his activities the training of evangelists at major international conferences. The result of this combination was recognized at the European counterpart to Wheaton held in Berlin in 1966, two decades after Graham's first arrival in Europe. For the first time, European journalists discovered 'evangelicals' as a coherent religious group with a unique selling point. Thanks to direct contacts and the educational projects—and soon-to-be mass media events—Europeans would get to know the American evangelicals better than the mainstream American churches. But the evangelicals had even higher ambitions.

---

[14] The approved text said "that create ecclesiastical organizations moving in the direction of a worldwide religious monopoly." For an example of visa problems in India caused by the agency not belonging to the NCC in India, see Taylor, Letter to Kirby.

[15] The partners included Horace Fenton, John Howard Yoder, Lesslie Newbigin, and Eugene Smith, but the evangelicals gave up when the WCC assembly in Uppsala approved violence for liberation purposes. Eugene Smith was appreciated by Taylor, but considered naive and not critical enough (Taylor Letter to Kirby 1964). Kirby had an article about evangelical cooperation but Taylor kept it private in order not to give its enemies an argument (Taylor to Kirby 1962).

The newest technological innovations, such as direct TV connections between European cities, were tested during Billy Graham's Earls Court Crusade in London, 1967. New media connections seemed to multiply Graham's presence everywhere and offered an alternative to addressing large audiences in person. American evangelicals' sense of urgency led to an efficient organization, which targeted diversified audiences in Europe.

The End of Monopoly Thinking: Diversification and Cooperation in the 1970s

After the first generation of American evangelical missionaries in Europe collected sufficient converts to launch new congregations, some coordinators of the mission agencies reviewed their stance toward the existing churches in Europe. They realized that a foreign-based mission would alienate Europeans from their natural environment. To avoid this isolation, they began to explore collaborations with European churches. These contacts would remove the stigma of being an American proselytizer. Furthermore, they would provide legal protection, leave converts less isolated, and open up two-way communication with European churches. This process could increase religious unity and make European churches share the responsibility for missions, which, in turn, would provide more continuity for young believers. Edwin E. Jacques, the overseas secretary of the Conservative Baptist Foreign Mission Society, summarized the findings of a summit of evangelical mission leaders in 1972, and concluded that staying culturally separate would harm, not help, the missionary cause (Jacques).

Yet even with this strategic turn away from isolation, it was difficult to find a European church that shared the basic ideas of American evangelicals. A survey of key issues confirmed the existence of a transatlantic divide, extending even among the free churches in Europe that had no government support. Many free churches rejected the American concept of the "word-by-word dictation" of the Bible and most orthodox Protestants in Europe strongly adhered to "baptismal regeneration" without an explicit conversion experience (Jacques 3).

Jacques concluded that finding European partners was an almost impossible task. The goal of collaboration was hindered by the low prestige of American missions, which they ranked well below the majority churches—whether Catholic or Protestant—and the free churches. So even an affiliation with the latter could not improve their acceptability. Moreover, these free churches displayed a great variety within their own affiliations: some had joined the WCC in order to survive; others resolutely rejected these ties, following American separatist sentiments. Even if European partners could be found, identification with them led to alienation from their American constituency, as relaxed use of alcohol and tobacco in Europe, for example, went against evangelical taboos (Jacques 4).

Self-critically, the report suggested that the main obstacle was American impatience with the survival strategy of European churches. What Americans considered a lack of spirit and vitality, Europeans felt as a respectable effort to survive centuries of pressure. The report saw few options for cooperation. European church bodies that allowed theological and political differences or were affiliated with non-evangelical organizations did not qualify as potential partners. Only after the essential issues had been cleared, could flexibility be granted. Yet even then the pace of affiliation was slow, requiring much time to build trust. Too often European pastors felt attacked by American missionaries and their claims of quick success. If a partner denomination could be found, the missionary needed to cooperate with the existing bodies of that church and identify responsibilities and tasks. This report revealed that evangelical missions to Europe had entered a new phase of reflection and calibration.

Not all American agencies were ready to embrace this new policy. The older mission groups organized in the IFMA, which was more conservative than the EFMA, held on to their strategy to keep converts away from the existing churches. They advised only affiliation with small free evangelical groups. Walter Frank of the GEM justified the separate churches in traditionally "Christian countries" in Europe. These churches were weak and in an "apostatized anemic condition" and needed American reinforcements, both spiritually and organizationally. He considered the risk of membership in the existing, (partly) state-supported churches too high, because believers would be absorbed without a trace and not allowed to belong and create "a N.T. self-supporting, self-governing and self-propagating church" (Frank, "IFMA Missions" 4).

When the GEM looked back on twenty-five years of service in 1974, its founder, Robert Evans, noted that missions in Europe were too relaxed and seemed satisfied with the 2,000 students that the GEM had trained ("As I see it"). His executive director, Don Brugman, responded in 1977 to voices calling for foreign missionaries to go home, reflecting that many functions had been handed over to Europeans, but "Europe is still at the pioneer stage of missions compared with many parts of the world. The need for missionaries is more critical than ever" (7). Two years later, in 1979, Wayne Detzler, GEM's associate director for Northern Europe, witnessed a new generation of European evangelical leaders and wrote more responses to the GEM's activities (1). Even so, Evans wanted to keep his workers from fully integrating in European churches: "we do not believe that the foreign missionary's role is best played when he independently joins the national church structure itself. He then is in the same position as a national pastor or Christian worker. He loses the very uniqueness inherent in the nature of the missionary task." In actuality, he saw that a true believer inevitably would have to leave his or her church because he or she was "trapped in a less than adequate group where he cannot grow." Moreover, the foreign missionary who joined a national church (even a non-liberal one) would lose his advantage, as "a different viewpoint, an optimistic outlook born of experience in a more active evangelical environment [read: America], mobility, knowledge of worldwide methods, the prayerful backing of expectant donors, biblical oversight and accountability, and many others" (Evans, "Our responsiblity" 3). He pleaded for a separation of roles; the foreign missionary must keep his or her distance, even to the free churches in Europe.

Billy Graham did not intend to establish new churches. However, a growing disappointment with European churches, which failed to take the gospel outside their sanctuaries, moved him to take matters into his own hands. While the number of evangelical American missionaries swelled worldwide, Graham prepared an even larger effort through a series of large international training conferences. He organized the first one in Amsterdam in 1971, where he told 1,200 Europeans that evangelism was not a project of a church, but rather, as the current Jesus Revolution in California showed, an attitude of each believer (Press conference).

This sentiment was echoed by a Dutch evangelist, Jan van Capelleveen, who characterized the situation of Western Europe in the 1970s as "The Church is out; the Bible is in" (151). He alluded to the unpopularity of institutionalized religion and the vitality of grass-roots religious activities. As evidence for his claim, Capelleveen contrasted the decline of the number of clergy to the growth of informal Bible study groups. The choice to invest more in individual outreach to others ignored the older religious institutions in Europe and was one way out of the dilemma over existing churches.

The growth of the evangelical presence in Europe allowed evangelicals to present themselves not only as antipodes to the WCC, but also as partners (Baker, Travelog 5). The big 1974 mission conference in Lausanne, Switzerland marked the maturity of a global evangelical network. Evangelicals succeeded in establishing an international podium and made themselves visible as a third force to be reckoned with in Christendom alongside the Roman Catholic Church and the World Council of Churches. The Lausanne conference broadened the social and political scope of the evangelicals, set the stage for indigenization, and opened American evangelicalism to global influences. The outcome of this decade was that technology offered an alternative network to churches and provided new methods of mobilization, making it possible to reach Europe as one market and Christians as individuals.

Recognition came from the other side as well. In 1976 the WCC circulated a plan for a joint evangelical, conciliar, Roman Catholic and Orthodox missiology conference. Evangelicals were beginning to realize that the WCC was theologically different, but also that there was common ground with the WCC that could serve evangelicals as well. This shift was a result of a new historical awareness. WEF president Waldron Scott expressed this new insight in 1976, noting, "this business of evangelical cooperation is always relative to the past and the future and is therefore evolutionary in character. I must keep this in mind. I am eager for broader evangelical cooperation" (Baker, Letter to Scott; Scott, Letter to Baker).

Yet the difference in scope and organization between WCC and WEF remained enormous. The WCC had a 1977 budget of $18 million while the WEF operated on a budget of $150,000 — not even one percent of the WCC's budget, and barely sufficient to keep the organization afloat. Of this money, $25,000 came from the Billy Graham organization.[16] Still, this money was needed to make the WEF a global organization. At the end of the 1970s, the Third World constituency became a stronger voice in the WEF, and Pentecostal and Charismatic Christians, including those in the Roman Catholic Church, were welcomed (Howard 116-24). Despite the continuing differences of opinion about the best way forward

---

[16] American churches contributed a third to the WCC budget, and German churches 40 percent. Two thirds of the WEF funds came from the United States and one third from Europe (also mainly from Germany) and Australia (Scott "Double Helix").

(either under the WEF or by continuing the Lausanne Committee), it was clear that evangelicals wanted to broaden both their scope and their constituency.

Conclusion: The 1980s and beyond

The growth of the evangelical missions in Europe continued in the 1980s. In 1985 ten percent of the 37,000 American missionaries worldwide were stationed in Europe. Not only were they overwhelmingly evangelical, they were also involved in their number one priority: evangelism. Missionary statistics would stay at this level, showing that Europe had become a standard mission field for Americans.[17]

Before American televangelists came to dominate the news and complicate European-American relations in the 1980s, many missionary organizations, including the Graham campaign, enriched Europe's religious market with a comprehensive evangelical network, which had reproduced itself through training programs and mass meetings. While American evangelicals did not accomplish their goal of re-Christianizing Europe, they did achieve their other goal of challenging the monopolistic power of the WCC without marginalizing themselves alongside their fundamentalist brethren. Thanks to the mobilization of staff, money, and organizational innovations, these evangelical agencies introduced the new category of the 'evangelical Christian' and consolidated American religious pluralism all over Europe. According to the EEA, evangelicals in Europe are presently estimated at 15 million souls.

The initial resistance to uniformity and mandatory organizational structures among evangelicals had encouraged the privatization of missions, but in the 1980s shifted to more cooperation. This trend achieved its climax early in 2011. What was unimaginable 70 years before happened that summer: on Tuesday, June 28, 2011, the World Council of Churches, The World Evangelical Alliance, and the Vatican reached agreement on a document calling for cooperation in world missions and a code of conduct. The market for Protestant religious services from the United States changed from a monopolistic construct to a real joint venture.

Acronyms

ACCC – American Council of Christian Churches
BGCA – Billy Graham Center Archives
BGEA – Billy Graham Evangelical Association
CBFMS – International Conservative Baptist Foreign Mission Society
EEA – European Evangelical Alliance
GEM – Greater European Mission

---

[17] Europe had proven to be the fastest-growing area in evangelical missions and it stayed close to the core activity of evangelism. In the 1960s evangelicals began to invest increasingly more money in humanitarian causes at the costs of direct evangelism and church planting, but this shift did not take place in Europe (Hamilton 118-19).

ICCC – International Council of Christian Churches
IFMA – Interdenominational Foreign Missionary Association
NAE – National Association of Evangelicals
WCA – Wheaton College Archives
WCC – World Council of Churches
WEA – World Evangelical Alliance
WEF – World Evangelical Fellowship
UEA – United Evangelical Association

Works Cited

"Auditor's Reports Greater Europe Mission, 1954-1968, 1973." BGCA col. 352 IFMA, box 38 file 8.
"Auditor's Reports European Evangelical Crusade, 1955-1970." BGCA col. 352, box 37f 16.
Baker, Milton. Travelog Dr. Baker 1974. BGCA col. 352, box 67 file 4. WEF.
---. Letter to Waldron Scott. 12 May 1976. BGCA col. 352, box 67 file 6.
Beaver, Pierce R. "Distribution of the American Protestant Foreign Missionary Force in 1952." *Occasional Bulletin from the Missionary Research Library* 4.10 (1953): 1-3. Print.
---. "The Expansion of American Foreign Missionary Activities Since 1945." *Occasional Bulletin from the Missionary Research Library* 5.7 (1954): 5-6. Print.
Brugman, Don. *Greater Europe Report.* 7.5 (1977). Print.
Bolten, John. Letter to Francis Schaeffer. 6 July 1948. WCA SP 113, box 1 file Clarens 1948.
Calleo, David. *Europe's Future: The Grand Alternatives.* New York: Horizon, 1965. Print.
Capelleveen, Jan van. "Western Europe in the Seventies." *Let the Earth Hear his Voice*: *International Congress on World Evangelization, Lausanne, Switzerland.* Minneapolis, MN: World Wide Publications, 1975. 151-52. Print.
Carpenter, Joel A. *Revive Us Again: The Reawakening of American Fundamentalism.* New York: Oxford UP, 1993. Print.
Crouse, Eric. R. "Popular Cold Warriors: Conservative Protestants, Communism, and Culture in Early Cold War America." *Journal of Religion and Popular Culture* 2 (2002): 1-18. Print.
Dayton, Edward R., ed. *Mission Handbook: North American Protestant Ministries Overseas.* 11th ed. New York: Missions Advanced Research and Communication Center, 1976. Print.
Decker, R.L. "Confidential Report." SC 113 NAE, box 1 file Clarens 1948.
---. "Confidential Resume and report of trip to Europe, July 30 – August 30, 1948." WCA SC 113 NAE, box 1 file Clarens 1948.
Detzler, Wayne. *Greater Europe Report.* 9.4 (1979). Print.
Dresselhuis, F., and A.H. Oussoren. "De gulden middenweg." National Association of the Evangelicals in the Netherlands 12 March 1949. BGCA col. 338, WEF, box 9 f 2 "Holland" 1948-1951.

"The Evangelical Alliance Mission Finances, 1964-1973." BGCA col. 352, box 39 file 19.

Evans, Robert P. "As I see it this month." *Together: A Family Newsletter* 19.3 (1975): 1. BGCA col. 352, IFMA, box 34 file 9.

---. "Can Europeans Evangelize the Continent?" *United Evangelical Action* (1963): BGCA col. 506, box 22 folder 13.

---. Interview by Robert O. Ferm. August 1971. BGCA col. 141, box 3 folder 35.

---. *Let Europe Hear: The Spiritual Plight of Europe*. Chicago: Moody, 1963. Print.

---. Letter to J. O. Percy of the IFMA. 22 November 1956. BGCA 352, IFMA, box 7 file 2.

---. Newsletter 28 October 1947. BGCA col. 20, box 72 folder 4.

---. "Our responsibility: disciple the weaker brother." *Greater Europe Report* (May-June 1980). Print.

Faircloth, Samuel. Field Letters, June 1949-December 1956. BGCA col. 658, Faircloth field letters.

---. Personal interview. 5 June 2011.

Ferm, Lois. Interview with Peter Schneider. BGCA col. 141, BGEA Oral History Project, box 62 file 13.

Frank, Walter. "General Director's Report, 1964." BGCA col. 352, box 21 file 10 GEM 1964-65.

---. "IFMA Missions and Church Planting in Areas Where Old Churches are Established." BGCA col. 352, IFMA, box 27 folder 4 GEM 1970-71.

---. *North American Protestant Foreign Mission Agencies*. New York: Missionary Research Library, 1964. Print.

Graham, Billy. Letter 12 November 1952. BGCA col. 338, box 29 file 22.

---. Press Conference. Congress on Evangelicalism, Amsterdam 26 August 1971. BGCA col. 24, news conferences, box 1 file 33.

Hamilton, Michael S. "More Money, More Ministry: The Financing of American Evangelicalism Since 1945." *More Money, More Ministry: Money and Evangelicals in Recent North American History*. Ed. Larry Eskridge and Mark A. Noll. Grand Rapids, MI: Eerdmans, 2000. 104-38. Print.

Hankins, Barry. *Francis Schaeffer and the Shaping of Evangelical America*. Grand Rapids, MI: Eerdmans, 2008. Print.

Herzog, Jonathan P. *The Spiritual-Industrial Complex: America's Religious Battle against Communism in the Early Cold War*. New York: Oxford UP, 2011. Print.

Hinklemann, Frank. *Die Evangelikale Bewegung in Österreich: Grundzüge ihrer historischen und theologischen Entwicklung 1945-1998*. Bonn: Verlag für Kultur und Wissenschaft, 2014. Print.

Howard, David. M. *The Dream that Would Not Die: The Birth and Growth of the World Evangelical Fellowship 1846-1985*. Exeter: Paternoster, 1986. Print.

IFMA News Bulletin. Interdenominational Foreign Mission Association, 1951-1960. Print.

Jacques, Edwin E. "Can Our Missions Collaborate with European Church Bodies?" EFMA Mission Executives Retreat, Europe Section, 26 September 1972. BGCA col. 218, Pulse Europe, box 8 folder 4.

Jongeneel, Jan. "European-Continental Perception and Critiques of British and American Protestant Missions." *Exchange* 30.1 (2001): 103-24. Print.

Kane, James H. "Major Concerns of Modern Missions." BGCA col. 182, box 1 file 20.

---. "Where are we in Foreign Missions?" BGCA col. 182, box 1 file 32.

Kessler, J. B. A. Jr. *A Study of the Evangelical Alliance in Great Britain*. Goes: Oosterbaan en le Cointre, 1968. Print.

Kirby, Dianne, ed. *Religion and the Cold War*. New York: Palgrave Macmillan, 2003. Print.

Loveland, Anne C. *American Evangelicals and the U.S. Military, 1942-1993*. Baton Rouge: Louisiana State UP, 1997. Print.

"Missions Situation Europe." Report CBFMS 1966, WCA, spec. col. 113, box 9.

Mott, John R. *The Evangelization of the World in this Generation*. New York: Student Volunteer Movement for Foreign Missions, 1900. Print.

Murch, James DeForest. "Amsterdam, 1948: An Evangelical View of the World Council of Churches." *United Evangelical Action* 7 (1 Feb.-15 May 1949). Print.

---. Letter to G. E. Hoek 22 June 1950. BGCA col. 338, WEF, box 9 f 2 "Holland" 1948-1951.

Noll, Mark. *The New Shape of World Christianity: How American Experience Reflects Global Faith*. Downers Grove, IL: IVP Academic, 2009. Print.

North American Protestant Foreign Mission Agencies. New York: Missionary Research Library, 1962. 117-19. Print.

North American Protestant Foreign Mission Agencies. New York: Missionary Research Library, 1964. 66-67. Print.

North American Protestant Ministries Overseas. New York: Missionary Research Library, 1968. 26-31. Print.

Postel, Charles. *The Populist Vision*. Oxford: Oxford UP, 2007. Print.

Preston, Andrew. "The Death of a Peculiar Special Relationship: Myron Taylor and the Religious Roots of America's Cold War." *America's 'Special Relationships': Foreign and Domestic Aspects of the Politics of Alliance*. Ed. John Dumbrell and Axel Schäfer. New York: Routledge, 2009. 202-16. Print.

Randall, Ian M. "American Influence on Evangelicals in Europe: A Comparison of the Founding of the Evangelical Alliance and the World Evangelical Fellowship." *Religion in America: European and American Perspectives*. Ed. Hans Krabbendam and Derek Rubin. Amsterdam: VU UP, 2004. 263-74. Print.

---. "Conservative Constructionist: The Early Influence of Billy Graham in Britain." *Evangelical Quarterly* 67.4 (1995): 309-33. Print.

"Report of European Youth for Christ conference, October 3-6, 1961." BGCA col 48, box 6 folder 23.

Scott, Waldron. Letter to Milton Baker. 14 May 1976. BGCA col. 352, box 67 file 6.

---. "Double Helix: A Missionary's Odyssey." N. p., n. d. Web. 16 Feb. 2012.

---. "Report to the WEF Executive Council, January 1, 1979." BGCA col. 352, box 67 file 6.

Shufelt, J. Stratton. "Report Sun. March 24 [1946]." "Youth for Christ, European Teams: Letters and Reports; March-April, 1946; May-June, 1947." The Papers of J. Stratton Shufelt, 1930-1979. BGCA col. 224, box 1 folder 17.

Shuster, Bob. Interview with Arthur F. Glasser. BGCA col. CN 421, tape T8.
Smith, Oswald. "The Miracle of Youth for Christ in Europe." *People's Magazine* 1 (1949): 10-21. Print.
Taylor, Clyde W. "Confidential NAE Report." WCA SP 113, box 1 file Clarens 1948.
---. Letter to Gilbert Kirby 5 August 1962. BGCA col. 165, box 6 file 10.
---. Letter to Gilbert Kirby 22 July 1963. BGCA col. 165, box 6 file 10.
---. Letter to Gilbert Kirby 5 May 1964. BGCA col. 165, box 6 file 10.
---. Letter to Charles Pitts 20 March 1964. BGCA col. 165, box 6 file 10.
---. "Implementing our Evangelical Unity." *United Evangelical Action* 22 (Dec. 1963): 14-16. Print.
"Tentative Preliminary Draft of proposition statements which might be included in an anticipated 'Declaration' eventuating from the Congress." BGCA col. 165, box 6 file 23.
Wagner, William L. *North American Protestant Missionaries in Western Europe: A Critical Appraisal*. Bonn: Verlag für Kultur und Wissenschaft, 1993. Print.
"The Wheaton Declaration." *Evangelical Mission Quarterly* 2 (1966): 231-44. Print.
Wilson, Samuel, ed. *Mission Handbook: North American Protestant Ministries Overseas*. 13th ed. Monrovia, CA: MARC, 1986. Print.
"Worldwide European Fellowship Finances, 1964-1966." BGCA col. 352, box 40, file 6.
Wright, J. Elwin. Letter to G. E. Hoek 18 March 1950. BGCA col. 338, WEF, box 9 f 2 "Holland 1948-1950.
---. Letter to G. E. Hoek 1 November 1950. BGCA col. 338, WEF, box 9 f 2 "Holland 1948-1950.
---. Letter to home, Utrecht 7 October 1949. BGCA col. 338 folder 8-1. Correspondence.
---. Letter to Arie Kok in Hilversum the Netherlands 16 April 1948. WCA SP 11, box 1 file Clarens 1948.
---. "Minutes of the Clarens Conferences of Evangelicals August 7-10, 1948. St. George's School, Switzerland." WCA SC 113.
---. "The Movement for Evangelical Cooperation part Two: International Developments." WCA SC 113, NAE, box 1 file Clarens 1948.
Youth for Christ Magazine. Youth for Christ International Chicago, January 1947. Print.
"Youth for Christ World Conference" BGCA 285, Torrey M. Johnson Papers box 25 f 1.
Zeilstra, Jurjen A. *European Unity in Ecumenical Thinking, 1937-1948*. Zoetermeer: Boekencentrum, 1995. Print.

Quaker Reform and Evangelization in the Eighteenth Century

GEOFFREY PLANK

ABSTRACT

When they first arrived in England's North American colonies, the Quakers enjoyed several competitive advantages over other Christian groups. Quaker Meetings were relatively inexpensive to run compared to more formal churches, and partly as a consequence Quakerism spread quickly. Things changed, however, in the mid-eighteenth century after Quaker reformers took control of the meetings' disciplinary structures. They condemned intermarriage between Quakers and non-Quakers, made greater demands on the Friends, and in general adopted a stance that in retrospect appears to have hurt Quakerism's ability to attract new adherents. Still, the reformers continued to proselytize even as they expelled the wayward from their meetings. Violence on the Pennsylvania frontier after 1763 made it politically and practically difficult for the Quakers to evangelize through conventional means. In response, the reformers redoubled their efforts to enforce severe disciplinary strictures against theater-going, horse-racing, excessive drinking, participation in warfare and slaveholding, always believing that moral purity would make Quakerism more attractive. Examining several leaders of the Quaker reform effort including Abraham Farrington, John Woolman, Israel and John Pemberton, and Anthony Benezet, this essay argues that these men never intended to abandon evangelization in the mid-eighteenth century, nor did they want the Quakers to become an insular, minority sect.

In 1652 George Fox, the most prominent founder of the Quaker movement, was traveling through northern England when he passed a peak called Pendle Hill. As he described the event in his journal, "I was moved by the Lord to go up to the top of it, which I did with much ado, it was so very steep and high. When I was come to the top, I saw the sea bordering on Lancashire. From the top of this hill the Lord let me see in what places he had a great people to be gathered" (66). Fox's vision is now celebrated as an original moment of discovery for Quakerism. Pendle Hill is something of a pilgrimage site for Quakers, and the content of Fox's vision illustrates the importance of evangelization as an energizing force driving the early Society of Friends.[1]

It is not clear how far across the terrain Fox was looking. At that moment he may have been concentrating on Lancashire and its coastline, but it is also possible that he was looking beyond the sea. Quaker missionaries arrived in Barbados within three years of Fox's vision, and Friends would come to Maryland, Rhode Island, and Massachusetts shortly thereafter.[2] Initially they did not cross the ocean in a large immigrant stream, but rather as a small, steady, and determined troop of evangelists. In Barbados, the Chesapeake colonies, and Rhode

---

[1] For the origins of Quakerism, see Moore.
[2] See Gragg; Pestana; and Jones.

Island, they were quickly successful. Most of the first Quakers in those colonies were converted by small bands of English missionaries in America.

Quakerism's Position on the American Religious Marketplace

Quakerism was well positioned to thrive in the American colonies in the seventeenth century. The Society of Friends made demands on its members. The adoption of plain speech, in particular—addressing individuals as 'thee' instead of 'you' and identifying the days of the week and the months of the year with numbers—placed a burden on Quakers and distinguished them from their neighbors. Nonetheless, as Jon Butler has written, "Quaker doctrines had the advantage of unique realism" in the context of seventeenth-century America. "The Quaker rejection of the Anglican liturgy of baptism, marriage, communion, and burial appeared perfectly reasonable in a society where those rites were so frequently unavailable and unpracticed" (53). The Quakers dispensed with expensive ritual, and with their devaluation of formal religious education and their unpaid ministers, they were well positioned to compete with other religious groups. Quaker Meetings were less expensive to run than more formal churches, and they proliferated partly because of that competitive advantage. American Quakerism received a major boost in the 1670s and 1680s with the founding of West Jersey and Pennsylvania, two colonies with Quaker leadership. By the early eighteenth century the Friends had become, in Patricia Bonomi's words, one of the four "hegemonic" religious groups in colonial America, alongside the Anglicans in the south, the Congregationalists in New England, and the Dutch Reformed Church in New York (96). But sometime in the eighteenth century—whether the change was sudden or gradual is open to debate—the Quakers lost their numerical prominence. Current conceptions of success in the religious marketplace would suggest that the Quakers should have thrived and flourished. The fact that they did not raises critical questions about those conceptions.

There are various possible explanations for Quakerism's decline. Under the influence of a reform movement that began in the middle decades of the eighteenth century, the meetings may have intimidated potential recruits and driven them away by making greater demands on their members with a stricter application of Quaker rules of discipline. As Jack D. Marietta notes, by prohibiting marriage outside of their religion, Quakers cut themselves off from an important source of potential converts (62-67). They also became increasingly unpopular as a result of their pacifism during the Seven Years War (Silver 191-226). There can be no doubt that America's Quakers made decisions in the mid-eighteenth century that hurt their recruiting efforts, and their share of the colonial population declined. The Friends could see what was happening to them, and in many respects, as Marietta suggests, they began to "behave like a self-conscious religious minority" (185).[3]

---

[3] The Quakers' sense of their declining prominence in Pennsylvania is evident in the decision made by many Quaker reformers to withdraw from formal participation in provincial politics.

Nonetheless, in order to understand their actions in this period we must distinguish between aims and unintended consequences. The reform-minded leaders who transformed Quakerism in the late colonial period did not intend to create a minority or insular sect. To the contrary, they believed that moral purity would make Quakerism more attractive, and they continued to proselytize even as they expelled the wayward from their meetings.

Reform Movement

Quaker reformers in the eighteenth century were striving toward two goals: maintaining a righteous community and spreading the truth. There was a great potential for conflict between these objectives, which manifested itself quickly and dramatically in the 1750s during conflicts over the propriety of marrying outside the Quaker fold. As Marietta has shown in detail, at mid-century the Quakers began disowning members who married outside the Society of Friends, and in doing so denied themselves access to non-Quaker spouses, which almost certainly had a negative effect on the expansion of their membership (46-73).[4] It is very clear from the historical record, however, that the newly rigorous enforcement of the discipline against marrying outside the religious society was never intended to signal an abandonment of evangelization. The proponents of the new policy included some of the Quakers' most ambitious and indefatigable evangelists. Consider, for example, the life and work of Pennsylvania-born Abraham Farrington.

Farrington was born in 1692 in a Quaker-dominated region of Pennsylvania. Both of his parents were Quakers, but his father died when Farrington was only nine months old. His mother proceeded to marry a non-Quaker; therefore, Farrington received what the Quakers later called 'a loose irregular education.' At the age of ten he was bound out for service in a non-Quaker family. During that period, as Farrington described it, he "seemed like one abandoned from good for several years." After he obtained his freedom at the age of 21 he took lodging in a household of Quakers and was reintroduced to the religious community his mother had left behind. He recalled that it felt like he was coming home. He "saw that the Lord had work for him to do" and eventually became a minister (*Collection of Memorials* 186-87, 189).

Farrington recounted his life story as an object lesson on the dangers of marrying outside the Society of Friends. In the 1750s he joined other Quaker ministers in visiting families in the Delaware Valley's meetings to make sure that their marriages were healthy, that the children were being raised in a Quakerly environment, and that no one was courting non-Quakers (Burlington 259). He also self-consciously presented himself as the head of a model Quaker family, and he was celebrated among the Friends as "an affectionate husband and parent." After he died his meeting published notes he had written for his children (*Collection of Memorials* 186).

---

[4] For more on the ideological and religious significance of the Quaker family, see Frost's *Quaker Family*; and Levy.

We know a fair amount about Farrington's work as a minister because in 1743 he served as a mentor to the famous Quaker journalist John Woolman. A few weeks after Woolman was formally recognized as a minister, Farrington approached him and asked him to come along on "a visit to Friends on the eastern side" of New Jersey. He told Woolman at the outset that the two men were going to visit "Friends." Woolman was therefore surprised that they went to New Brunswick, New Jersey, which was, as Woolman described it, "a town in which none of our Society dwells." There were no Quaker homes in New Brunswick to host meetings, and certainly no available meetinghouses. The two men arranged to hold worship in a tavern. The event seemed to go well. At least, Woolman reported, "The room was full and the people quiet." In total the ministers spent two weeks on the road and Woolman was continuously impressed by the number of non-Quakers they were able to gather around them. As they went through Woodbridge, Rahway, and Plainfield, they convened six or seven meetings among people Woolman identified as Presbyterian. At these gatherings Farrington did more talking than Woolman. Farrington was "frequently strengthened to hold forth the Word of Life amongst them" (Woolman, *Journal* 34).

Farrington's evangelical impulses ultimately tore him from his family. Like several other Quaker ministers of the era, he left his wife and children behind in order to preach in Britain and Ireland. He knew that the trip would be dangerous and declared ahead of time that he expected to "lay down his body" in England and "not see his friends in America more." This proved prophetic. After he died, the London Quakers held a "large and solemn" meeting for worship and organized a procession with his body through the streets of the city to the Quaker burial ground containing the remains of George Fox (*Collection of Memorials* 190, 193-94).

Woolman learned a great deal from Farrington, and in 1746 when he began his own travels as a minister, he sought out opportunities to worship with non-Quakers. On Long Island he convened a general meeting "chiefly made up of other societies" (*Journal*, 41-42). Later he traveled along the coasts of southern New Jersey "to visit some people in those parts amongst whom there is no settled worship" (144). During the rest of Woolman's career in America, he repeatedly sought out opportunities to worship with sympathetic non-Quakers. Occasionally he expressed his hope that those who "professeth nearly the same principles as our Society" would correct their "irregularities" and accept guidance from "skillful fathers" to make their practices more fully conform to Quaker norms (145-46).

In 1772 Woolman obtained certificates authorizing him to travel as a minister to Britain, Ireland and Holland (London Minutes June 8, 1772 qtd. in Cadbury 49). On the ship that carried him to London he proselytized among the non-Quakers, convincing "most of the sailors" to attend impromptu Quaker meetings in the cabin (Woolman, *Journal* 169, 172, 178, 179). In England he created a small sensation because in his eagerness to serve as a "sign to the people" and visibly oppose the prevailing currents of "pride and extravagancy," he wore clothing that he made himself from undyed cloth, and he traveled on foot from London to York (Journal of Deborah Morris qtd. in Cadbury 95-96). On his way he held meetings in private houses, some of which were "near full," though few of the attendees were Friends. In Chesterfield he worshiped with "Friends and the better sort of others," and according to a witness who saw him there, the house where he gathered this group was "near full," though "few there could understand him" (Cadbury 91, 92). Woolman died of smallpox in York, but even on his deathbed he continued to reach out to non-Quakers. He deeply moved the apothecary who had been summoned to treat him in his illness. That apothecary never formally became a Friend, but he wrote a poem after Woolman's death declaring that Woolman had exhibited an "unbounded love" that embraced "all sects, all nations." There were "thousands" who could testify that "his words were powerful and divinely sweet" ("On the death").

Woolman's career suggests that America's Quaker reformers did not—at least not as a group—abandon proselytizing in the late colonial period. Nonetheless an important shift in their tactics occurred in the aftermath of the Seven Years' War. In the two decades immediately following the war, the Quakers relied much more heavily on creating and maintaining model communities and waiting for God's help in directing others to notice and emulate the example they set for their neighbours. This shift in strategy can be observed in the story of Woolman's most celebrated missionary effort, his journey to visit the Munsee religious leader Papunhank in 1763. Since the early 1960s, scholars have counted Papunhank among the prophets who arose within Native communities in the northern Appalachians and the Ohio Valley during the Seven Years' War and its aftermath (Wallace 177; Hunter 39-49; Dowd, *A Spirited Resistance* 32; Cave 15; Irwin 127, 373-76). Most of those prophets preached some form of resistance to colonial culture. Papunhank, however, was different. He reached out to the Quakers and sought common ground with them (Benezet qtd. in Brookes 479-85; *An Account of a Visit*; "Minutes" 8:486-90).

Papunhank arrived in Philadelphia unexpectedly in 1760. He sought out Israel Pemberton, the de facto leader of the Quakers' "Friendly Association for the Gaining and Preserving Peace with the Indians by Pacific Measures," and with his help, Papunhank met the provincial governor and council and attended several Quaker meetings for worship. He did not speak English, but by all accounts he spoke with impressive gravity and apparent conviction. When translated for a Quaker audience, his words were dazzling. He made pleas for peace, and he described his own religious experiences in terms that seemed to resemble Quakerism. After hearing Papunhank speak, many Quakers came to believe that he had acquired their beliefs and practices spontaneously, through the direct intervention of God, when alone in the woods. Pemberton described the implications of this in cosmic terms. In a note he chose to keep to himself, he suggested that Papunhank's arrival amongst the Quakers was a sign pointing toward the "fulfilling of the many glorious prophesies of the general spreading of the gospel of our Lord and Savior in the dark corners of the Earth, when the wilderness and the solitary places will be made to rejoice and become as the Garden of the Lord" (Pemberton, Draft of a letter 4:263).

In 1761 Woolman met Papunhank in Philadelphia and shortly thereafter resolved to visit him in his village (Woolman, "The substance of some conversation" 122).[5]

---

[5] For an account of Woolman's meeting with Papunhank see Woolman, "The substance of some conversation." More generally for Papunhank's 1761 visit to Philadelphia see Brookes 485-92.

Woolman was busy, however, and years would pass before he undertook the journey. He set out in the late spring of 1763, coincidentally at the start of Pontiac's War. Though it had not been his intention, Woolman rode into a region of armed conflict. It proved to be a frightening trip, and consequently, Woolman's understanding of the purpose of his mission changed. Even before he left home the journey had become for him a test of his faith. He decided that he had to demonstrate his obedience to God's will. On his last Sunday afternoon before he departed, he stood in his meetinghouse and quoted a Psalm, declaring that although he faced danger, he took comfort from the knowledge that the "the angel of the Lord encampeth round about them that fear him" (Woolman, *Journal* 123-24). On his way to Papunhank's village his principal concern was to demonstrate the "all sufficiency of God," and God's "care in providing for those that fear him." As he explained in a letter to his wife Sarah, during his travels it was his "daily labor" to achieve "full resignedness" to God's will, as he felt certain that if he did so all would "end well." Woolman relied on God's protection, and in effect he performed a practical demonstration of the efficacy of trusting Providence. He had a short, quiet visit with the Indians, and after his safe return, he believed he had reasserted a truth that had been demonstrated earlier by the first Quaker settlers in New Jersey and Pennsylvania (Woolman, *Journal* 124; Woolman to Uriah Woolman; Woolman to Sarah Woolman; Woolman to Israel Pemberton 1763).

Woolman long maintained that God sheltered and strengthened the original Quaker colonists in the Delaware Valley, not only by sustaining them "through the difficulties attending the improvement of a wilderness," but also by finding a place for them "in the hearts of the natives." "It was by the gracious influence of the Holy Spirit," he suggested, that the Quakers had found a way to "work righteously and walk uprightly one toward another and toward the natives, and in life and conversation manifest the excellency of the principles and doctrines of the Christian religion" (Woolman, *Journal* 98-99).

The prospects for peace between Pennsylvania and the Indians deteriorated rapidly after Woolman's visit with Papunhank. Frontier violence was spreading eastward, and on his return home Woolman passed through an old Indian settlement where "the Indians were mostly gone" (Woolman, *Journal* 135). A few months later Papunhank and all the other residents of his village were evacuated and taken to an island in the Delaware River near Philadelphia, ostensibly for their own protection. Papunhank survived a long subsequent ordeal, as he and his fellow internees were removed from the island, marched northward through New Jersey, and then brought back to Philadelphia and confined in the city barracks after hundreds of angry settlers, known to posterity as the 'Paxton Boys,' threatened to kill them (Dowd, *War Under Heaven* 194-96; Kenny 128-29; Merritt 305-06).

Woolman's only comment on these circumstances in his journal is an entry about an incident in 1764 in which he discussed both his dismay and his stubborn resolution in the face of worsening conditions in the west. In the fall of that year he hired a man who had previously been captured by Indians. The man had seen two other captives tortured to death. One of the captives had been pierced with wooden splinters that were subsequently set on fire, and the other had been forced to run around a tree dragging his entrails behind him. Hearing these stories saddened Woolman, but he wrote in his journal that after a good night's sleep he awoke the next day "with a fresh and living sense of divine love." Warfare, Woolman reminded himself, began when "pride" led to "vanity," which in turn prompted "men to exert their power in requiring that of others" which they themselves would "rather be excused from." He wrote a note to himself, asking whether coercion generated "hard thoughts." Do "hard thoughts when ripe become malice? Does malice when ripe become revengeful," and in the end lead men to "inflict terrible pains on their fellow creatures and spread desolations through the world?" The solution, he concluded, was to remember that "the Prince of Peace is the Lord, that he communicates his unmixed wisdom to his family that they, living in perfect simplicity, may give no offence to any creatures, but may walk as he walked" (Woolman, *Journal* 142-43).

The Paxton Boys threatened Quakers as well as Indians in part because they accused pacifists within the Society of Friends of exerting excessive political influence and leaving Pennsylvania defenseless. In February 1764, with angry rioters massed just north of Philadelphia, several Quakers took up arms to defend themselves from the mob (Silver 191-226; Eustace; Kenny 147-45; Sloane). This episode shook the Quaker community. Friends feared reprisals from their non-Quaker neighbors, but they were also frightened by the prospect of continuing internal discord, a loss of their sense of moral direction, and the destruction of their distinctive identity as a people favored by God. Prudence seemed to dictate that the Quakers withdraw for a time from active engagement in Indian affairs.

The Significance of Quaker Outreach to Indians

Outreach to Indians was only one branch of Quaker evangelization in the eighteenth century, and it had never been the most vigorous. Nonetheless, it was ideologically significant for a number of reasons. William Penn's supposed treaty with the Indians during the founding of Pennsylvania assumed a central place in the Delaware Valley Quakers' celebratory conception of their own history.[6] The Quaker colonists cited their alleged ability to live well with Indians as a sign of their righteousness and God's favor toward them. Additionally, Papunhank's story suggested the power of divine intervention. It seemed that God was ready to bring the teachings of the Quakers into virgin regions. As Israel Pemberton and others recognized, Papunhank's religious awakening therefore had the potential to carry global and eschatological import. It was a story worth spreading. Within months of Papunhank's first visit to Philadelphia, the reformer Anthony Benezet prepared an account of the event with an evaluation of Papunhank's religious experience, which was printed in London and also translated for distribution among German-speaking colonists (Benezet, "An Account of Behavior"; Schultze).

The Quakers' withdrawal from Indian affairs after 1763 did not signal an abandonment of their evangelical aspirations. On the contrary, many Quakers like

---

[6] For more on this point, see Smolenski; Frost "Wear the Sword."

Woolman retained a millenarian sense of optimism despite their setbacks. Anxious to retain God's favor in the face of an escalating series of crises, those Quakers who had once been in contact with Indians turned their attention to questions they thought were more closely related to their own personal morality. Some protested against theatrical performances and horse races. Others campaigned against alcohol and indulgent fashion, concentrated on the regulation of marriage, or, like Woolman, some devoted most of their energy to the controversies that continued to divide Quaker communities over the slave trade, slaveholding, and the meaning of emancipation.

The complex interplay between the Quakers' sense of wartime and post-war crisis, their perceived need to put their own house in order, and their aspirations to reach out to others can be seen in the early history of Philadelphia Yearly Meeting's 'Meetings for Sufferings,' which were first convened, partly under Woolman's initiative, in 1756. In the traumatic early years of the Seven Years' War, Woolman and twenty-nine like-minded reformers had proposed that a new standing committee of twelve Philadelphia Friends be appointed to address the "distressed state of the frontier settlements of these provinces," and to consider appeals from Quakers in need, "especially such as suffer from the Indians or other enemies" (Philadelphia Minutes 1756-1775, 85-90; Philadelphia Meeting for Suffering 1756-1775, 27-29). Philadelphia Yearly Meeting responded positively to this proposal, and the committee of twelve was established. Its sessions eventually became known as the 'Meetings for Sufferings.' The committee's agenda expanded, its term of service was extended indefinitely, and its work became a lasting feature of American Quakerism. While the Meetings for Sufferings initially concentrated on the ordeals of the Quakers living in war zones, within a year the committee was seeking to ameliorate the suffering of other apparent victims of the conflict including Indians and Acadian deportees. Interpreting its responsibilities broadly, the Sufferings committee also sponsored efforts to procure and distribute religious books in French and German, and to prohibit allegedly immoral theatrical performances in Philadelphia. The aim of these projects was to promote Quaker ideals and to convince all the people in the region to place their trust in God in the hope that they might secure God's favor and lasting peace (James 172-74).

The 'Friendly Association' for peace with the Indians grew moribund and dissolved in the 1760s, but its leading spirit, Israel Pemberton, remained convinced of the vitality of the organization's core principles. In 1773 he helped bring a lawsuit on behalf of a woman identified as an Indian slave. The suit was unsuccessful, but the resulting controversy led to the formation of America's first antislavery society, the "Society for the Relief of Free Negroes Unlawfully Held in Bondage" (Gerona; Thayer 200; Turner 94; and Sword 315-43). During the Revolutionary War, Pemberton became one of the Friends' most articulate and controversial pacifists. Facing banishment in Virginia for his views, he published an "Address to the Inhabitants of Pennsylvania" in which he claimed that he stood for the procedural rights of all Americans. Pitching his argument to the widest possible audience, he protested that he and his fellow pacifists should not have been arrested without formal legal charges, their homes should not have been searched or their property seized without warrants, and they should not be punished unless they were found guilty at the end of a regular criminal trial. But more was at stake than any list of procedural rights. Pemberton made a general plea for peace:

> We are clearly convinced, from the precepts of Christ, the doctrine of his Apostles, and the example of his followers in primitive ages of Christianity, that all outward wars and fightings are unlawful for any cause whatever. We cannot but remind you that we are by the same principles restrained from pursuing any measures inconsistent with the Apostolic advice, 'to live peaceably with all men,' under whatever powers it is our lot to live, which rule of conduct we are determined to observe whatever you, or any others, may determine concerning us. (Pemberton, *An Address*)[7]

Anthony Benezet's Outreach to Non-Quakers

In the early 1760s the Quaker reformer Anthony Benezet was deeply involved in outreach to the Indians. He hosted Papunhank in his home and did more than any other Quaker to publicize Papunhank's visits to Philadelphia. After 1764, however, Benezet directed his attention elsewhere. His greatest work as an abolitionist was still ahead of him, and he found time to campaign against other evils close to home (Jackson). For example, in 1774 Benezet produced one of the first temperance tracts ever published in America, *The Mighty Destroyer Displayed, in Some Account of the Dreadful Havock made by the Mistaken Use, as well as Abuse of Distilled Spirituous Liquors*. Benezet addressed this pamphlet to a wide colonial audience. He began by citing medical treatises, and through its first eighteen pages he offered a few mere hints that he was a Quaker. He devoted the second half of his treatise to the importance of good exemplary behavior, however, and it was in this section that his Quakerism revealed itself. Quoting Benjamin Rush, Benezet reminded his readers of Pennsylvania's earlier, if mythical, virtuous times, when rum was unknown and Quaker principles prevailed: "The food of the inhabitants was then simple; their only drink was water; their appetites were restrained by labour; religion excluded the influence of sickening passions; private hospitality supplied the want of public hospitals; nature was their only nurse; temperance their principal physician" (20). Turning to the present day, Benezet told the story of Joshua Evans, a New Jersey Quaker who had broken with prevailing tradition by harvesting his wheat without drinking rum or offering the drink to his workers. Evans, as Benezet presented him, was an original paragon, a man who alone had "apprehended it to be his duty, to become an example in opposition to this pernicious custom" (23; Evans). Encouraging his readers to follow in the footsteps of Evans and serve as models for those around them, Benezet went on to suggest that good people should only drink water, or if needed, substitute water for coffee or tea. He described tea as "but an infusion in water of an innocent plant" (Benezet, *Mighty Destroyer* 39). With a tone-deafness that was becoming typical among the Quakers in 1774, he ignored the escalating taxation controversy.

Israel Pemberton's brother, John, was another prominent Quaker reformer who had taken a keen interest in Papunhank. He had walked with Woolman on the first leg of his journey to Papuhank's village, and he had debriefed Woolman

---

[7] See also Gilpin, Thayer 215-233; Marietta 240-41.

after he returned (Woolman, *Journal* 124-25; John Pemberton Letter to Israel Pemberton). Along with his brother, John Pemberton had been deeply concerned with Indian affairs for several years, but after 1763 he devoted more of his time to a futile effort to suppress betting races and theatrical plays. In 1768, when John Pemberton learned that theatrical performances and horseraces had been scheduled for Philadelphia, he appealed to Pennsylvania's governor to stop them. Along with three others, he signed a petition directed to the Quaker parents of Philadelphia, pleading with them to "manifest" their obedience to God "by integrity, sobriety, and circumspection of life." Specifically he and his partners told the parents to warn their children away from the "ensnaring diversions of the horse races and stage-plays." They simultaneously sent a message to the Quaker youths themselves, advising them to "attend to the restraints of the divine grace." If they did so they would be "preserved from the evils of this world," "become serviceable" in their "several stations," and "obtain true peace" (*Life and Travels of John Pemberton* 49-52). In contrast to Benezet's temperance pamphlet, these pleas were aimed exclusively at Quakers, though their purpose in the long run was to encourage moral reform in the entire colonial population. Philadelphia Quarterly Meeting articulated this more ambitious aim in a statement against horse racing and idle attendance at fairs. The meeting declared that by "steadily and carefully avoiding every appearance of evil and all temptations, [avoiding] lightness, extravagance and wantonly spending our time, we may have humble hope that others will follow us" (Philadelphia Minutes 1723-1772, 292). Woolman described the reform effort in similar terms, contending the meetings' ultimate goal as the restoration of the "True Harmony of Mankind."

In an essay published under the title *Considerations on the True Harmony of Mankind*, Woolman addressed himself to all good Christians, and warned them not to "indulge a desire to imitate our neighbors in those things which harmonize not with the true Christian walking." "Strong are the desires I often feel," he wrote, "that this holy profession may remain unpolluted, and the believers in Christ may so abide in the pure inward feeling of his spirit, that the wisdom from above may shine forth in their living, as a light by which others may be instrumentally helped on their way." He admonished his readers to be "true patterns of the Christian life, who in living and walking may hold forth an invitation to others." In order to send a message through their way of living, the Christians should "come out of the entanglements of the spirit of this world." By visibly avoiding the corrupting influence of "the world" they could transform it. Indeed Woolman suggested that if the faithful set a good examples, their influence would ultimately span the globe, reaching "all nations and tongues" to "the utmost parts of the earth" (Woolman, *Considerations of the True Harmony* 3-4, 5, 17-18, 25-26).[8] Woolman wrote *Considerations on the True Harmony of Mankind* in 1770 and submitted it to the Quaker Overseers of the Press in Philadelphia. They approved the piece for publication and arranged for the printer Joseph Crukshank to produce several hundred copies. Woolman wrote an advertisement for the work and with the help of the Philadelphia Quakers he sent his ad to every Quaker Meeting

---

[8] See Isaiah 66:18; Psalm 2:8.

in Pennsylvania and New Jersey. He explained that he wrote the essay "under an apprehension of duty" and encouraged the meetings to buy multiple copies, advising them that Crukshank would sell the pamphlets in bundles of twelve (Woolman to Israel Pemberton 1771, 22: 87). In support of these efforts, Philadelphia Yearly Meeting took an active role in distributing the pamphlet, sending it to "distant places" where it was thought Woolman's message might have a "salutary effect." In 1772 a committee of the Yearly Meeting wrote to Quaker meetings in New York, Rhode Island and Massachusetts, encouraging them to buy copies of Woolman's essay and give them along with other religious writings to their children, their servants, and any "new settlers" who came to visit them. The Pennsylvania Quakers took note of the general increase of "settlement" in the various colonies and "the poverty of many who may be religiously concerned for the right instructing of their children in the principles of truth, as professed by us." They asserted that Woolman's essay could be read for "profit," unlike those "vain books that amuse the thoughtless youth, and lead such who love to read them [away] from the simplicity of the truth" (Philadelphia Meeting, Meeting for Suffering 1756-1775, 367-68). The uncompromising advice contained within *Considerations on the True Harmony of Mankind* and the pamphlet's widespread distribution highlight Woolman's belief in the universality of his precepts.

The Effect of Reform on Recruitment

Avoiding alcohol, horse races, plays, and fairs did not in the short run bring many converts to the Quakers. The religious society's opposition to slaveholding and its pacifism did not help its recruitment efforts either. In the long run, especially in the years following the American Revolution, Quakerism suffered a dramatic decline in numbers relative to other American religious sects. One could argue that Quakerism abandoned the pragmatic advantages it had enjoyed in America in the seventeenth century. As Friends became rigorous in the demands it made on each other, their praxis no longer exhibited that "unique realism" that Jon Butler noticed in seventeenth-century Quakerism. Nonetheless, there is no reason to conclude that the strategy of attracting members through austere righteousness was inevitably doomed. Similar tactics would later be adopted by Shakers, Amish, Mormons, Black Muslims, and Hasidic Jews. Sometimes recruitment success comes to those religious groups that make the requirements for membership hard.

Dean M. Kelley observes that the religious groups in America that were expanding their membership were generally those that made the greatest demands on their members. He argues that this was so because a central function of religion is to provide for people a sense that their lives have meaning. The espousal of unusual beliefs, and the adoption of distinctive and difficult ways of living, facilitates the development of a communal sense of dramatic, important peculiarity. "Strong" religions can be distinguished from weak ones by their adherents' level of commitment, discipline, and missionary zeal. Kelley associates "strong" religions with "absolutism" and insularity, self-absorption and intolerance. He lists Fox among those charismatic religious leaders who claimed to have discovered "the authoritative teaching of Truth for all time." Kelley continues, "At its worst, such absolutism leads the faithful to hatred and persecution of competing truths and their adherents; at best, they are simply not interested in what, in their view, can only be error" (*Why Conservative Churches* 79-80). Kelley confesses that he initially had difficulty locating the Quakers on the spectrum of "strong" and "weak" religious groups. After further examination, though, he concluded that Fox and the reformers of Woolman's era were "strong" and absolutist. By the twentieth century, however, run-of-the-mill Quakers had become more ecumenically minded, tolerant and weak (86-87).

Kelley's work does not dominate the historiography of Quakerism, but the dichotomy he draws between insular, demanding, strong religious movements and less demanding, ecumenically-oriented, weaker groups has exerted considerable influence on the writing of American religious history generally.[9] Kelley's scheme may have real explanatory power for the study of many religious movements, including America's Quakers after 1827, when the Society of Friends splintered into several groups, each with its own interpretation of Quaker discipline. After the breakup, the various factions' overriding concern for the maintenance of discipline led nearly all of them to denounce those who cooperated with non-Quaker abolitionists.[10] The mid-eighteenth-century Quakers were different, however. They maintained an uncompromising discipline and exhibited most of the traits that Kelley associates with strong religious movements. Yet at the same time, they remained passionately and effectively engaged with the affairs of their neighbors, including those who showed no inclination to adopt Quaker practices or beliefs.

In their work among non-Quakers, America's eighteenth-century Quaker reformers may have exhibited a degree of tolerance, but it was not the sort of tolerance that undermined the strength of their convictions. They remained confident that they belonged to a special community with a divinely inspired historical mission, and they were sustained by a millenarian hope that in the future their understanding of truth would prevail. They were waiting for God to touch the hearts of those around them. If the reformers were tolerant, it was only because they believed that tolerance was necessary for a limited time. It is more accurate to describe them as simultaneously committed and patient.

Works Cited

An Account of a Visit Lately Made to the People Called Quakers in Philadelphia, by Papoonahoal, an Indian Chief. London 1761. Print.
Benezet, Anthony. "An Account of Papunhank's Second Visit to Friends the 4th of 8th month, 1761." *Friend Anthony Benezet*. Ed. George S. Brookes. Philadelphia: U of Pennsylvania P, 1937. 485-92. Print.

---

[9] See Iannaccone; Kelley, "Why Conservative Churches."
[10] See Jordan. Also, the religious basis for anti-abolitionism within antebellum Quaker meetings is discussed in several essays in Carey and Plank.

---. "Account of the Behavior." *Friend Anthony Benezet*. Ed. George S. Brookes. Philadelphia: U of Pennsylvania P, 1937. 479-85. Print.

---. *The Mighty Destroyer Displayed, in Some Accounts of the Dreadful Havock made by the Mistake Use, as well as Abuse of Spirituous Liquors*. Philadelphia, 1774. Print.

Bonomi, Patricia U. *Under the Cope of Heaven: Religion, Society, and Politics in Colonial America*. Oxford: Oxford UP, 1986. Print.

Brookes, George S., ed. *Friend Anthony Benezet*. Philadelphia: U of Pennsylvania P, 1937. Print.

Burlington Monthly Meeting Minutes, 1737-1756. Friends Historical Library, Swarthmore.

Butler, Jon. *Awash in a Sea of Faith: Christianizing the American People*. Cambridge, MA: Harvard UP, 1990. Print.

Cadbury, Henry J. John. *Woolman in England: A Documentary Supplement*. London: Friends Historical Society, 1971. Print.

Carey, Brycchan and Geoffrey Plank, eds. *Quakers and Abolition*. Champaign-Urbana: U of Illinois P, 2014. Print.

Cave, Alfred A. *Prophets of the Great Spirit: Native American Revitalization Movements in Eastern North America*. Lincoln: U of Nebraska P, 2006. Print.

A Collection of Memorials Concerning Divers Deceased Ministers. Philadelphia, 1787. Print.

Dowd, Gregory Evans. *A Spirited Resistance: The North American Indian Struggle for Unity, 1745-1815*. Baltimore: John Hopkins UP, 1992. Print.

---. *War Under Heaven: Pontiac, The Indian Nations and the British Empire*. Baltimore: John Hopkins UP, 2002. Print.

Erben, Patrick M. *A Harmony of the Spirits: Translation and the Language of Community in Early Pennsylvania*. Chapel Hill: U of North Carolina P, 2012. Print.

Eustace, Nicole. "The Sentimental Paradox: Humanity and Violence on the Pennsylvania Frontier." *William and Mary Quarterly* 66.1 (2008): 29-64. Print.

Evans, Joshua. "Journal.". *Friends Miscellany*. Ed. John Comly and Isaac Comly Philadelphia 1831-39. 33-36. Print.

Frost, William. *The Quaker Family in Colonial America*. New York: St. Martin's, 1973. Print.

---. "'Wear the Sword as Long as Thou Canst': William Penn in Myth and History." *Explorations in Early American Culture* 4 (2000): 13-45. Print.

Fox, George. *Journal*. London, 1765.

Gerona, Carla. "Pemberton, Israel." *Oxford Dictionary of National Biography*. Oxford: Oxford UP, 2013. Print.

Gilpin, Thomas, ed. *Exiles in Virginia, with Observations on the Conduct of the Society of Friends during Revolutionary War*. Philadelphia, 1848. Print.

Gragg, Larry. *The Quaker Community on Barbados: Challenging the Culture of the Planter Class*. Jefferson City: U Missouri P, 2009. Print.

Hunter, Charles E. "The Delaware Nativist Revival of the Mid-Eighteenth Century." *Ethnohistory* 18.1 (1971): 39-49. Print.

Iannaccone, Lawrence R. "Why Strict Churches are Strong." *American Journal of Sociology* 99 (1994): 1180-211. Print.

Irwin, Lee. *Coming Down from Above: Prophecy, Resistance, and Renewal in Native American Religions*. Norman: U of Oklahoma P, 2008. Print.

Jackson, Maurice. *Let This Voice Be Heard: Anthony Beneze, Father of Atlantic Abolitionism*. Philadelphia: U of Pennsylvania P, 2009. Print.

James, Sydney V. *A People Among Peoples: Quaker Benevolence in Eighteenth-Century America*. Cambridge, MA: Harvard UP, 1964. Print.

Jones, Rufus. *The Quakers in the American Colonies*. London: Macmillan, 1911. Print.

Jordan, Ryan P. *Slavery and the Meetinghouse: The Quakers and the Abolitionist Dilemma, 1820-1865*. Bloomington: Indiana UP, 2007. Print.

Kelley, Dean M. *Why Conservative Churches are Growing*. New York: Harper, 1972. Print.

---. "Why Conservative Churches are Still Growing." *Journal for Scientific Study of Religion* 17 (1978): 165-72. Print.

Kenny, Kevin. *Peaceable Kingdom Lost: The Paxton Boys and the Destruction of William Penn's Holy Experiment*. Oxford: Oxford UP, 2002. Print.

Levy, Berry. *Quakers and the American Family: British Settlement in the Delaware Valley*. Oxford: Oxford UP, 1992. Print.

The Life and Travels of John Pemberton, A Minister of the Gospel of Christ. London, 1844. Print.

Marietta, Jack D. *The Reformation of American Quakerism, 1748-1783*. Philadelphia: U of Pennsylvania P, 1984. Print.

Merritt, Jane T. *At the Crossroads: Indians and Empires on a Mid-Atlantic Frontier*. Chapel Hill: U of North Carolina P, 2003. Print.

"Minutes of Meetings with a Delegation of Minisink, July 11-16, 1760." *Minutes of the Provincial Council of Pennsylvania*, 10 vols. HM 8249 Huntington Library. Harrisburg, 1852.

Moore, Rosemary. *The Light of Their Consciences: The Early Quakers in Britain, 1646-1666*. University Park: Pennsylvania State UP, 2000. Print.

"On the death of John Woolman." Catchpool mss. vol. 2:218. Friends House Library. London.

Pemberton, Israel. Draft of letter to Benjamin Hersey, and others, January 14, 1762. Friendly Association Minutes. Haverford College Library.

---. *An Address to the Inhabitants of Pennsylvania*. Philadelphia, 1777.

Pemberton, John. Letter to Israel Pemberton July 2, 1763. Pemberton Papers 16:109. Historical Society of Pennsylvania.

Pestana, Carla Gardina. *Quakers and Baptists in Colonial Massachusetts*. New York: Cambridge UP, 1991. Print.

Philadelphia Yearly Meeting Minutes 1723-1772. Haverford College Library.

---. 1747-1779. Harverford College Library.

Philadelphia Yearly Meeting, Meeting for Suffering Minutes 1756-1775. Friends Historical Library. Swarthmore.

Plank, Geoffrey. *John Woolman's Path to the Peaceable Kingdom: A Quaker in the British Empire*. Philadelphia: U of Pennsylvania P, 2012. Print.

Schultze, Christian. Letter to Israel Pemberton. December 1, 1760. Friendly Association Minutes 4:59. Special Collections, Haverford College Library.

Silver, Peter. *Our Savage Neighbors: How Indian War Transformed Early America*. New York: Norton, 2008. Print.

Sloan, David. "'A Time of Sifting and Winnowing': The Paxton Riots and Quaker Non-Violence in Pennsylvania." *Quaker History* 66.1 (1977): 3-22. Print.

Smolenski, John. *Friends and Strangers: The Making of a Creole Culture in Colonial Pennsylvania*. Philadelphia: U of Pennsylvania P, 2010. Print.

Sword, Kirsten. "Remembering Dinah Nevil: Strategic Deceptions in Eighteenth-Century Antislavery." *Journal of American History* 97.3 (2010): 315-43. Print.

Thayer, Theodore. *Israel Pemberton: Kind of the Quakers*. Philadelphia: Historical Society of Pennsylvania, 1943. Print.

Turner, Edward Raymond. "The First Abolition Society in the United States." *Pennsylvania Magazine of History and Biography* 36.1 (1912): 92-109. Print.

Wallace, Paul A.W. *Indians in Pennsylvania*. Harrisburg: Pennsylvania Historical and Museum Commission, 1961. Print.

Woolman, John. *Considerations of the True Harmony of Mankind, and How it is to be Maintained*. Philadelphia, 1770. Print.

---. *The Journal and Major Essays of John Woolman*. Ed. Phillips P. Moulton. Richmond, ID: Friends United P, 1971. Print.

---. Letter to Israel Pemberton June 16, 1763. Pemberton Papers. Historical Society of Pennsylvania.

---. Letter to Israel Pemberton January 1771. Pemberton Papers. Historical Society of Pennsylvania.

---. Letter to Sarah Woolman June 8, 1763. Woolman Collection Box 1, 7. Historical Society of Pennsylvania.

---. Letter to Uriah Woolman June 4, 1763. Gratz Mss, Case 8 box 25. Historical Society of Pennsylvania.

---. "The Substance of some conversation with Paponahoal the Indian Chief at AB of Jo. W-n AB Etc." Pemberton Papers, 13:23. Historical Society of Pennsylvania.

California 'Zen': Buddhist Spirituality Made in America

INKEN PROHL

ABSTRACT

Focusing on the United States as a contact zone for transcultural flows, this article examines how Zen Buddhism was imported into the United States; remade and remarketed there; and then re-imported back into Japan. Beginning with the impact of D.T. Suzuki, the article presents important cultural brokers, institutions, and popular discourses that spread the narratives and practices of both Zen Buddhism and 'Zen.' The examination illustrates the importance of the United States as a religious marketplace in itself and as a productive and creative refinery of and for ideas, lifestyles, and products—in this case, Zen Buddhism.

The United States as a Contact Zone for Transcultural Flows

This essay examines how Zen Buddhism, one of the sets of ideas and practices lumped under the umbrella term 'Spirituality,' is in many respects an exemplary product of translocative flows. In what follows, I employ Thomas Tweed's framework of the translocative, which he has designed to account for the importance of transnational exchange and flows and the dynamics of religious practice in an era of global exchange and mobility ("Theory and Method"). As this analysis of the transformation of Zen Buddhism in the United States in general, and Calfornia in particular, shows, the United States plays a crucial role as a catalyst of religious change and a contact zone for interactions among agents, ideas, and material culture, turning Zen Buddhism into a new religious brand: California 'Zen.'

Transforming Zen Buddhism

The strange career of Zen Buddhism in the United States illustrates the way America functions as a transcultural contact zone. Until the last third of the nineteenth century, one could describe Japanese Zen Buddhism as a small, rather conservative Japanese religion. Zen monks played important administrative roles in the wake of the 1868 Meiji Restoration, but apart from that, their duties consisted chiefly of conducting traditional funeral rites and performing rituals dedicated to the emperor's safety and welfare, as well as that of the country as a whole—rituals that helped legitimate the emperor (Williams). With the opening of Japan to the West following the Convention of Kanagawa (1854), however, Zen Buddhism began to be captured by the same global translocative flows that led to new forms of Buddhism elsewhere. These new forms of Buddhism are highly dynamic conglomerations of Buddhist ideas and practices merged with concepts of democracy, capitalism, the modern individual self, and Protestant notions of interiorized religion. These new forms of Buddhism are what David McMahan refers to as "Buddhist Modernism." Buddhist Modernism—those forms that "emerged out of an engagement with the dominant cultural and intellectual forces of modernity" (McMahan 6)—centers on meditation, individual experience, and the compatibility of Buddhism with science, democracy, and classical humanistic ideals. Numerous encounters between Asian Buddhists and Western audiences led to transcultural hybridization, which transformed understandings of Buddhism for Westerners and Asian Buddhists alike and led to ongoing processes of exchange and conceptual synthesis among Europe, Asia, and other parts of the world, including the United States. The Zen Buddhism that emerged from these manifold transformations was the epitome of a highly experiential, mystical religious tradition with a strong focus on meditation practices (Sharf, "Zen").

The emergence of Modern Buddhism created a continuum between more traditional forms of Zen Buddhism and the modern variants, with a diverse field of meaning, practices, and aesthetics between these two poles developing over the course of the twentieth century. This is the field that is referred to in the contemporary discourse simply as 'Zen.'[1] 'Zen' typically refers to an 'exotic' means of optimizing and reforming the self. 'Zen' combines different allegedly Zen Buddhist ideas and practices into schemas for attaining a balanced, successful life. Books, lectures, and workshops promise 'Zen' as the optimal tool for fashioning a new life via the improvement and realization of the self. Gary R. McClain and Eve Adamson's *The Complete Idiot's Guide to Zen Living* is but one example of the 'Zen' lifestyle's influence on postmodern marketplaces around the world. For the American market, Inez Stein's *The Magic of Zen* is an example of self-optimization through the refinement of personal skills, as are the nearly innumerable books dedicated to 'Zen and the Art of X,' a range that includes such famous topics as "Motorcycle Maintenance" and "Happiness" and workshops focusing on "Zen and the Art of Self-Transformation through Mindfulness."[2]

These commercially successful manifestations of 'Zen' have been supplemented by the expansion of 'Zen' into the world of wellness. A huge array of products, diets, techniques, and practices for catering to one's lifestyle and needs are sold under the label of 'Zen.' With these end results in mind, I will now focus on the way a traditional, conservative, local Japanese religion—Zen Buddhism—transformed into a global, consumer-oriented religious brand: 'Zen.' What factors and mechanisms led to this fundamental transformation, breathtaking in its scope and speed? Answering this question requires an examination of the role the United States played in this transformation as a dynamic marketplace and a refinery of ideas, products, and agents, particularly in the field of religion.

---

[1] As I show in this essay, 'Zen' is a highly flexible and adaptable signifier, thus I typographically distinguish 'Zen' from Zen Buddhism.
[2] See Pirsig; Prentiss; Stein; and Hutter.

Importing and Refining

The metaphor of the refinery explains this transformation, in that refining a product requires both the raw product as well as technology for the refining. In the case of the transformation of Zen in America, the raw materials were imported from Japan, partly through early American converts and aficionados such as William Sturgis Bigelow (1850-1926) and Ernest Fenollosa (1853-1908), but chiefly through D.T. Suzuki (1870-1966).[3] The refinement, meanwhile, came via the translation of the product for a new audience and their consumption tastes, principally in northern California and New York, and particularly in the postwar decades as the 'Zen' brand continued to expand.

D.T. Suzuki, one of the most famous and beloved Buddhist intellectuals in the first half of the twentieth century, arrived in the United States in 1897. He worked with the German Paul Carus (1852-1919), a philosopher, publisher, and advocate of world religion. In 1893, when Carus was at work translating several Buddhist texts, he met Sōen Shaku (1860-1919), Suzuki's teacher, at the World's Parliament of Religions in Chicago in 1893. Shaku later sent Suzuki to the United States, putting the latter in position to serve as Zen Buddhism's principal mediator and representative in the American West. Suzuki's form of Zen Buddhism was a highly individualist and interiorized form of Zen Buddhism, where the individual seeks their own path to a salvation that must be directly experienced and cannot be expressed in words; Suzuki called this experience *satori*. *Satori* is the revelation of a new world to the practitioner. It is a radical transformation of self, in which the practitioner undergoes a total epistemological readjustment as a result of the revelation.

Scholars have shown that Suzuki's form of Zen Buddhism had little in common with contemporary Japanese Zen Buddhism.[4] Suzuki's Zen Buddhism, which he described in a number of commercially successful books and lectures, was the product of a number of translocative flows—his readings in a variety of Western traditions and personal encounters with the Western intellectuals he met during his time in Illinois, New York, and California. In addition to his work with Carus, who was a believer in the essential unity of all religions, Suzuki also translated the writings of Swedish mystic Emanuel Swedenborg and met with a number of different American intellectuals, including Transcendentalists, literary figures, and members of the Theosophical Society.[5] These encounters influenced Suzuki's conception of Zen Buddhism, which he saw as a pure, unmediated, non-dualistic, highly individual religious experience. Suzuki thus echoed and creatively incorporated a religious paradigm that was and remains influential in the American religious marketplace, that of religion as predominantely individual-driven. Although European and American intellectuals such as Friedrich Schleiermacher,

---

[3] See Rosenstone; and Tweed, "American Occultism and Japanese Buddhism."
[4] On Suzuki's Japanese context, see Faure, *Chan Insights and Oversights*; Ketelaar; and Snodgrass.
[5] On Suzuki's numerous encounters with Western intellectuals, see Fields; Offermans; Jaffe; Sharf, "Experience"; Sharf, "Uses and Abuses"; Suzuki, *Swedenborg*; and Tweed, "United States."

Ralph Waldo Emerson, William James, and Rudolf Otto had contributed to the idea of religion as an individual endeavor, practice, or state of mind, the religious marketplace in the United States was a major force in developing and exporting the idea of religion as an individual path to salvation (Sharf, "Experience"). As Robert Sharf notes, Suzuki's form of Zen Buddhism, with its highly experiential personal access to truth, adapts this integral component of American religious history and identity. Suzuki thus helped create the paradigm of modern spirituality and paved the way for the later export of other forms of American-grown religiosity, including New Age (Sharf, "Uses and Abuses").

The Market for *Zazen*

Suzuki's 'Modern Zen' emerged out of the 'Buddhist Modernism' of the late nineteenth and early twentieth centuries (Jaffe). For his American customers, however, only Suzuki's Zen Buddhism offered the Zen experience; they either did not appreciate the broader context within which Suzuki's form was developing or, more likely, were unaware of it. They flocked to Suzuki and other Zen priests, like Sokei-an (1882-1945), in search of *satori*, hoping for a fundamental transformation of their lives. An example will illustrate the powerful influence American practitioners had on what has come to be called Zen Buddhism, especially in the contemporary West. A follower of the Rinzai school of Zen Buddhism, Sokei-an came to the United States in 1906 and brought with him a rather plain, unspectacular teaching style. This baffled his early customers. How, they wondered, could they achieve this overwhelming, radical, self-transformative experience simply sitting in a chair listening to an admittedly shy teacher lecture to them? It was Sokei-an's wife, Ruth Fuller-Sasaki (1892-1967), who saw the potential in the market and convinced her husband to alter his teaching style. Fuller-Sasaki, who became aquainted with Zen Buddhism on her travels through Japan, persuaded Sokei-an to teach his American students *zazen*, the practice of 'ritual sitting' or 'meditation' (depending on how it is translated). Sokei-an at first balked at the idea; he refused to teach the strict, highly regulated practice of *zazen*, which he saw as little more than a subtle form of physical and psychological abuse of young novices in the monastery. Eventually, however, Fuller-Sasaki prevailed and Sokei-an began teaching *zazen*, to the delight of his American customers, who were thrilled about their new lessons and who showed up at 8 am to practice the only 'real' Zen (Fields).

After Suzuki's brand of Zen found its success in the early decades of the twentieth century, the 1950s and 60s provided the cultural ferment for further refinement and growth. In these decades, the United States' power, rivaled only by the Soviet Union, was undisputed but not universally welcomed. For many, around the world as well as domestically, the United States represented a particularly Western, Christian-oriented focus on technology and the accumulation of material wealth. Individuals ontologically wary of this orientation found an alternative in the various Asian religious traditions, which were beginning to receive a great deal of attention at this time. These traditions were widely perceived as inherently peaceful, anti-materialist, and non-dualistic, and were hailed for their allegedly deep and exotic wisdom. The Beats, for example, who emerged in Berkeley and the greater San Francisco Bay area and came to prominence in the 1950s, celebrated their own take on Zen Buddhism in their novels, poems, and articles and thus served as one of the catalysts for the development of 'Zen.'[6]

Another major force in the development of 'Zen' was Alan Watts. Watts, a former Episcopal priest and follower of Suzuki, purged many of the traditional elements from what he understood as the only correct form of Zen Buddhism, transforming it into a set of practices and techniques directed toward individual salvation. Watts's 1957 bestseller, *The Way of Zen*, helped define 'Zen' as an atemporal religious orientation toward the immanent world around us. One result of this radical decontextualization was that 'Zen' was no longer tied to a particular time, place, or even practice and instead came to be used as a label for everything from literature to modern art to poetry, music, or dancing. By 1960 Fuller-Sasaki could describe it as a kind of shibboleth deployed at cocktail parties or certain bohemian gatherings. 'Zen' became a popular buzzword in contemporary psychology and psychotherapy (Fields 205).

It was in this context—psychology and psychotherapy—that the 'Zen' created by people like Suzuki and Watts became especially successful. The 1950s and '60s saw the birth of what Eva Illouz has termed 'therapeutic culture,' a term that she uses in her explanations of the profound impact that the therapeutic discourse has had on the lives of modern individuals and the centrality of psychology to contemporary notions of identity. This therapeutic culture was the product of figures such as Carl Rogers and Abraham Maslow, who developed concepts of 'self-actualization' and created the human potential movement (Gamble). Rather than seeking to mend old emotional wounds, this movement redefined psychotherapy as a means for pursuing personal growth and, thereby, happiness. Human potential psychology saw the inner self as the sole source of happiness and well-being and thus necessarily in need of constant attention and maintenance. As Illouz and Nikolas Rose argue, this new focus on the "regime of the self" is one of the hallmarks of Western modernity and has led to the dominant role of therapists, doctors, personal coaches, and motivational trainers in determining what is beneficial to the proper development of the self (Rose 100).

With its focus on the transformation of the self, Suzuki's Modern Zen was a comfortable fit with this emerging therapeutic culture. Examining the latter, moreover, shows us another respect in which Suzuki's Zen Buddhism incorporated a dominant American cultural narrative. Suzuki's stress on techniques of self-development and on 'unleashing the hidden potential of the self' via transformative practices designed to remake one's life and make the individual happier and more successful merged with the teachings of Watts and his followers. Another example is the Esalen Institute, founded in 1962 in Big Sur, California. Easlen provided a social space and contact zone for a broader exchange of ideas and techniques among like-minded practitioners. Esalen was designed to be an experimental center that dealt with spiritual growth and human potential by

---

[6] For context, see Ellwood; Roof; and Wuthnow.

combining Eastern thought, humanistic psychology, and psychedelics with meditation practices, therapeutic works, and bodily practice. Watts brought Suzuki's Zen Buddhism to Esalen, where he worked with others to psychologize Zen Buddhism, thus refining it into the prototype of modern spirituality and demonstrating the power of Esalen to be a refinery of 'Asian spirituality made in America.'[7]

From the nineteenth century on, wealthy Americans had funded projects exploring or research into religion and spirituality. The history of Zen Buddhism and emergent 'Zen' in California, particularly the development of the Esalen Institute, fits within this pattern. Esalen provided a network that brought representatives of Zen Buddhism, Modern Zen, and 'Zen' together with wealthy supporters, who in turn funded the organizations. An example of this is Laurence Rockefeller, who donated millions to Esalen in deference to his mother's interest in Zen Buddhism. Rockefeller also donated millions to the San Francisco Zen Center (Goldman 143-44).

If the wealthy enjoyed the advantages of their connections, however, they were not the only beneficiaries. As Marion Goldman has convincingly shown, Esalen democratized "spiritual privilege," i.e., the ability to devote time and resources to working with the religious notions and practices that had formerly been restricted to the few. According to Goldman, who focuses on spiritual privilege throughout her book, Esalen played an important role in diversifying the American religious marketplace by extending this spiritual privilege beyond the wealthy and deeper into American society more broadly. The fusion of humanistic psychology and alternative spiritualities, like yoga or 'Zen,' morphed spiritual practices into "pathways to better mental and physical health" (Goldman 4). This in turn made 'Zen' a tool for personal growth, a tool that was legitimized by the contemporary Western uses of psychology. These psychological perceptions of 'Zen' were concurrently disseminated via other Esalen-derived practices like gestalt therapy, meditation, and self-psychology. The result was the transformation of "spiritual privilege" into something perceived as the inherent right of every American: the right to maximize their potential in mind, body, spirit, and emotion.

This 'Asian spirituality made in America' was congruent with other semantic fields like health, body, mind, self-improvement, and recreation. As several authors have pointed out, by the 1960s, Asian spirituality had shifted from countercultural margins to the cultural mainstream in Western societies (Ellwood; Kripal). The mid-twentieth century field of cultural production in the United States participated in the therapeutic reconfigurations of Asian traditions and became one of the most important channels for their dissemination into a wider cultural and global context. The transformations and disseminations of 'Zen' through the institutional and social networks at Esalen illustrate this point convincingly.

---

[7] On Esalen, see Goldman; Kripal; Kripal and Shuck.

The Marketing Potential of Zen Buddhist Rhetoric

One further point to consider is what made the synthesis between Zen Buddhism and prevailing concepts of self-optimization so natural. To answer this, one needs to take a closer look at the specific rhetorical content of Zen Buddhism, of which one of the prime characteristics is an ambiguous stance toward defining 'truth.'[8] The truth that can be found through and in Zen Buddhism is ineffable—it cannot be reduced to words, but can only be hinted at, circumscribed, or ritually staged. Questions of truth-testing, and the ontological and theological questions that mingle with and stand behind them, are properly beyond the interest of scholars of religious studies. Of interest, rather, are the ways traditional Zen Buddhism and its modern apologetics attract so many practitioners by answering their existential questions—"Who am I?," "What do I really want?"—without actually offering any concrete explanations or spiritual guidelines.

Ambiguity in Zen Buddhism—a paradoxical combination of the vagueness of traditional Zen Buddhist rhetoric and the elite inclusivity of its many apologists—is one of the most attractive elements of modern 'Zen.' This traditional rhetoric is characterized by a deep suspicion of words and a fondness for a style that uses paradox, irony, absurdity, sarcastic insult, and descriptions of extreme physical gestures and body language (Heine 39). This is the rhetoric typical of the Koan literature to which many of the apologists of Zen Buddhism refer in their own writings. One famous example of this is the exchange between a monk who asks, "What is Buddha?" and the master, who answers, "Three pounds of flax." In another instance, a monk asks, "Does a dog have Buddha nature or not?," to which the master replies, "Wu," which means "nothing" or "no" (*Blue Cliff Record*; Yamada).

The 'truth' behind these words, Zen Buddhists proclaim, can be felt and known only by enlightened minds—it remains inaccessible for those who have not yet reached the state of enlightenment. Following this logic, the rhetoric of 'Zen' is both shielded from any kind of critical examination and also remarkably capacious: anything can be proclaimed 'Zen' or adorned with that label, including the arts of archery, dieting, falling in love, becoming an emotionally balanced manager or CEO, or living a stress-free, joyful life. Again, however, our question is not whether 'Zen' is an appropriate signifier or meaning carrier for all of these different 'lifestyle techniques' but rather why it can be deemed so. What is it that for so many people makes 'Zen' such a natural, ideal meaning carrier for notions of sacralizing the self and focusing on a balanced, happy life free of suffering?

'Zen' is popularly understood as a highly individual effort to give one's life a deeper meaning by optimizing and sacralizing the self. I suggest that this process is made possible because the rhetoric of Zen Buddhism helps package the modern project of the self in religious rhetoric, thereby turning it into a commendable pursuit that resembles and strengthens the allegedly natural order of things. By focusing on the construction of a successful life while legitimizing this construction by

---

[8] On the rhetorical characteristics of Zen Buddhism, see Faure, *The Rhetoric of Immediacy*; Heine; McRae.

linking it to the hidden transcendental value of 'Zen,' individual practitioners can view their efforts as linked with the deep secrets and metaphysical truth behind all things as revealed through 'Zen.' These hidden transcendences include, for example, beliefs in the transmission of the Buddha Dharma down through the lineage of the great masters, the golden age of Zen Buddhism, and the possibility of achieving enlightenment through paradoxical dialogues or unexpected gestures as described in the Koans. The nebulous aura of sacrality that 'Zen' created and has maintained reinforces these 'hidden transcendences,' which give 'Zen' the power to consecrate activities, notions, and goods with which it is associated in a way that appears natural. This allegedly natural order of things makes 'Zen' a highly attractive consumer good that can be branded and sold through books, seminars, meditation courses, or 'Zen' art. 'Zen' is thus a powerful tool for regulating the 'technologies of the self'[9] and thus can help shape individual actors who are highly adapted to the requirements of modern societies.

Traditional Zen Buddhist Schools Enter the Field of 'Asian Spirituality' in the United States

These reconfigurations of Asian traditions—or refinements, depending on your perspective—were further intensified by the arrival of a number of offshoots from traditional Zen Buddhist schools in Japan. One of the most successful of the Zen priests to arrive in America and spread Zen Buddhism was *Shunryū Suzuki* (1904-1971) (Chadwick). "Little Suzuki," as he called himself to avoid confusion with his famous predecessor, D.T. Suzuki, was a priest in the Soto-Zen school who arrived in San Francisco in 1959 and set out to teach his followers traditional *zazen*. By the time Little Suzuki arrived at the end of the 1950s, San Francisco had become a hotbed for the emerging counterculture and a magnet for those interested in Asian traditions and thus offered the immigrant priest a receptive environment and potential following. Little Suzuki gathered many followers and students, taught them the sequence of events in Japanese monasteries, and began importing traditional material objects like mats made from rice straw, meditation cushions, and other paraphernalia used in the monasteries.

Little Suzuki continued to expand and went on to found the San Francisco Zen Center, which grew into one of the largest Zen associations in the West. The Center is an excellent case study as both a pioneering institution and a representative example of other Zen Buddhist centers in the United States, especially California, and Europe. In these centers, the arrival of Zen priests from Japan and their attempts to bring with them a traditional, highly formalized, and often very strict form of Zen Buddhism lent credibility and authenticity to the more popular, non-institutionalized, therapeutic notions of 'Zen.' The result—a combination of D.T. Suzuki-inspired techniques of self-optimization with the authority of an

---

[9] In a narrow sense, this refers to the Foucauldian concept of "technologies of the self." See Foucault et al. In a broader sense, however, I mean all kinds of techniques and practices aimed at self-optimization. See Reckwitz.

authentic, centuries-old Japanese tradition—was the culturally and commercially prominent California 'Zen.' Thus legitimated, California 'Zen' was also able to become a powerful tool driving and shaping teachings in fields of practice related to the body. The proliferation of yoga centers, the success of Buddhist- and Hindu-inspired forms of meditation, and the vitality of Asian healing traditions within the many postmodern marketplaces attest to the attractiveness of practices catering to the body and the senses.

In addition to adorning various practices and products with the 'Zen' label, the Zen Buddhist centers in the United States served as influential importers of elements and aesthetic 'trademarks' of Japanese culture. Thanks to the impact of California 'Zen,' 'Zen gardens,' 'Zen art,' and 'Zen cooking' have become powerful stylistic devices for shaping and branding such diverse products as houses, hotels, food, clubs, restaurants, fitness studios, celebrity biographies, and even a city's public profile. Taking a material religion approach to such phenomena, Jane Iwamura has recently shown that many Americans have come to know and experience Asian religions via mass-mediated representations that are primarily visual in nature (see also Meyer et al.). This visual mediation and resulting visual orientation has several significant social effects. Iwamura presents D. T. Suzuki as the prototypical 'oriental monk,' whose teachings and personality profoundly influenced popular notions of Zen Buddhism. As Iwamura shows, these notions are embedded and transmitted via material objects, social practices, aesthetic representations, and religious agents who have the ability, social capital, and legitimacy to define a religious tradition. Zen Buddhism offers a wide range of materialities, be they in the form of the 'oriental monk,' the tradition's aesthetics, or the practices that have contributed to its credibility and marketability.

The United States as a Producer of Religious Brands

Having seen how raw materials were imported and refined into a new product, we can see the importance of treating the United States as a dynamic, powerful cultural refinery and contact zone for ideas, material objects, and global agents. Such an approach helps us better understand the mechanics of interchange between religions and the various American marketplaces, but also to situate the ways these interactions in the U.S. marketplace function within a broader global marketplace. The American marketplace, as we have seen, has accommodated and helped produce three distinct forms of Zen: therapeutic 'Zen,' which is closely related to other therapeutic practices catering to sensual and bodily needs; institutionalized Zen Buddhism, which has carved out a comfortable niche in California, from which it has spread throughout the United States and across Europe, Australia, and other Western societies; and 'Zen,' which is increasingly used as a compelling, commercially successful label for a modern but reflective lifestyle centered on the development of the self.

These forms of Zen Buddhism 'made in America' allow us to look at an idea I have hinted at above—faith branding—from the theoretical perspective developed by Mara Einstein. As Einstein has shown, religious products are branded in much the same ways as other consumer goods, and, as with other consumer goods, these faith brands help consumers build and maintain a personal connection with the products they consume. In today's overcrowded religious marketplace, a brand's narratives, symbols, and aesthetics help it attract attention, increasing its chances of being consumed. From this theoretical perspective, 'Zen' undoubtedly qualifies as a faith brand, since it helps market the different forms of 'Zen' that I have described. 'Zen' could perhaps be called an *über-brand*, a mega-brand, since it can be readily deployed in nearly all fields of Western consumer culture and overlays virtually any product or practice with an attractive narrative matrix. Important elements of this narrative matrix, as we have seen, were born in California. The result of the refining process, in which the raw materials were changed via translocative flows and hybridizations, was California 'Zen,' or, perhaps more accurately, a uniquely Californian discourse on 'Zen.' This Californian discourse on 'Zen' is itself a brand that is applied to the various forms, practices, and products that are marketed under that label. Refined via this Californian discourse, 'Zen' was re-exported and made commercially and culturally significant inroads into a number of marketplaces; it has spread not only throughout the West but, vitally and informatively, also back to Japan, where the re-import of American-made 'Zen' demonstrates the reach of this successful global brand.

As noted above, the most important duties of traditional Japanese Buddhist temples are those involved with conducting rituals dealing with death and grief and rituals aimed at procuring worldly benefits. Repeated surveys of temple visitors have shown that very few visitors come to seek a Buddhist priest for advice.[10] My fieldwork in Japan confirmed this pattern; I often encountered visitors who told me, "Well, I go to the temple because I'm going to need it when I'm dead."[11] Many Japanese, in fact, see financial support of their family temple as little more than an administrative way of dealing with death.

The 1980s, however, saw a change in how the Buddhist tradition was seen in Japan. The rise of the 'spiritual world' (*seishin sekai*)—the Japanese equivalent of the Western New Age (Shimazono; Prohl)—transformed Zen from the religion of a small intellectual elite into 'Zen,' a religious practice designed to help enhance the inner self of all who seek it. Meditation came to be seen as a way of leading to a more balanced and conscious life and thus as a means for achieving self-enhancement. In Japan, as in other modern societies, recent decades have seen the publication of many magazines dealing with the spiritual world. These Japanese magazines feature titles such as *Tama* ("spirit"; "soul") or English titles like *Inner Voice*, *Conscious*, or *Star People*. In 2005, *Conscious* featured an article about *zazen* that stresses the 'Zen experience' and illustrates the shift in perceptions:

> I could hear the sound of the wind sweeping through the trees, the flutter of insects and chirping of little birds. Then there was the symphony of the cicadas at the beginning of fall. The veneration of all living creatures is soaking through my skin and slowly entering my body. I feel as if I am turning into a tree full of life's energy [...]. The living splendor of the flowers in a tree's shadow is meeting my eyes. I sit and I indulge. In the temple

---

[10] See Reader; and Rowe.
[11] Fieldwork conducted in Nagano, Japan, from fall 2005 through summer 2006.

the pure morning means freshness for my mind and my spirit. This is pure happiness. (Kitazawa 52)

As this quotation shows, Japanese Zen Buddhism has changed from being chiefly a provider of rituals concerning death and worldly benefits to a set of practices aimed at creating happiness. There is also a growing number of books and seminars offering ideas for how to use 'Zen' to refine one's lifestyle and thereby create a more meaningful life, such as Yutaka Ikeda's *Zen: Kokoro to karada ga girei ni naru suwarikata* ("The 'Zen' Style for a Beautiful Life"). The re-importation to Japan of a therapeutic 'Zen' has led to the emergence of a religious marketplace offering many different books and seminars selling 'Zen' as a powerful tool for becoming more professionally successful and as a means of dealing with stress, loneliness, suffering, sickness, and personal crises. In Japan, one can now find virtually the same 'Zen' products and services as are available in the West. Traditional Zen Buddhist practices and ideas have morphed into means of self-improvement, self-optimization, and coping strategies along the California 'Zen' model.

The 'Zen' Brand

The fact that the 'Zen' brand made its way back to Japan is just one example of its global spread, which can be explained via the dynamics of transcultural flows and confluences as well as the potential of certain cultural climates—in this case, the United States—to act as contact zones for translocative fusion and exchange. Other factors accounting for the global spread of 'Zen' are the importance of 'regimes of the self' in highly industrialized societies, the specific aesthetic dimensions associated with 'Zen,' and 'Zen's' elaborate religious rhetoric. Whether this global brand is the result of an ongoing process of the "corporatization of spirituality, that [leads] to the tailoring of individualized spiritualities to fit the needs of corporate business culture," as Jeremy Carette and Richard King intriguingly suggest, is up for debate (29). What is not debatable, however, is that California 'Zen' is one of the most successful and influential religious exports the United States has ever seen.

I would like to conclude by briefly addressing the following question: is there any Zen left in the various forms of Modern 'Zen'? Absolutely there is. For many scholars, the history of Zen Buddhism in the West is little more than a sequence of misunderstandings and false interpretations. Instead of speaking about these misunderstandings or incorrect interpretations, I think that we would do better to see the emergence of Modern Zen and the various formations that developed in highly industrialized societies under the 'Zen' mega-brand as further examples of the creativity and innovation that goes into processes of religious transformations. To think that 'Zen' is somehow an exception to these processes would be to misinterpret thousands of years of religious history that have shown us, and continue to show us, that these transformations and innovations are one of the constants nothing more in the histories of religious traditions.

Works Cited

Blue Cliff Record. Trans. J.C. Cleary and Thomas Cleary. Boston, MA: Shambhala Publications, 2005. CD.
Buswell, Robert E., ed. *Encyclopedia of Buddhism*. New York: Macmillian Reference, 2004. Print.
Carrette, Jeremy and Richard King. *Selling Spirituality: The Silent Takeover of Religion*. London: Routledge, 2008. Print.
Chadwick, David. *Crooked Cucumber: The Life of Zen Teaching of Shunryū Suzuki*. New York: Broadway Books, 1999. Print.
Einstein, Mara. *Brands of Faith: Marketing Religion in a Commercial Age*. London: Routledge, 2008. Print.
Ellwood, Robert S. *The Sixties Spiritual Awakening: American Religion Moving from Modern to Postmodern*. New Brunswick, NJ: Rutgers UP, 1994. Print.
Faure, Bernard. *Chan Insights and Oversights: An Epistemological Critique of the Chan Tradition*. Princeton: Princeton UP, 1993. Print.
---. *The Rhetoric of Immediacy: A Cultural Critique of Chan/Zen Buddhism*. Princeton, NJ: Princeton UP, 1991. Print.
Fields, Rick. *How the Swans Came to the Lake: A Narrative History of Buddhism in America*. Boston, MA: Shambhala Publications, 1992. Print.
Foucault, Michel, et al. *Technologies of the Self: A Seminar with Michel Foucault*. Amherst: U of Massachusetts P, 1988. Print.
Gamble, John W. "When East Meets West: The Rise of Meditation." *Religion as Entertainment*. Ed. C.K. Robertson. New York: Lang, 2002. 79-104. Print.
Goldman, Marion. *The American Soul Rush: Esalen and the Rise of Spiritual Privilege*. New York: New York UP, 2012. Print.
Heine, Steven. *Zen Skin, Zen Marrow: Will the Real Zen Buddhism Please Stand Up?* Oxford: Oxford UP, 2008. Print.
Hutter, Jeffrey. "Zen and the Art of Self-Transformation through Mindfulness." UCLA Extension, Los Angeles. 21 Feb. 2009. Workshop.
Ikeda, Yutaka. *Zen: Kokoro to Karada Ga Kirei Ni Naru Michi*. Tokyo: Ikedashoten, 2005. Print.
Illouz, Eva. *Saving the Modern Soul: Therapy, Emotions, and the Culture of Self-Help*. Berkeley: U of California P, 2008. Print.
Iwamura, Jane Naomi. *Virtual Orientalism: Asian Religion and American Popular Culture*. New York: Oxford UP, 2011. Print.
Jaffe, Richard M. Introduction to the 2010 Edition. *Swedenborg: Buddha of the North*. By Daisetsu Teiterō Suzuki. Trans. Andrew Bernstein. West Chester, PA: Swedenborg Foundation, 1996. xxviii. Print.
Ketelaar, James Edward. *Of Heretics and Martyrs in Meiji Japan: Buddhism and Its Persecution*. Princeton, NJ: Princeton UP, 1990. Print.
Kitazawa, Anri. "Seijaku He No Michi (The Path to Silence)." *Conscious* 1.1 (2005): 52-53. Print.
Kripal, Jeffrey J. *Esalen: American and the Religion of No Religion*. Chicago: U of Chicago P, 2007. Print.

Kripal, Jeffrey J. and Glenn W. Shuck, eds. *On the Edge of the Future: Esalen and the Evolution of American Culture.* Bloomington: Indiana UP, 2005. Print.
McClain, Gary R., and Eve Adamson. *The Complete Idiot's Guide to Zen Living.* Indianapolis, IN: Alpha P, 2001. Print.
McMahan, David L. *The Making of Buddhist Modernism.* Oxford: Oxford UP, 2006. Print.
McRae, John R. *The Northern School and the Formation of Early Ch'an Buddhism.* Honolulu: U of Hawai'i P, 2005. Print. Studies in East Asian Buddhism 3.
Meyer, Brigit, et al. "The Origin and Mission of Material Religion." *Religion* 40.3 (2010): 207-11. Print.
Offermanns, Jürgen. *Der lange Weg des Zen-Buddhismus nach Deutschland.* Lund: Almquist & Wiskell International, 2002. Print.
Pirsig, Robert M. *Zen and the Art of Motorcycle Maintenance.* New York: Bantam, 1974. Print.
Prentiss, Chris. *Zen and the Art of Happiness.* Los Angeles: Power, 2006. Print.
Prohl, Inken. "The Spiritual World: Aspects of New Age in Japan." *Handbook of New Age.* Eds. James R. Lewis and Daren Kemp. Vol. 1 Leiden: Brill, 2007. 359-79. Print.
Reader, Ian. "Zazenless Zen? The Position of Zazen in Institutional Zen Buddhism." *Japanese Religions* 14.3 (1986): 7-27. Print.
Reckwitz, Andreas. *Subjekt.* Bielefeld: Transcript, 2008. Print.
Robertson, C. K., ed. *Religion as Entertainment.* New York: Lang, 2002. Print.
Roof, Wade Clark. *Spiritual Marketplace: Baby Boomers and the Remaking of American Religion.* Princeton, NJ: Princeton UP, 2001. Print.
Rose, Nikolas S. *Inventing Our Selves: Psychology, Power, and Personhood.* Cambridge, MA: Cambridge UP, 1996. Print.
---. *The Politics of Life Itself: Biomedicine, Power, and Subjectivity in the Twenty-First Century.* Princeton, NJ: Princeton UP, 2007. Print.
Rosenstone, Robert A. *Mirror in the Shrine: American Encounters with Meiji Japan.* Cambridge, MA: Harvard UP, 1991. Print.
Rowe, Mark. *Bonds of the Dead: Temples, Burial, and the Transformation of Contemporary Japanese Buddhism.* Chicago: U of Chicago P, 2011. Print.
Seager, Richard Hughes. *Buddhism in America.* New York: Columbia UP, 1999. Print.
Sharf, Robert H. "Buddhist Modernism and the Rhetoric of Meditative Experience," *Numen* 42.3 (1995): 227-83. Print.
---. "Experience." *Critical Terms for Religious Studies.* Ed. Mark C. Taylor. Chicago: U of Chicago P, 1998. 94-116. Print.
---. "The Uses and Abuses of Zen in the Twentieth Century." *Zen, Reike, Karate: Japanese Religiosität in Europa.* Eds. Inken Prohl and Hartmut Zinser. Hamburg: LIT, 2002. 143-54. Print.
---. "The Zen of Japanese Nationalism." *History of Religions* 33.1 (1993): 1-43. Print.
Shimazono, Susumu. "'New Age Movement' or 'New Spirituality Movements and Culture'?" *Social Compass* 46.2 (1999): 121-33. Print.

Snodgrass, Judith. *Presenting Japanese Buddhism to the West: Orientalism, Occidentalism, and the Columbian Exposition.* Chapel Hill: U of North Carolina P, 2003. Print.

Stein, Inez. *The Magic of Zen: Pathway to Self-Transformation.* Atlanta, NC: Humanics, 1996. Print.

Suzuki, Daisetsu Teiterō. *Swedenborg: Buddha of the North.* Trans. Andrew Bernstein. West Chester, PA: Swedenborg Foundation, 1996. Print.

---. *Zen and Japanese Culture.* Princeton, NJ: Princeton UP, 2010. Print.

Tweed, Thomas A. "American Occultism and Japanese Buddhism: Albert J. Edumunds, D.T. Suzuki, and Translocative History." *Japanese Journal of Religious Studies* 32.2 (2005): 249-81. Print.

---. "Theory and Method in the Study of Buddhism: Toward the 'Translocative' Analysis." *Journal of Global Buddhism* 12 (2011): 17-32. Print.

---. "United States." *Encyclopedia of Buddhism.* Ed. Robert E. Buswell. New York: Macmillian Reference, 2004. 864-70. Print.

Watts, Alan. *The Way of Zen.* New York: Pantheon, 1956. Print.

Williams, Duncan Ryūken. *The Other Side of Zen: A Social History of Sōtō Zen Buddhism in Tokugawa Japan.* Princeton, NJ: Princeton UP, 2004. Print.

Wuthnow, Robert. *After Heaven: Spirituality in America since the 1950s.* Berkeley: U of California P, 1998. Print.

Yamada, Koun. *The Gateless Gate: Classic Zen Koans.* Somerville, MA: Wisdom Publications, 2004. Print.

Evangelicals and Catholics Together: How it Should Have Been in the Roaring Twenties Marketplace of Ideas

BARRY HANKINS

ABSTRACT

The presidential election of 1928 was merely the most glaring example of Protestant-Catholic tension in America's Roaring Twenties. Catholics understood that they could not fully embrace American freedom, and Protestants viewed them as un-American for holding such a view. In the late twentieth century, evangelical Protestants broke with their liberal brethren and joined Catholics in critiquing a culture that left virtually all moral questions to choice. The elements for this common ground between evangelicals and Catholics already existed in the twenties, but the marketplace of ideas made an alliance impossible. Only later did evangelicals begin to understand that the liberal conception of freedom is based on the autonomy of the individual. As a result, they joined Catholics and now live in tension with American freedom.

On the heels of the U.S. presidential election of 1928, the liberal Protestant journal *Christian Century* ran a remarkable editorial. The editor denounced bigoted anti-Catholicism, but framed the election as a contest between those who believe a candidate with a "conscience formed under ecclesiastical authority" was better fit for office than a candidate with a "conscience individually formed." "A conscience formed under ecclesiastical authority" was a reference to Democratic candidate Al Smith, the first Roman Catholic to run for president of the United States. There was little doubt that the *Christian Century* preferred "a conscience individually formed" and therefore had supported the Protestant Republican candidate Herbert Hoover during the election. Likewise, most Protestants outside the solidly Democratic South supported Hoover. Whether fundamentalist or modernist, evangelical or liberal, Protestants agreed that their kind of freedom was the American kind of freedom. By contrast, the Catholic Church's hierarchical view of authority and communitarian view of the individual threatened the American way of life. Protestants were wrong on both counts. Their kind of freedom was not American freedom, and the Catholic Church was no threat ("What elected").[1]

In a time long before the advent of two-year presidential campaigns, the election of 1928 nevertheless started in spring 1927. In April the *Atlantic Monthly* magazine published an essay by little-known American attorney Charles C. Marshall, titled "An Open Letter to the Honorable Alfred E. Smith." A full year and

---

[1] This essay is adapted from Barry Hankins, *Jesus and Gin: Evangelicalism, the Roaring Twenties and Today's Culture Wars* (New York: Palgrave Macmillan, 2010); used by permission. A different version of the essay also appeared as "Liberty, Conscience & Autonomy: How the Culture War of the Roaring Twenties Set the Stage for Today's Catholic-Evangelical Alliance," *Touchstone*, 24:6 (2011), 42-48; used by permission.

a half before the election, it was widely rumored that Al Smith would receive the Democratic Party's nomination. A highly successful governor of New York, Smith was a career politician who had held public office almost continuously since 1895. His political genius lay in his ability to blend the patronage of the infamous Tammany Hall political machine with the reform-mindedness of the Progressive Era. In bipartisan fashion, Smith worked well with both Democrats and Republicans while serving in the New York state legislature. By the 1920s Smith was a nationally known politician who narrowly missed out on his party's nomination in 1924. The astute twentieth-century journalist and social commentator Walter Lippmann described Smith by saying he "holds these crowds as no man can hold them. He holds them without promise of a millennium, without a radical program, without appeal to their hatreds, without bribes and doles and circuses." In posing the rhetorical question as to how Smith retained the support of the masses of working-class people, Lippmann wrote, "The answer, I think, is that they feel he has become the incarnation of their own hope and pride." In doing so, Smith had lifted "their secret sense of inferiority" (7).[2]

Catholic American and the "New Immigrants"

Smith was a product of Catholic America. Hailing from New York's Bowery neighborhood on the lower east side of Manhattan, he grew up in St. James Parish, where the entire neighborhood revolved around the activities of the Church. Oftentimes, at 9 p.m. in the evenings, when it was time to get off the streets, Father Keen shooed the neighborhood children to their homes, shouting at them from a second-floor window in one of the parish buildings. Religion infused virtually every aspect of Smith's boyhood. St. James parish consisted of roughly 16,000 communicants, with more than fifteen social clubs, offering everything from drama to rifle shooting. As a Catholic from a city where immigrants abounded, Smith represented what Lippmann called the "new immigrants," i.e., those whose ancestors arrived in America as late as the mid-nineteenth century. Writing in 1925, Lippmann foresaw a looming conflict between Smith and "that older American civilization of town and country which dreads him and will resist him." Lippmann called the new immigrant class "half enfranchised Americans," who, personified by Al Smith, were making their first bid for presidential power. "Here are the new people, clamoring to be admitted to America," Lippmann wrote, "and there are the older people defending their household gods" (1-4, 9).

When this contest between the old and new America took place in 1928, it provided an abundance of anti-Catholicism in defense of those household gods. Charles Marshall's 1927 open letter in the *Atlantic Monthly*, however, raised legitimate questions that Smith would need to answer. Marshall's first and foremost query addressed the Catholic doctrine of the 'two swords,' which dates at least from the fifth century pope Gelasius I. In this political theory, if there should be a

---

[2] Lippmann used the term "millennium" in a secular sense. He seemed to be saying that Smith promised no grandiose political program that would lead to utopia.

clash between the two swords of church and state, the church is supreme. Inherent in this is the idea that the Catholic Church itself is not merely one expression of Christianity among others, but indeed the one true Church. In conjunction with the two swords theory, Marshall drew attention to Pius IX's Syllabus of Errors (1864) and Leo XIII's encyclical of 1885. Both documents condemn separation of church and state, in part because separation means that the state has no interest in adjudicating a preferred faith. Moreover, Pius's Syllabus of Errors rejects democracy along with socialism, communism, and other dangerous modern -isms. Under the U.S. constitution, Marshall argued correctly, all religions are equal before the law. What then to make of the Catholic claim of church supremacy? As Marshall wrote, "We are satisfied if [Catholics] will but concede that those claims unless modified and historically redressed, precipitate an inevitable conflict between the Roman Catholic Church and the American State irreconcilable with domestic peace" (548).

Al Smith's Answer

In 1960 John F. Kennedy faced similar questions when running as the second Catholic presidential candidate. He famously replied to the ministerial association of Houston, Texas, that being Catholic and being president presented no dilemma because his religion was a private matter. "I believe in a President whose views on religion are his own private affair," Kennedy told the Houston ministers. This was not Al Smith's position in 1928. Rather, Smith argued that being a religious person, indeed a Catholic Christian, was no disadvantage to being president because the nation itself was founded on Christian principles. The *Atlantic Monthly* rushed Smith's response into print. While addressing specific points Marshall raised, Smith stated his case most succinctly when he wrote, "The essence of my faith is built on the commandments of God. The law of the land is built on the commandments of God. There can be no conflict between them" (2). He sounded more like an evangelical Protestant of the Christian Right in our own time than did John F. Kennedy in 1960.

Once the campaign was underway in earnest, reporters hounded Smith about the nineteenth-century papal encyclicals that seemed to reject separation of church and state. On one occasion, Smith allegedly exclaimed in exasperation, "Will someone please tell me what the hell an encyclical is?" Addressing Pope Pius's Syllabus of Errors more seriously in his response to Marshall, however, Smith relied on the 'thesis-hypothesis' political theory of Father John Ryan of Catholic University in Washington, D.C. Smith quoted Ryan as having written, "Pope Pius IX did not intend to declare that separation [of church and state] is always unadvisable, for he had more than once expressed his satisfaction with the arrangement obtaining in the United States" (2). The thesis part of Ryan's thesis-hypothesis held that the Catholic Church is the one true church and should therefore be preferred by the state. Such a view goes back historically at least to Thomas Aquinas. The hypothesis, however, was that in America Catholics were the minority, and so it would be unjust for the state to prefer the Catholic Church.

This view, of course, led to Marshall's charge that Catholics did not really believe in the First Amendment, which was based on the equality of all religions before the law, all the time. Rather, many Protestants reasoned, Catholics believe in religious liberty only as a necessary but insufficient condition, given America's Protestant majority. The ultimate goal of Catholics, Protestants reasoned, was to someday become the majority then rewrite American law so as to prefer the Catholic Church. Ryan answered this line of reasoning, stating, "[T]he danger of religious intolerance toward non-Catholics in the United States is so improbable and so far in the future that it should not occupy their time or attention." Ryan suggested that only "zealots and bigots" could possibly worry about an occurrence that was "five thousand years hence" (Ryan and Millar 39). Still, the idea that a Catholic-supported state was preferable to the First Amendment, even if impractical at the moment, troubled Protestants such as Marshall.

In addition to citing Ryan, Smith also quoted St. Paul, Minnesota Archbishop Dowling as saying, "[Father Ryan's] thesis may well be relegated to the limbo of defunct controversies," and he quoted Dowling's predecessor Archbishop Ireland, a leading Americanist Catholic, as saying, "Religious freedom is the basic life of America, the cement running through all its walls and battlements, the safeguard of its peace and prosperity" (2).[3] Smith also employed the writings of America's ranking Catholic and leading Americanist, James Cardinal Gibbons, quoting him as saying, "American Catholics rejoice in our separation of church and state, and I can conceive of no combination or circumstances likely to arise which would make a union desirable to either church or state. For ourselves, we thank God that we live in America" (2). In other words, Smith wanted to show that while Ryan's thesis-hypothesis theory may have been academically sound for the university seminar room, most Catholics, even in the Church hierarchy, had pretty much made peace with the First Amendment as a practical matter. Smith's most direct statement, indeed his church-state creed, read: "I believe in the absolute freedom of conscience for all men and in the equality of all churches, all sects, and all beliefs before the law as a matter of right and not as a matter of favor." He continued, "I believe in the absolute separation of church and state and in the strict enforcement of the provisions of the Constitution that Congress shall make no law respecting the establishment of religion or prohibiting the free exercise thereof." He ended his essay by concluding, "In this spirit I join with fellow-Americans of all creeds in a fervent prayer that never again in this land will any public servant be challenged because of the faith in which he has tried to walk humbly with his God" (2).

---

[3] The Americanist party within the Catholic Church in America consisted of those who advocated for greater accommodation with American ways of life. They sought to harmonize church teaching with American forms of democracy and religious liberty.

Fundamentalist Responses to Smith's Campaign

Smith's "fervent prayer" was not answered in the election of 1928. There was religious bigotry aplenty that year, and many Protestants opposed him because he was Catholic, or, more precisely, because they presumed that Catholic theology could not be reconciled with American freedom. While moderate and liberal Protestants attempted, for the most part, to take the high road in their opposition to Smith, fundamentalists such as J. Frank Norris in Texas and John Roach Straton in New York City hit Smith hard and often below the belt. On many occasions Norris referred to immigrants as "the dregs of southern Europe," Catholics as "toe-kissing, Tammnanyites," and those who opposed Prohibition as "lowdown whiskey-soaked imps of Hell" (qtd. in Hankins 54-63). He issued headlines in his newspaper such as, "The Conspiracy of Rum and Romanism to Rule This Government," and he told at least one crowd that if Smith were elected it would be the St. Bartholomew's Day Massacre all over again (referring to the 1572 slaughter of Huguenots during the French Wars of Religion). In one sermon Norris remarked in race-baiting exasperation, "What a conglomeration, Tammany Hall, Roman Catholicism, bootleggers, carpet bag politicians and negros [sic]. What will the white people of Texas do?" (4).[4]

New York City's leading fundamentalist, John Roach Straton, also tried to tie the corruption of Tammany Hall to Smith. Smith responded with a demand for equal time to defend himself before Straton's Calvary Baptist congregation. There ensued a weeks-long debate between the two carried out through the pages of the *New York Times*. Smith challenged Straton to a debate. The fundamentalist pastor accepted, only to have the idea nixed by his board of deacons. Straton then suggested the debate take place at Madison Square Garden or St. Patrick's Cathedral, only to be reminded by a priest's op-ed that a non-Catholic could not speak from a Catholic pulpit. On and on raged the war of words between preacher and governor through August and into September of the campaign. The preacher and the candidate finally had their debate—or, at least the closest thing to a debate they would garner. By luck or design, they appeared on consecutive nights at a coliseum in Oklahoma City in late September. An estimated 70,000 Oklahomans standing several rows deep on the city's sidewalks greeted the candidate enthusiastically when he arrived in their capital on the twentieth. Emboldened, Smith used his evening campaign speech to tackle the religion issue head-on for the first time since his reply to Marshall. Referencing the "whispering campaign" against his religion emanating from certain elements in the Republican party, Smith exclaimed, "[A]ny person who votes against me simply because of my religion is not, to my way of thinking, a good citizen" (qtd. in "Smith Assails" 1-2). He then parallely condemned the Ku Klux Klan, and little wonder, given that his campaign train had passed a burning cross on the Arkansas-Oklahoma border the night before.

Straton took the same stage the following night, saying he was in town to "do some more whispering," a remark that must have had his audience howling with

---

[4] The *Fundamentalist* was Norris's own weekly newspaper published in Fort Worth, Texas

laughter given that Straton never whispered anything. Rather, Straton was on a swing through the South loudly denouncing the corruption of Tammany Hall and Smith's association with that notorious political machine. As Straton put it, "I have had quite an interesting time 'whispering' to people about the present presidential campaign, not only up in New York but down through Dixie as well" ("Straton Raps" 4). Straton headed south from Oklahoma City and preached a few days later at J. Frank Norris's First Baptist Church in Fort Worth. Straton told Norris's congregation he had "double-dog dared" candidate Smith to a debate back in New York, implying that Smith feared a face-to-face meeting but ignoring the fact Smith had volunteered—actually, practically demanded—to appear at Straton's church. Straton injected race into the campaign, telling the Fort Worth Baptists that in the "negro heaven" of Harlem, "all the corrupt Negroes are behind Smith." In response, Norris gave a hearty shout, "Good bye Al" ("Star-Telegram Account" 2).

Liberal Protestants opposed Smith like their fundamentalist counterparts but with less rancor, prejudice, or bigotry. Much of the opposition from both groups of Protestants came on the issue of Prohibition, which Al Smith opposed. Prohibition and fundamentalist anti-Catholicism aside, however, there was something else going on in the election of 1928, and the editor of the *Christian Century* came closest to the mark when he pitted the Protestant "conscience individually formed" against the Catholic "conscience formed under ecclesiastical authority." The issue was freedom, and the editor had latched onto something important, perhaps more important than he could have known at the time. Historian John McGreevy argues convincingly in his 2003 book *Catholicism and American Freedom* that there has always been a tension between Catholicism and the American notion of freedom because American freedom (that is, liberal freedom) is premised on the autonomy of the individual. A product of the Enlightenment, autonomy posits the right of individuals to make up their own minds, even about deeply moral matters, unencumbered by external authority. Popes Pius and Leo may have seen this, or something like it, as the undergirding of the U.S. Constitution's First Amendment, and so rejected separation of church and state. Likewise, late twentieth-century secular liberals in America often interpret the First Amendment this way. Essentially, in their view, the First Amendment is premised on the idea that religion remains beyond the reach of the state because religion is a private matter and therefore left to the choice of autonomous individuals.

A New Understanding of the Separation of Church and State

A quarter century after the election of 1928, John Courtney Murray argued that it is not necessary to interpret the First Amendment this way. In what became the basis for Vatican II's 1965 Declaration of Religious Freedom, Murray argued that the kind of separation of church and state condemned by Pope Leo was a separation based on continental liberalism in Europe that relegated religion to the private, individual sphere where it would have little impact on society. Murray started his argument with the medieval conception of church and state. In the middle ages, the Church was the "Great Society," free to carry out its own law. The secular power of the state, by contrast, was but a minor order distinct from the Great Society. The rise of absolutism during the early modern era (sixteenth and seventeenth centuries) reversed the relation of church and state. Rather than the Church being independent and supreme and the state small and limited, the absolutist state of France's Louis XIV and other European monarchs became increasingly powerful and was eventually identified with the nation itself. The state became the Great Society within which all other institutions existed in subservient form. The result was what Murray called the "society-state," "the one all-embracing omnicompetent form of human association" (149). Here, the state aspect of power and law quickly assumed primacy over the society aspect of family, education, and religion. This was clearly an unacceptable situation for the transcendent Church.

Beginning in France, liberal revolutions overthrew absolutist monarchy but left intact an absolute state that Murray and others called "totalitarian democracy." Since the state was still the 'society-state,' encompassing all that was considered important in life, separation of church and state really meant that the Church had no substantial role within society. All important matters took place in the society-state, within which the Church was allowed to play but a small role. Religion became a purely private, individual, and subjective matter (Murray 149). Little wonder that after nearly a century under totalitarian democracy, Pope Leo condemned separation of church and state. Murray argued, however, that the above history had no bearing on America. America was untouched by either absolutism or the type of revolutions that had taken place in France and then across Europe. Instead, the American founders crafted a constitutional government that kept society and state distinct from one another. Rather than a society-state where state power overrides the society aspects, in America the state has limited powers and is interior to society. Society, or civil society, as it is often called, encompasses all institutions—family, churches, voluntary organizations, the state, and so forth. As merely one of the institutions within civil society, the state has a limited role, allowing other institutions to do their work freely and intervening with coercive power when necessary. Spiritual life is located in civil society and is ultimately more important than the state, which is why the state should for the most part leave the church untouched. The church, therefore, not the state, is the most important institution in civil society. What all this meant for Murray was that the essential spirit of the medieval arrangement, which Catholics extolled, had been preserved better in America than in the Catholic countries of Europe. "In the American case," Murray wrote, "the essential lines of the medieval structure of politics are still somehow visible; in the Continental case they are destroyed utterly" (152).

Murray's critique of twentieth-century American liberals was essentially that they were establishing secularism, which would relegate religion to the realm of unimportance and elevate politics and the state to the realm of the ultimate, much as totalitarian democracy had. Within a proper understanding of the First Amendment, by contrast, there was no suggestion that politics was the realm of ultimate meaning or salvation. Instead of insisting that religious matters were wholly individual, private, and subjective, with no bearing on matters of the state, the American system placed matters of the spirit within the realm of society where the state could not touch them. Rather than state and society being off limits to religion, religion was off limits to the state. The requirement that the state leave religion alone allowed religion free reign within society. This was all accomplished by the First Amendment, which Murray summarized as follows: "The First Amendment has no religious overtones whatever; that is it does not imply any ultimate vision of the nature of man and society. [...] It is a legal rule, not a piece of secular ecclesiology" (152-53).

While Murray's historical understanding of religious liberty in America can be contested, the upshot was that American-styled separation of church and state freed the church to exercise ultimate authority over the individual conscience because the state was denied that domain. For Catholics, this arrangement meant that individuals were free from the state's ultimate authority so they could submit to a Catholic Church that has already decided the important issues. By Murray's interpretation, therefore, Catholics could accept religious freedom, properly understood as freedom from state power.

Protestant Critiques of Individual Conscience

The *Christian Century* editor was right when he said Catholics believed in a "conscience formed under ecclesiastical authority." John Courtney Murray merely pointed out later, though much too late to do Al Smith any good, that in order for this to happen, the state had to stop defining what was ultimate and step aside. The *Christian Century* editor was wrong, however, when he assumed that Protestants believed in a "conscience individually formed." Or rather, at least he was mistaken for evangelicals and fundamentalists, whether or not they knew it at the time.[5] We can see this more clearly when we throw two other Roaring Twenties issues into the mix: prohibition and obscenity. Liberal Protestants of the *Christian Century* stripe and fundamentalist Protestants supported Prohibition laws and laws against obscene literature, both of which, of course, restricted individuals. Prohibition had been enforced for eight years by the time Smith ran for president, and the *Christian Century*, like nearly all liberal Protestant entities, consistently joined fundamentalists in vigorous support of its continuation. Prohibition was as central to the election as was Catholicism, largely because in 1923 Governor Smith signed into law the Mullen-Gage Act, which essentially ended the state of New York's enforcement of Prohibition, leaving matters to an understaffed federal police force. Fundamentalists and many liberal Protestants may have sup-

---

[5] It would be fair to say that in the 1920s there was virtually no distinction made between evangelicals and fundamentalists. The term "fundamentalism" applied to virtually all conservative or orthodox Protestants who defended the fundamental tenets of historic Christianity and opposed liberal Protestantism in the northern denominations. Beginning in the 1940s, moderate fundamentalists weary of the militant spirit of fundamentalism, consciously set out to refashion conservative Protestantism. These moderate fundamentalists preferred the name "neo-evangelical" or simply "evangelical." See Carpenter.

ported Prohibition because they had religious scruples against alcohol, but Prohibition was not actually premised on such scruples. Rather, Prohibition existed as a Progressive Era reform movement based on the very real societal degradation caused by the abuse of alcohol. As liberal Protestant reformer Charles Stelzle put the case, "Prohibition was brought about because large numbers of the nearly two hundred thousand saloons and places where liquor was sold in this country had become a distinct menace" (192-93). For him, as for most Prohibitionists, the movement aimed to protect the public, not police private morality. Notwithstanding, however, in this case protecting the public required a restriction on individual freedom to consume—or at least to manufacture, sell, or purchase—alcoholic beverages.[6]

The *Christian Century* frequently editorialized support of Prohibition, especially as the movement for repeal increased in the late twenties. The magazine's editor consistently said that any argument against Prohibition based on freedom alone was insufficient. Only a few 'wets' (those who opposed Prohibition) fought for freedom in order to build a better society, he said, as "more of them were fighting for a personal privilege regardless of public welfare." By contrast, "The drys were fighting for a policy and a program which they conceived to have deep moral significance and to which they attached the sanctions of religion. [...] Religious conviction attaching itself to a practical program for social betterment is both legitimate and indispensable" ("What Elected Hoover?"). This view of a corporate and communal morality to which all individuals must submit for the maintenance of a good society seemed strangely out of sync with the "conscience individually formed" that the *Century* editor extolled when squaring off against Al Smith. To the question, "from whence comes communal or corporate morality," the Catholics had an answer: the Church, which stood in authority over the individual conscience and was responsible for its formation as well as the formation of a good society. The *Christian Century* editor, by contrast, could only assume or hope that "consciences individually formed" would arrive at a consensus concerning what a good society is.

As was the case with Prohibition, the *Christian Century* editors stood opposed to individual freedom when it came to salacious literature where here again they stood on the same side of an issue as fundamentalist Protestants. Ironically, on the issue of obscenity, liberal and fundamentalist Protestants stood together with Catholics over against secular cultural liberals in the American Civil Liberties Union (ACLU) who argued for the right of authors to discuss sex. The obscenity wars of the Roaring Twenties started in earnest in 1926 with the arrest of *American Mercury* editor and nationally famous journalist H. L. Mencken. Mencken published an article by Herbert Asbury titled "Hatrack," the allegedly true story from a small Missouri town where a prostitute lived who was so thin locals said she was a skinny as a hat rack. Also dubbed "Fanny Fewclothes," she attended the local Methodist church, where parishioners shunned her as a sinful and un-endearing

---

[6] Prohibition actually criminalized the manufacture and sale of alcoholic beverages, not their private consumption. Still, in many places it became extremely difficult, and always illegal, to obtain alcohol for private consumption, which, of course, was the whole point of the legislation.

member of a low-class moral station. Following Sunday night services, Hatrack walked across town to the local cemetery where she plied her trade, advertising to men on the street corners that she was open for business (Asbury 479-83).

The story "Hatrack" ran afoul of Boston's liberal Protestant reform organization called the Watch and Ward Society, which in 1915 helped create a Booksellers Committee that made judgments on the obscenity of literature sold in Boston. When the Booksellers Committee deemed a book or magazine obscene, the group put local stores on notice not to carry the item for sale, warning that they could run afoul of Massachusetts's state obscenity law. Boston police usually accepted the judgment of the Booksellers Committee and when necessary enforced the law against obscenity. Mencken wished to challenge this cooperation between religion and law, which in his view amounted to a suppression of individual freedom to say, write, and publish what he wanted. He agreed, therefore, to travel from his home in Baltimore to sell a copy of his own magazine to the head of the Watch and Ward Society at Boston's famous Brimstone Corner, allegedly nicknamed for the fire and brimstone sermons preached there for more than a century. The corner is also the site of the city's renowned Park Street Congregational Church.[7]

Mencken's arrest marked the beginning of a series of legal battles that pitted authors, publishers, the ACLU, and Boston's secular elites against liberal Protestant reformers in and beyond the Watch and Ward Society. Fundamentalist Protestants and key Catholic spokespersons offered their tacit and sometimes overt support for the Watch and Ward Society. This Roaring Twenties culture war went national when the U.S. Postmaster banned obscene materials, including "Hatrack," from the U.S. mail. Additional enforcement of anti-obscenity came from U.S. Customs agents who seized imported books deemed obscene. This federal ban on obscene materials was based on the 1870 Comstock Act, which banned the mailing of both obscene materials and birth control devices. Authors such as Sinclair Lewis (*Elmer Gantry*), Theodore Dreiser (*An American Tragedy*), and, especially, D.H. Lawrence (*Lady Chatterley's Lover*) all ran afoul of obscenity laws over the next few years. Collectively, the obscenity wars marked the beginning of the end for liberal Protestant policing of public morality that marked Victorian America throughout the nineteenth and early twentieth centuries. One historian frames the obscenity battles as America's "repeal of reticence" (Gurstein), arguing that from the Gilded Age (1877–1900) through the 1930s the party of reticence sought to uphold public decorum while the party of exposure worked to maximize freedom for individual expression regardless of the coarsening and vulgarizing of society that might ensue.[8] One might also see this episode as a battle between individual autonomy and a communitarian understanding of the good.

The Watch and Ward Society was to censorship what the Anti-Saloon League was to Prohibition. Both organizations sought to outlaw something they believed was injurious to the good of society. Prohibition and censorship, therefore, were

---

[7] Another theory is that the corner got its nickname as a result of the War of 1812 when the Congregationalists allegedly stored in the church basement brimstone and sulfur for the making of gunpowder.

[8] For an excellent discussion of this and other similar incidents see Gurstein, and Kemeny.

centered on what kind of freedom America should have. The ACLU argued against censorship using the liberal notion of American freedom based on individual autonomy. Some arguments for the repeal of prohibition ran along similar lines, although this was not the argument advanced by Catholics. The ACLU's version of freedom appeared as license to those who favored a more communitarian notion of society—a group that included fundamentalists, liberal Protestants, and Catholics as well. The struggle against individual autonomy as license saw fundamentalist and liberal Protestants on the same side, working as allies against Catholics, ethnic Protestants, and secular liberals who argued for the personal freedom to drink alcohol.[9] On the issue of censorship, however, the lines were more clear between those who believed in individual autonomy and those with communitarian views. Liberal Protestants led the way, with both fundamentalists and Catholics cheering from the sidelines. All three groups believed at least implicitly that individual autonomy led not to liberty, but rather to license. Opposing this coalition were cultural liberals (also called cultural modernists). Cultural liberals differed from theological liberals precisely on this issue of censorship. Theological liberals retained the Protestant idea that they were the custodians of society and responsible for public morality, while cultural liberals believed that an individual's freedom of expression trumped communitarian views. For cultural liberals, individual autonomy was the essence of personal liberty.

The *Christian Century* editor was conflicted, extolling "the conscience individually formed" in the election of 1928 while nevertheless arguing that such a view of freedom in matters of alcohol and obscenity remained insufficient for the maintenance of a good society. But how can "a conscience individually formed" advocate restrictions on other consciences individually formed? To what authority would one appeal in limiting another's freedom? The *Christian Century* editor assumed, but would not acknowledge, that such authority existed—an authority to which individual consciences were responsible. On the issues of Prohibition and obscenity, the editor referred to the common good of society but was loath to identify the source of the common good. He seemed to assume, but not acknowledge, an authority that defined the common good for everyone; or he believed that the common good emanated from multiple consciences individually formed deciding together what they wanted, with the added assumption that somehow this would turn out to be something good. One might have asked the editor: to what standard consciences individually formed would measure their collective will and deem it good?

Beginning in the 1970s, John Rawls and other liberal theorists argued that individual freedom, based on autonomy, makes it impossible for a society even to deliberate over what constitutes the good, let alone enforce such a vision. Politcal liberalism argues that notions of the good must be left to individuals—to the consciences individually formed. By contrast, liberal Protestants in the twenties want-

---

[9] One could argue that for many urban, working class Catholics drinking alcohol was a communal enterprise as workers came together in the local saloon to imbibe. Saloons often served as community centers with a variety of informal services to help families in need or individuals in trouble.

ed to have their cake and eat it too. They wanted consciences individually formed, which is none other than the autonomy of the individual, while still having a communitarian society where everyone lives under the authority of some entity that defines the common good. Yet one cannot have it both ways.

Fundamentalist or evangelical Protestants were not less conflicted, but just conflicted in a different way. They chimed in with liberal Protestants against Catholics when it came to discussions of freedom, but when faced with a choice between an individually formed conscience and a conscience formed under ecclesiastical authority, fundamentalist Protestants should have sided with Catholics, if with a slight twist. Fundamentalists believed in consciences formed under "biblical" authority, which made them much more like Catholics than liberal Protestants. It would take more than a half century and a major shift in the marketplace of ideas, however, for fundamentalists (who would later be called evangelicals), to see who their real brothers and sisters were. By the 1970s, the "political liberalism" described and advocated by Rawls became the dominant way of understanding freedom. The autonomy of the individual, or the conscience individually formed, meant that individuals had the right to do anything so long as it did not interfere with the right of other individuals to do anything. In other words, political liberalism advocates not freedom from the state in order to submit to proper authority (the Bible, the Church, or both), but freedom of conscience in order to decide everything for oneself unencumbered by authority. This sort of freedom is most clearly visible in the present-day abortion controversy that has wracked American politics for more than three decades. As McGreevy puts it, "Intermittent discussion of privacy rights extends backward into the nineteenth century, but only debates over contraception and abortion would make 'privacy' and 'autonomy' keywords in the modern liberal vocabulary" (260). McGreevy cites Michael Sandel, a key critic of political liberalism, who argues that the right of privacy that undergirds the right to an abortion is "grounded in notions of individual autonomy," which includes the right to "choose and adopt a lifestyle which allows expression of [one's] uniqueness and individuality" (qtd. in McGreevy 260). The *Christian Century* editor certainly did not advocate individual freedom to decide all moral issues, as his support for Prohibition and obscenity laws shows.

A Shift in the Marketplace of Ideas

In 1993, twenty years after *Roe v. Wade* espoused the autonomy of the individual to abortion, evangelicals and Catholics could finally "come together" and issue the Evangelicals and Catholics Together document (ECT) ("Evangelicals and Catholics Together"). The document was made possible because evangelicals, or at least a few of them, saw that "freedom of choice," like the "conscience individually formed," is premised on the autonomy of the individual. It took a ideological shift for evangelicals to come to this new understanding. In the broadly Protestant marketplace of the twenties, communitarian notions of the good were too easily taken for granted, leaving liberal and fundamentalist Protestants to focus solely on freedom within those assumed parameters. By the 1990s, with the liberal view of autonomy clearly the dominant way of conceiving democracy, evangelicals could see what Catholics intuited all along: that a conscience formed under the authority of God (as taken in scripture, the Church, or both) stood in stark contrast to "a conscience individually formed." One of John Courtenay Murray's contemporaries, Jesuit scholar Wilfrid Parsons, wrote in 1942, "[T]here is vastly more in common between the modern Catholic and the colonial Protestant than between the old colonial Protestant and the modern secularized product of public education" (qtd. in McGreevy 192). The specific reference to "public education" in the quote serves to obscure the broader point. Evangelicals see themselves as the heirs of the eighteenth-century Protestant revivals, and, beginning in the 1990s, key evangelical leaders began to see themselves as more like Catholics than liberal Protestants or secular liberals. In other words, evangelicals, or at least some of them, finally understood the tension identified by John McGreevy between Catholicism and American freedom. Today, evangelicals feel that same tension, or at least they should. The last line of McGreevey's 2004 book reads as follows: "Perhaps the final assessment of the long Catholic encounter with American ideas of freedom will rest here: on whether twenty-first-century Catholics can convince their fellow citizens, and themselves, that associations and ties with the strangers in our midst satisfy our deepest, most common aspirations" (295). It is not altogether clear just what McGreevy means, but if his conclusion can be taken to mean that Catholics have an interest in convincing others that individual autonomy is not the best way to conceive of freedom or produce a good society, then they have succeeded in convincing evangelicals.

Works Cited

Asbury, Herbert. "Hatrack." *American Mercury* Apr. 1926: 479-83. Print.
Carpenter, Joel. *Revive Us Again: The Reawakening of American Fundamentalism*. New York: Oxford UP, 1997. Print.
"Evangelicals and Catholics Together." *First Things*. The Institute on Religion and Public Life, May 1994. Web 12 Apr. 2013.
Gurstein, Rochelle. *The Repeal of Reticence*. New York: Hill, 1996. Print.
Hankins, Barry. *God's Rascal: J. Frank Norris and the Beginnings of Southern Fundamentalism*. Lexington: UP of Kentucky, 1996. Print.
Kemeny, P. C. "Power, Ridicule, and the Destruction of the Religious Moral Reform Politics in the 1920s." *The Secular Revolution: Power, Interests and Conflict in the Secularization of American Public Life*. Berkeley: U of California P, 2003. 216-68. Print.
Kennedy, John F. "Address to the Greater Houston Ministerial Association." 12 September 1960. *American Rhetoric*. AmericanRhetoric.com. Web 2 May 2013.
Lippmann, Walter. *Men of Destiny*. New York: MacMillan, 1927. Print.
Marshall, Charles. "An Open Letter to the Honorable Alfred E. Smith." *Atlantic Monthly* Apr. 1927: 540-49. Print.
McGreevy, John T. *Catholicism and American Freedom: A History*. New York: Norton, 2004. Print.

Muarry, John Courtney. "Leo XIII: Separation of Church and State. *Theological Studies* 14 (1953): 149-53. Print.
Norris, J. Frank. "Al Smith and the Negro." *Fundamentalist* 19 Oct. 1928: 4. Print.
Ryan, John A., and Moorhouse F. X. Millar. *The State and the Church*. New York: Macmillan, 1922. Print.
Stelzle, Charles. *A Son of the Bowery: The Life Story of an East Side American*. 1926. Freeport: Books for Libraries P, 1971. Print.
Smith, Alfred E. "Full Text of Governor Smith's Reply on Religious Issue." *New York Times* 18 Apr. 1927: 2. Print.
"Smith Assails Intolerance, Answers Foes on Record, Oklahoma Crowd Cheers." *New York Times* 21 Sept. 1928. Print.
"Star-Telegram Account of Straton's Address." *Fundamentalist* 28 Sept. 1928: 2. Print.
"Straton Raps Smith in Oklahoma City." *New York Times* 22 Sept. 1928: 4. Print.
"What Elected Hoover?" *Christian Century* 15 Nov. 1928: 1388. Print.

Forum

Amerikastudien als "kooperatives Experiment":
60 Jahre Deutsche Gesellschaft für Amerikastudien*

HANS-JÜRGEN GRABBE

Meine Mitgliedschaft in der Deutschen Gesellschaft für Amerikastudien währt jetzt sechsunddreißig Jahre. 1980 kam ich in den Beirat als Repräsentant des sogenannten wissenschaftlichen Nachwuchses. 1984 wurde ich mit breiter Unterstützung insbesondere der weiblichen Mitglieder wiedergewählt. Es gab ja schon den Women's Caucus, der Wahlen zu entscheiden vermochte. Aus dessen Umfeld wurde mir damals erklärt, man schätze mich, weil ich nicht als bedrohlich wahrgenommen werde. Ich habe lange überlegt, ob ich das als Kompliment begreifen sollte. Mittlerweile denke ich, es war eines. 1993 wurde ich Schatzmeister, im zweiten Anlauf, denn es gab damals noch Kampfkandidaturen. Neun Vorstandsjahre, bis 2005, habe ich insgesamt absolviert. Die DGfA war ein zentraler Bestandteil meines Berufslebens, war zu Zeiten nicht mehr nur Ehrenamt, sondern kam an erster Stelle. Darum erfüllt es mich mit Stolz und Freude, heute abend zu Ihnen sprechen zu dürfen.

Worum wird es im Folgenden gehen? Nicht um die Fortsetzung meines Aufsatzes von 2003 zum fünfzigjährigen Jubiläum der Deutschen Gesellschaft für Amerikastudien (Grabbe) mit der Maßgabe: 'Berichten, was danach geschah.' Übrigens ist mir kritisch vorgehalten worden, ich hätte in diesem Jubiläumsaufsatz nicht alle Vorsitzenden der DGfA namentlich erwähnt. Ich bitte um Nachsicht, wenn dies auch hier nicht geschieht. Es ging mir damals und es geht mir heute nicht um eine Chronik, sondern um eine Auseinandersetzung mit dem, was diesen Verband in seinem Wesenskern ausmacht.

Anknüpfen möchte ich aber doch an meinen Aufsatz von 2003, weil er mich in den, ich möchte sagen, Genuß einer wichtigen Lektion gebracht hat: Kurz nach Erscheinen des Jubiläumsheftes erhielt ich einen Brief von Martin Christadler. Herr Christadler war von 1968 bis zu seiner Emeritierung 1996 Professor für amerikanische Literaturwissenschaft an der Johann Wolfgang Goethe-Universität Frankfurt am Main gewesen und schrieb mir nun aus seinem französischen Refugium. Er dankte mir zunächst für die Schilderung der Auseinandersetzung zwischen Literatur- bzw. Kulturwissenschaftlern und Historikern, setzte aber hinzu:

> Manchmal hatte ich [...] den Eindruck, daß Sie die Mühen, Schwierigkeiten und Anstrengungen der [Historiker] mit etwas mehr Sympathie betrachten als die der sog. Phi-

---

* Der Text des Vortrags folgt dem Duktus des gesprochenen Wortes. Er blieb im wesentlichen unverändert, wurde aber um einige Teile erweitert, die in Marburg aus Zeitgründen weggelassen werden mußten. Ich danke Frau Dipl.-Ang. Anke Hildebrandt-Mirtschink und Herrn Dipl.-Ang. Carsten Hummel für wertvolle Hinweise.

lologen [...]. In der Tat waren, wie Sie zeigen, die amerikabezogenen Historiker fach- und institutionengeschichtlich benachteiligt [...]. Allerdings ist mein erinnerter Eindruck auch der, daß sich die Historiker länger gegen neue Wissenschaftsorientierungen und Forschungsthemen gesträubt haben, gerade weil sie an dem überkommenen Disziplinpurismus festhielten und [...] Fächerüberschreitungen oder -amalgamierungen [...] mit Mißtrauen wahrnahmen. Es waren daher eher 'gebürtige' Literaturwissenschaftler, die den Übergang zur Amerikanistik als interdisziplinärer Kulturwissenschaft im Sinne von American Studies vorantrieben.[1]

Aus dem Nachdenken über Christadlers Monitum entstand dieser Vortrag. Der Titel stammt aus Arnold Bergstraessers programmatischem Referat auf der DGfA-Gründungsversammlung am 13. Juni 1953, gedruckt im ersten *Jahrbuch für Amerikastudien* von 1956. Darin benannte der Freiburger Politikwissenschaftler vier Möglichkeiten, die wissenschaftliche Beschäftigung mit den USA an deutschen Universitäten zu verankern. Ich möchte diesen Passus in Gänze zitieren:

> Es ist denkbar, mit der Einrichtung von Amerikastudien die Begründung einer neuen Disziplin ins Auge zu fassen oder, zweitens, sie als eine Erweiterung der Forschung und Lehre auf den Gebieten der englischen Philologie, Sprache und Literatur aufzufassen, oder, drittens, Amerikastudien in Spezialgebiete aufzuteilen und an Einzeldisziplinen wie die Sozialwissenschaft, das Staats- und Völkerrecht und die Geschichtswissenschaft anzugliedern, oder aber, viertens, die Amerikastudien als einen kooperativen Versuch verschiedener wissenschaftlicher Disziplinen zu betreiben. (9)

Bergstraesser favorisierte die Variante 4, die er im weiteren Verlauf seiner Rede zum Experiment latinisierte. Daß eine glückliche Kooperation aller mit den USA befaßten Wissenschaftlerinnen und Wissenschaftler den Königsweg darstelle, ist seitdem immer wieder vorgetragen worden. Aber Experimente, das wissen wir aus dem Physikunterricht, können mißlingen. Amerikastudien als institutionalisierte Kooperation unterschiedlicher Disziplinen zu betreiben, war von allen Konzepten das ambitionierteste und—das muß unbedingt hinzugefügt werden— das teuerste, weil es mehr Planstellen erforderte als die anderen Varianten. Ich glaube übrigens nicht, daß man diese Variante 4, das kooperative Experiment, als Forderung nach einer kulturwissenschaftlich-interdisziplinären Integration der Amerikastudien verstehen kann (Hebel 1). Aber dazu später mehr.

Wer sind wir, wer sind die Mitglieder der Deutschen Gesellschaft für Amerikastudien? Oder, frei nach Schiller: Was heißt und zu welchem Ende betreiben wir Amerikastudien? Udo Hebel hat bekanntlich 2008 eine *Einführung in die Amerikanistik/American Studies* publiziert und will mit diesem Titel "vor allem die mit der Bezeichnung American Studies bzw. Amerikastudien verbundene interdisziplinäre Grundlegung und kulturwissenschaftliche Ausrichtung der Disziplin in Forschung und Lehre" betonen (2). Das ist ein Satz, dem sich vermutlich die meisten Amerikanistinnen und Amerikanisten anschließen können. Ich hingegen

---

[1] Christadler an Grabbe, 2.2.2004, Privatarchiv Grabbe.

hege Bedenken, und zwar wegen der Konjunktion "beziehungsweise": "American Studies bzw. Amerikastudien." Laut Duden kann "beziehungsweise" stehen für "oder," für "oder vielmehr" und für "genauer gesagt." American Studies und Amerikastudien wären demnach ein und dasselbe. Die als American Studies begriffene Amerikanistik ist heute an fast an allen deutschen Universitäten ein gut etabliertes Fach und vielerorts auch ein Studiengang. Aber sind American Studies und Amerikastudien deshalb wirklich synonym? Sind wir, die ca. eintausend Mitglieder der nunmehr sechzig Jahre alten Deutschen Gesellschaft für Amerikastudien, alle in American Studies aktiv? Werden Amerikastudien mit American Studies gleichgesetzt, dann würde in der Tat gelten, daß die Begriffe als Synonyme anzusehen sind und für beide—ich zitiere noch einmal Udo Hebel—eine "interdisziplinäre Grundlegung und kulturwissenschaftliche Ausrichtung [...] in Forschung und Lehre" konstitutiv wäre (2).

Winfried Fluck und Thomas Claviez haben American Studies beschrieben als "joint, interdisciplinary academic endeavor to gain systematic knowledge about American society and culture in order to understand the historical and present-day meaning and significance of the United States" (Fluck und Claviez ix). Das ist, so scheint mir, eine offenere Definition, denn es wird nicht gesagt, daß das gemeinsame interdisziplinäre Unterfangen zwingend oder gar exklusiv kulturwissenschaftlich ausgerichtet sein muß—und schon gar nicht in dem weitgehenden Sinne, in dem Klaus Lubbers, Vorsitzender der DGfA von 1981 bis 1984, Amerikastudien/American Studies in Abgrenzung zur philologischen Amerikanistik definierte, nämlich als "synthetisches, interdisziplinäres Kulturfach" (zit. nach Hebel 1).

Bevor ich der Frage "Wer sind wir?" weiter nachgehe, stelle ich eine andere, nämlich "Woher kommen wir?" Dazu gehe ich zunächst exemplarisch auf die Anfänge der Amerikastudien in München ein, weil es dort die zunächst umfassendsten Anstrengungen gab, fachlich übergreifende Amerikastudien als kooperatives Experiment im Nachkriegsdeutschland, oder besser gesagt, in den Westzonen und der späteren Bundesrepublik, zu etablieren. Am Anfang stand die Initiative von Heinz Peters, der Schüler eines der angesehensten Anglisten der Vorkriegszeit, des Münchener Ordinarius Karl Förster, gewesen war (Huber 3). Peters' Konzeption gemäß und dem Wunsch der amerikanischen Militärregierung entsprechend, sollten in München neben der Kulturgeschichte der USA (die Literatur und Kultur gewissermaßen vermählte) auch Staats- und Wirtschaftswissenschaften gelehrt werden. Dieses Konzept entsprach recht gut den Vorstellungen, wie sie Arnold Bergstraesser parallel für Erlangen entwickelte, wo er seit 1951, neben seiner hautamtlichen Tätigkeit an der University of Chicago, als Gastprofessor wirkte (Paulus 244).

Nach Bekanntwerden dieser Pläne bat die Philosophische Fakultät der Ludwig-Maximilians-Universität den Rektor und den Akademischen Senat, "unter keinen Umständen den Namen 'Institut für Amerikanistik' zuzulassen," und plädierte für die Bezeichnung Amerika-Institut. Das klang nicht schlecht, aber die Begründung war pikant: Werde eine so umfassende, nach allen Seiten hin offene Lehre über

Amerika eingerichtet, so falle der größere Teil in den Zuständigkeitsbereich anderer Fakultäten. Man wolle nicht mit einem Institut belastet werden, "das vielleicht zu drei Vierteln Fremdkörper wäre" (Huber 27). Aber nicht nur die Philosophische Fakultät mauerte, sondern auch das bayerische Kultusministerium, dessen Bereitschaft, Haushaltsmittel für den Betrieb eines Amerika-Instituts und gegebenenfalls für den Bau oder die Herrichtung eines Gebäudes zu zahlen, nicht groß war. Bestenfalls sei man bereit, einen Bauplatz zu beschaffen, falls die darauf zu errichtenden Gebäude mit amerikanischen Geld finanziert würden (Huber 20–21).

Ich beschreibe hier Vorgänge aus den Jahren 1948 und 1949. Die Bundesrepublik war noch nicht gegründet. Es galt das Besatzungsstatut, das heißt Bayern war de facto ein Protektorat der USA. Hinzu kam, daß der Wunsch der Amerikaner, die wissenschaftliche Beschäftigung mit ihrem Land möglichst breit anzulegen, dauerhaft zu verankern und materiell zu fördern, für jedermann offensichtlich sein mußte. Dennoch zeigt die Chuzpe, mit der Kultusminister Hundhammer im März 1949 die Militärregierung aufforderte, auch noch die personelle Ausstattung des geplanten Instituts sicherzustellen, daß die Einrichtung einer oder mehrerer Professuren, die USA-bezogen lehren und forschen würden, für die bayrische Politik keine besondere Priorität besaß. Und die Amerikaner lieferten! Die Rockefeller-Stiftung sagte 1949 für zwei Gastprofessuren 50.000 Dollar auf drei Jahre zu. Das wären nach heutigem Geld[2] beachtliche 482.000 Dollar (Huber 25).

Am 7. November 1949 wurde das Münchener Amerika-Institut gegründet. Ein Blick auf die Zusammensetzung des mehrheitlich mit Amerikanern besetzten Kuratoriums zeigt deutlich, welche Ausrichtung der Amerikastudien amerikanische Regierungsstellen und NGOs präferierten: Howard P. Becker war Soziologe, Luther H. Evans Politologe und Direktor der Library of Congress, Cornelis de Kiewit war Professor für Europäische Geschichte der Neuzeit. Weiterhin zählten die Politikwissenschaftler Harold Laswell und Peter H. Odegard zu den Kuratoriumsmitgliedern—und als einziger Kulturwissenschaftler Henry Nash Smith, der Begründer der Myth and Symbol School, dessen Buch *Virgin Land: The American West as Symbol and Myth* (1950) als eine erste bedeutende Forschungsleistung der American Studies gilt.[3]

Das bayerische Kultusministerium erklärte schließlich 1951 seine "Geneigtheit," Arnold Bergstraesser als Ordinarius zu berufen, doch die Philosophische Fakultät mochte sich mit ihm nicht "befreunden" (Huber 43). Es erging dann 1952 ein Ruf an Eric Voegelin, ebenfalls Politologe und ebenfalls seit seiner Emigration aus Deutschland in den USA lebend. Voegelin lehnte ab. Ende 1952 gab es eine zweite Berufungsliste, die der 1949 aus dem amerikanischen Exil zurückgekehrte

---

[2] Berechnet für das Jahr 2013. Siehe Morgan Friedman, *The Inflation Calculator*, Web 2 July 2014.

[3] Neben den amerikanischen Gästen gab es zunächst keine deutschen Hochschullehrer. Allerdings hatte das Institut zwei Assistenten. Einer war der Slawist Heinrich Stammler, der 1953 in die USA auswanderte, und der andere war der rechtsextrem-revisionistische Eiferer David L. Hoggan, dessen Harvard-Dissertation über den Konflikt von 1939 zwischen der 'neuen Ordnung' in Deutschland und der polnischen Ostmitteleuropaidee den Verantwortlichen wohl verborgen geblieben war. Hoggans revisionistisches Opus magnum über die Ursachen des Zweiten Weltkriegs, *Der erzwungene Krieg*, erschien erst 1961.

Philosoph Helmut Kuhn anführte, bei dem George N. Shuster, Präsident des Hunter College und 1950/51 amerikanischer Landeskommissar für Bayern, sich allerdings fragte "ob er ein tiefer Kenner Amerikas" sei (Huber 46). Die Frage war nicht unberechtigt. Im Grunde konnte man bei vielen Wissenschaftlern, die nach 1933 in die USA geflohen waren und nach 1945 für USA-spezifische Professuren vorgeschlagen wurden, die wissenschaftliche Kompetenz für inneramerikanische Themen anzweifeln. Arnold Bergstraesser zum Beispiel hatte in Chicago eine Professur für Deutsche Literatur und Geschichte inne. Dietrich Gerhard, DGfA-Vorsitzender von 1959 bis 1961, war 1936 Professor für europäische, speziell osteuropäische Geschichte an der Washington University in St. Louis geworden und behielt diese Stelle bei, als er 1955 den Lehrstuhl für amerikanische Geschichte an der Universität zu Köln erhielt.

In München wurde 1953 schließlich Helmut Kuhn, DGfA-Vorsitzender von 1957 bis 1959, zum Professor für amerikanische Kulturgeschichte und Philosophie ernannt. Das Amerika-Institut verfügte nur über diese eine Professur, die pikanterweise einen KW-Vermerk hatte, der zu greifen drohte, als Kuhn 1958 auf den Lehrstuhl Philosophie II der Ludwig-Maximilians-Universität berufen wurde (Huber 42–53). Erst zwei Jahre später wurde ein Extraordinariat etatisiert, ausgewiesen für Nordamerikanische Kulturgeschichte und besetzt mit Friedrich Georg Friedmann, der 1960 aus dem amerikanischen Exil zurückgekehrt war. Ab 1965 Ordinarius, blieb Friedmann bis zu seiner Emeritierung im Jahre 1979 am Amerika-Institut. Er war Philosoph, wie Kuhn, und Kultursoziologe. Diesen Bereichen—und nicht USA-spezifischen Fragen—hat er seine wichtigsten Schriften gewidmet. Friedmann stand aber auch für lebendige, interdisziplinäre Amerikastudien, die ab 1981 von Berndt Ostendorf fortgeführt wurden und den guten Ruf des Instituts begründeten. Die dauerhafte Etablierung eines Lehrstuhls für American Studies mit interdisziplinärer Grundlegung und kulturwissenschaftlicher Ausrichtung im Sinne Udo Hebels zog sich also über siebzehn Jahre hin. So zeigt das wohldokumentierte Beispiel der Vorgänge um die Münchener Gründung besonders eindringlich, welche enormen Schwierigkeiten bei der Etablierung kooperativer Amerikastudien im Westdeutschland der ersten Nachkriegszeit zu überwinden waren.

Es gibt aber noch einen zweiten Grund für meine ausführliche Beschäftigung mit dem Münchener Amerika-Institut: Ich möchte ein Wagnis eingehen, indem ich den kontroversen, von manchen auch als verletzend empfundenen Satz, "The Munich institute, as far as American History was concerned, was an almost total failure" (Doerries 114), aufgreife und, wenn möglich, ins Versöhnliche wende. Dieses harsche Urteil steht in dem von Reinhard R. Doerries, DGfA-Vorsitzender von 1987 bis 1990, verfaßten Aufsatz über das Fach amerikanische Geschichte an deutschen Universitäten. Der Beitrag erschien 2005 als Teil der Jubiläums-Doppelausgabe der Zeitschrift *Amerikastudien/American Studies*. Ich erinnere mich mit Schaudern an die der Publikation folgende Sitzung des DGfA-Beirats und an die Tagung der Historikerinnen und Historiker in der DGfA im Februar 2006 in Tutzing, das ja im weiteren Sinne ein Vorort von München ist. Liest man den Aufsatz sorgfältig und ohne dem Autor ehrabschneiderische Absichten zu unterstellen, so wird deutlich, daß Doerries einen "proper chair for American History" vermißte (114). Oder, anders gesagt, daß er sich ein kooperativ arbeiten-des Institut nicht ohne die Berufung habilitierter Historiker oder Historikerinnen vorstellen konnte. Dazu kam es in München erst 2004 und 2007 mit den Berufungen Michael Hochgeschwenders und Christoph Mauchs.[4]

Übrigens hätte sich Doerries in seiner Einschätzung durchaus auf Bergstraesser berufen können. Sie kennen das Phänomen, daß gute Zitate immer wieder gern aufgegriffen werden und schließlich ein Eigenleben entfalten. So verhält es sich auch mit dem eingangs zitierten Passus über die vier Möglichkeiten, Amerikastudien zu betreiben. Er steht in der gedruckten Fassung von Bergstraessers Rede auf Seite 9. Nur drei Seiten weiter betont der Autor aber—und das wird meist übersehen—, daß ein kooperatives Experiment "die Qualitäten und Klarheit der wissenschaftlichen Methode in den Einzeldisziplinen" nicht beeinträchtigen dürfe: "Es kann sich nicht darum handeln, in die Leistungen und das Gefüge der Disziplinen von altem Bestand grundsätzlich ändernd einzugreifen" (11–12). Genau dies aber war in München geschehen, und daran entzündete sich die Kritik eines, wenn ich so sagen darf, in der Wolle gefärbten Historikers.[5]

Die Berliner Variante eines kooperativen Experiments geht bekanntlich auf Ernst Fraenkel zurück, der 1962 in einem Memorandum zur Gründung eines interfakultativen Amerika-Instituts, des späteren John F. Kennedy-Instituts für Nordamerikastudien, postulierte, das Studium des "Phänomens der Vereinigten Staaten" bedürfe verschiedener Methoden und Disziplinen.[6] Das war eine klare Absage an American Studies. In seiner vertraulichen Korrespondenz gab ihr Fraenkel noch deutlicher Ausdruck, als er in einem Brief an Dietrich Gerhard schrieb, die Etablierung von American Studies in Berlin müsse verhindert werden, weil es sich dabei um eine Wissenschaft in Anführungszeichen handele, "die im Grunde niemand ernst nimmt und die man nur toleriert, weil der Ami Geld gegeben hat."[7] Starker Tobak, aber wohl Konsens unter vielen Historikern und Sozialwissenschaftlern in den 1960er Jahren und zum Teil darüber hinaus.

Dauerhaft durchsetzen konnte sich Fraenkel nicht. 1986 wurden "Vorschläge zur Weiterentwicklung des John F. Kennedy-Instituts und seiner Bibliothek" von dessen Institutsrat veröffentlicht, die mit folgenden Ausführungen beginnen:

> Das JFKI dient der Forschung, der Lehre und dem Studium Nordamerikas in den Fachgebieten Literatur, Kultur, Sprache, Geschichte, Politik, Soziologie, Wirtschaft und Geographie. Als Kernbereich des Instituts konnte bisher die Amerikanistik (Amerika-

---

[4] Doerries erwähnt positiv das Wirken von Gerd Raeithel (114, fn65), der aber—und das war für den Nürnberger Historiker der springende Punkt—keinen Lehrstuhl innehatte. Daß der ehemalige Direktor des Deutschen Historischen Instituts in Washington (1999–2007), der in Köln bei Jürgen Heideking habilitierte Historiker Christoph Mauch, Nachfolger Berndt Ostendorfs auf der Professur für Kulturgeschichte werden würde, konnte Doerries nicht absehen.

[5] Das Herausgebergremium der Zeitschrift *Amerikastudien / American Studies* reagierte auf die Kontroverse, indem es den Vorschlag des Regensburger Historikers Volker Depkat aufgriff, die Vielfalt der in Deutschland praktizierten Formen USA-bezogener Geschichtsschreibung in einem thematischen Sonderheft zu dokumentieren (Depkat, "American History/ies in Germany"). Vgl. auch Depkats 2010 erschienene *Bibliographie raisonnée* zur jüngeren historischen USA-Forschung in Deutschland ("Literaturbericht").

[6] Memorandum zum Aufbau eines interfakultativen Amerika-Instituts an der Freien Universität Berlin, 28.11.1962, Archiv der FU Berlin.

[7] Fraenkel an Gerhard, 19.1.1961, Archiv der FU Berlin.

studien) mit den Disziplinen, Literatur, Kultur und Sprache gelten. Durch ihn war und ist das Kennedy-Institut in den wissenschaftlichen Zusammenhang der nationalen und internationalen Amerikastudien eingebunden. Um diesen Kernbereich gruppieren sich die sozialwissenschaftlichen Fachgebiete einschließlich Geschichte und Geographie.[8]

Zumindest im Selbstverständnis des damaligen Institutsrats bildeten also die Kulturwissenschaften am Kennedy-Institut den Kernbereich, die Sonne, umkreist von den historischen und sozialwissenschaftlichen Planeten. Damit bestätigte der Institutsrat unfreiwillig eine Studie des Aspen-Instituts vom Januar 1986, in der eine Unterrepräsentation der Sozialwissenschaften beklagt wurde: "Research and teaching remain skewed toward literary and cultural aspects of American life." Für München kam der Aspen-Bericht übrigens zu ähnlichen Schlußfolgerungen: "The faculty [...] remains modest and heavily oriented to literary/cultural aspects of American life."[9] Der Fairness halber muß aber hinzugefügt werden, daß sich insbesondere die Sozialwissenschaften in jenen Jahren vielerorts—also keineswegs nur in Berlin—mit großem Eifer selbst marginalisiert hatten.

Lassen Sie mich jetzt einen Blick auf die Alternativen zum kooperativen Experiment werfen, die Bergstraesser auf der DGfA-Gründungsversammlung genannt hatte. Die Beschäftigung mit den Vereinigten Staaten von Amerika könne "als eine Erweiterung der Forschung und Lehre auf den Gebieten der englischen Philologie, Sprache und Literatur" implementiert werden. Das war die Variante 2. Eine Angliederung der Amerikanistik an Anglistische Institute und deren Erweiterung zu Instituten für Anglistik und Amerikanistik war die pragmatische und am ehesten zur Verwaltungs- und Fächergliederung der deutschen Universitäten passende Lösung. Walther Fischer zum Beispiel optierte in Marburg für den Ausbau der amerikanistischen Lehre und strebte darüber hinaus eine lose "Arbeitsgemeinschaft" aller an Amerikastudien interessierten Wissenschaftler an (Strunz 201–09). Er widersetzte sich nicht der Einführung eines Teilfaches Amerikanistik, hielt dieses aber nur in enger Verbindung mit der Anglistik, also als Philologie, für möglich (Fischer 417). Egmont Zechlin, der Historiker im ersten DGfA-Vorstand, lehnte es ab, seine Forschung und Lehre unter dem Begriff Amerikanistik zu subsumieren. Nur der Begriff Amerikastudien gebe Anspruch und Ausrichtung der neuen Disziplin adäquat wieder.[10] Zechlin ging in Hamburg den Weg der Angliederung an ein etabliertes nichtphilologisches Fach, optierte also für die Variante 3. Wie Zechlin verfuhren mehr oder minder alle historisch und sozialwissenschaftlich geprägten Gründungsmitglieder der DGfA.

Eine Mischform der Varianten 1 und 4 (neue Disziplin und kooperatives Experiment) gab es in Frankfurt am Main. Da das dortige Amerika-Institut genau

---

[8] 20 hekt. S. und 2 unpag. S., Berlin: Februar 1986, 2, Privatarchiv Grabbe.

[9] Daniel Hamilton, The Status of University-Based American Studies Programs in Germany, Report from Aspen Institute Berlin on a Workshop, 10–12 Jan. 1986, o.D., 9. hekt. S., 2, 8–9, Privatarchiv Grabbe.

[10] Zechlin an Walther Fischer, 6.8.1952, Korrespondenz 1952–1962, DGfA-Archiv Wittenberg.

wie das spätere Zentrum für Nordamerika-Forschung (ZENAF) mit der Koordinierung aller wissenschaftlichen Aktivitäten in den Amerikastudien befaßt war, aber keine eigenständige Forschung und Lehre betrieb, kam es dem kooperativen Experiment nahe, wies aber unter dem ersten, kommissarischen Leiter, Fritz Meinecke (Schatzmeister der DGfA von 1953 bis 1956), auch Elemente der Variante 1 auf, denn Meinecke verstand American Studies im amerikanischen Sinne als eigenständige Disziplin.[11] Nachhaltig konnten sich American Studies in Frankfurt aber erst ab dem Wintersemester 1971/72 etablieren, als das Amerika-Institut— wie das *DGfA-Mitteilungsblatt* in schönstem Bürokratendeutsch vermerkt—eine "vorläufige Verwaltungseinheit" im Fachbereich Neuere Philologien wurde.[12]

Während der ersten zwanzig Jahre nach Gründung der DGfA war in Westdeutschland eine in der Anglistik beheimatete Amerikanistik der Regelfall wissenschaftlicher Beschäftigung mit den USA. Die Weichen dafür waren spätestens mit der Gründung der DGfA gestellt worden. Im Wittenberger DGfA-Archiv liegen Protokolle der Gründungskonferenzen, aber sie sind naturgemäß spröde. Ich möchte darum Sigmund Skard zu Wort kommen lassen, den norwegischen Polyhistor und Chronisten der europäischen wissenschaftlichen Beschäftigung mit den USA. Skard hatte als Beobachter an den Gründungskonferenzen von 1953 teilgenommen. Dies war Teil einer europaweiten 'fact-finding mission,' unternommen im Auftrag der Rockefeller-Stiftung, und bildete die Grundlage für sein 1958 publiziertes zweibändiges Werk *American Studies in Europe: Their History and Present Organization*:[13]

> Often I listened to the debates with a divided heart. I felt scant sympathy with *die alten Herren*, the elder *ordinarii* professors, often with a somewhat dubious political past, spokesmen of the traditional hierarchical system of German universities, for which the country had paid dearly, and of a rigid Anglicist approach, which I knew to involve considerable dangers to a newcomer like American studies. The survival of the ingrained system of academic power often was obvious. I noticed with pity the silence in the presence of their elders of many young scholars wary of their careers, and their demand that our private conversations not be quoted in my book. But neither was I always captivated by the champions of an 'interdisciplinary' study pleasant to the Americans, where the programs did not always inspire confidence, and where the 'integration' sometimes meant little more in reality than listing lectures on the Civil War, Ezra Pound, and American patent law under one American heading in the university catalog. (Skard, *Trans-Atlantica* 140)

"Dubious political past"—in der Tat. Ich möchte den Festcharakter nicht stören, aber auch nicht verschweigen, daß einige der damals in Marburg versammelten

---

[11] Christadler an Grabbe, 2.2.2004.

[12] *Mitteilungsblatt der Deutschen Gesellschaft für Amerikastudien* 19 (1972): 13.

[13] Noch heute staunenswert sind Skards durch die Rockefeller-Stiftung ermöglichten Vermarktungserfolge: Ca. 3000 Exemplare von *American Studies in Europe* wurden zunächst an Bibliotheken, Wissenschaftler, Politiker und Verwaltungen verschenkt; die Buchhandelsausgabe wurde mehr als 1000mal verkauft. Außerdem publizierte Skard mit *The American Myth and the European Mind: American Studies in Europe, 1776–1960*, eine popularisierte Form seiner Forschungsergebnisse oder, in Skards eigenen Worten, "the same porridge, served in a bowl instead of in a bathtub" (*Trans-Atlantica* 151). Dieses Buch erlebte zwei Auflagen in den 1960er Jahren und erschien 2012 noch einmal als Reprint.

Wissenschaftler sich durch Kooperation mit dem Nationalsozialismus kompromittiert hatten.[14]

Ursula Brumm hat die Amerikanisten der frühen Nachkriegszeit rückblickend in drei Gruppen eingeteilt (Brumm 9–11): Die erste Gruppe habe aus "Renegade-*Anglisten*" bestanden. Dieser Begriff ist meines Erachtens nicht so glücklich, denn im Wortsinn abtrünnig wurden sie nicht. Sie blieben Philologen und sahen die amerikanische Literatur als Erweiterung eines auf der englischen Literatur und Sprache basierenden Faches an. Nicht von ungefähr trägt Walther Fischers Geschichte der amerikanischen Literatur den Titel *Die englische Literatur der Vereinigten Staaten von Amerika* (Hervorhebung d. Vf.). Die zweite Gruppe in Frau Brumms Klassifizierung bildeten die in den Jahren nach 1945 aus der Emigration zurückgekehrten Wissenschaftler. Sie galten, wie schon gesagt, oft nur deshalb als Amerikaexperten, weil sie in den USA gelebt und meist an amerikanischen Universitäten gearbeitet hatten. Ihre Bindung an die Amerikastudien blieb in zahlreichen Fällen schwach. In München, auch das habe ich schon erwähnt, kehrte Helmut Kuhn nach fünf Jahren der amerikanischen Kulturgeschichte den Rücken und wechselte auf einen Lehrstuhl für Philosophie. Arnold Bergstraesser verschmähte die ihm angebotene Professur für nordamerikanische Geschichte in Köln und widmete sich auf seiner politikwissenschaftlichen Professur in Freiburg amerikanischen Themen eher am Rande. Dietrich Gerhard verließ den Kölner Lehrstuhl 1961 zugunsten des Max-Planck-Instituts für Geschichte in Göttingen. Kuhn und Gerhard legten überdies ihre DGfA-Vorstandsämter vorzeitig nieder, als sie ihre amerikabezogenen Stellen aufgaben.[15]

"Odd fellows, birds of strange feather," die durch Launen des Schicksals in der Kriegs- und Nachkriegszeit zu den Amerikastudien gestoßen waren, bildeten Frau Brumms dritte Gruppe. Dieser Kreis war sehr klein. Fritz Meinecke gehörte dazu, der in einen amerikanischen Kriegsgefangenenlager als Externer einen Harvard-Abschluß in American Civilization erlangte (Christadler 33). Das bunteste Gefieder trug zweifellos Ursula Brumm selbst, die in Mediävistik promoviert worden war und als Redakteurin der *Monumenta Germaniae Historia* mittelalterliche lateinische Urkunden ediert hatte, bis sie über einen Besuch des Salzburg-Seminars zu einem Commonwealth Fund-Stipendium kam, das sie nach Harvard führte. The rest, as they say, is history.

---

[14] Der Gründungsvorsitzende Walther Fischer war 1937 der NSDAP beigetreten, wurde aber von der Entnazifizierungsspruchkammer entlastet. Hellmut Bock (1957 bis 1961 Zweiter Vorsitzender der DGfA) war seit 1934 in der SA gewesen und 1937 NSDAP-Mitglied geworden. 1945/46 in Jena entlassen, konnte er 1948 seine Laufbahn in Kiel fortsetzen. Hans Galinsky (Zweiter Vorsitzender der DGfA von 1962 bis 1966), NSDAP-Mitglied seit 1933, wurde 1941 an die sog. Kampf-Universität Straßburg berufen und hielt dort seine Antrittsvorlesung in SA-Uniform. 1945 entlassen, wurde er dennoch 1952 Extraordinarius und 1957 Ordinarius in Mainz. Vgl. Hausmann, 410, 443, 455, 458–59. Eine rühmliche Ausnahme bildete Theodor Spira, DGfA-Vorsitzender 1956, der 1940 wegen seiner politischen und religiösen Überzeugungen als Ordinarius in Königsberg zwangsemeritiert worden war. Spira wurde 1947 in Frankfurt am Main anglistischer Ordinarius und Leiter des dortigen Amerika-Instituts. Vgl. Hausmann 510.

[15] DGfA-Beiratsprotokolle 21./22.8.1958 und 26.5.1961, Privatarchiv Ursula Brumm.

Bei der Bewertung der Erfolgschancen von Amerikastudien als kooperativem Experiment ist es unerläßlich, sich die ungleiche fachliche Distribution der in Marburg versammelten Wissenschaftler vor Augen zu halten. Die Amerikanistik an Englischen Seminaren, vertreten durch Inhaber anglistischer Lehrstühle, *mußte* zum Kern der Amerikastudien in Deutschland werden. Nur diese Institute lieferten zunächst die für den Erfolg notwendige kritische Masse. Und doch trugen auch andere Fächer zum Aufblühen der Amerikastudien in den 1960er und 1970er Jahren mehr als nur ein Scherflein bei. "There is no nation outside the United States today where the study of American Civilization shows so many facets and is so multifold in its scholarly organization as in present-day Germany," schrieb Sigmund Skard 1962 und fuhr fort, die Vielseitigkeit der Amerikastudien in Deutschland drücke sich in einer sehr weitgefächerten, nicht-derivativen Forschung aus. Zudem gebe es seit 1953 eine aktive Gesellschaft für Amerikastudien, deren Publikationsorgane Forschungsergebnisse verbreiteten, welche die Grenzen der Individualdisziplinen sprengen (*Trans-Atlantica* 103). Skards Urteil bezog sich auf das *Jahrbuch für Amerikastudien* und dessen *Beihefte*, die Vorläufer der Zeitschrift *Amerikastudien / American Studies* und der *Monograph Series*. Im *Jahrbuch* waren zwei Drittel der in den 1950er und 1960er Jahren erschienenen Aufsätze im engeren Sinne literaturwissenschaftlichen Themen gewidmet. Bei den *Beiheften* aber verblüfft noch heute eine enorme Bandbreite der Disziplinen, die seither nicht wieder erreicht wurde: Mit Monographien vertreten waren unter anderem Literatur, Geschichte, Politik, Philosophie, Sprache, Journalistik und das amerikanische Recht.

Lassen Sie mich die Frage "Wer sind wir?" noch einmal anders angehen: Auf der Tagung zum 25. Jubiläum des Kennedy-Instituts bezeichnete Ursula Brumm "Amerikastudien" als "German equivalent of American Studies" und führte weiter aus:

> In the most general sense, of course, research in any of the traditional fields such as history, literature, economics, or geography, which deals with American phenomena, qualifies as "American Studies." In a specific sense, American Studies is a new kind of research which developed when American literature was made instrumental to the interpretation and elucidation of the whole range of American culture. This involves an extension of the study of literature (in the widest sense), and it is something which happened in America not so long before the European discovery of American literature: There is something in American literary works which makes them intensely interpretative of the life in this country. (11–12)

Im weiteren Verlauf derselben Tagung sprach auch Manfred Jonas, der aus Hitlerdeutschland emigriert war, nicht dauerhaft zurückkehrte, aber eine Zeitlang am Amerika-Institut der Freien Universität als Gastprofessor gewirkt hatte. Jonas begann seinen Vortrag mit folgenden Worten: "My name is Manfred Jonas, and I am a historian. If this sounds like the confessional formula made famous by Alcoholics Anonymous, that is intentional, for it may well be important to the proper understanding of the remarks on American Studies that follow, to know that I am a historian, admit that I am one, and accept the perceptual parameters that state imposes" (76). Jonas lehrte mehrere Jahrzehnte am Union College in Schenectady, New York, und war dort Direktor interdisziplinärer American Studies-Programme ("Professor Manfred Jonas"), was zeigt, daß dieses Insistieren auf einem reinen Historikertum—von der Muse Clio geküßt und stets ein gut lutherisches 'Hier stehe ich ...' auf den Lippen—seiner Lebenswirklichkeit nicht entsprach, daß er aber das Gefühl hatte, sein Recht, Geschichtswissenschaft sozusagen in Reinform zu betreiben, immer wieder bekräftigen zu müssen.

Wie wollen und können wir uns in Deutschland mit den USA beschäftigen? Sollen wir American Studies im Sinne einer eigenständigen wissenschaftlichen Disziplin zur Regel machen oder aber sollen wir für Amerikastudien als koordinierte Zusammenarbeit unterschiedlicher geistes- und sozialwissenschaftlicher Fächer optieren? Zur Beantwortung dieser Grundfrage, die ich heute abend bereits einige Male variiert habe, rufe ich nun nach Bergstraesser einen weiteren Zeugen auf, nämlich Robert E. Spiller von der University of Pennsylvania. Spiller war 1954/55 Präsident der American Studies Association gewesen, und der Vorstand der DGfA hatte ihn eingeladen, den Eröffnungsvortrag auf der Jahrestagung 1959 in Köln zu halten. Das Thema seiner Ausführungen lautete: "Value and Method in American Studies: The Literary Versus the Social Approach." Ich beabsichtige nicht, diesen Vortrag zu referieren, sondern greife zunächst eine Anekdote auf.

Spiller beschreibt sehr amüsant, wie er und der Wirtschaftshistoriker Thomas C. Cochran 1954 ein großzügig von der Carnegie Corporation finanziertes Seminar abhielten, bei dem experimentell geklärt werden sollte, ob Geschichte und Literaturwissenschaft ihre Konzepte und Methoden im Interesse eines gemeinsamen American Civilization-Ansatzes synthetisieren könnten (17). Schon nach einem Monat zeigte sich ein nicht antizipiertes tiefes Schisma, weil jede Seite die Validität der von der anderen angewandten Methoden anzweifelte. Das Experiment wurde abgebrochen. Ein Jahr später unterrichtete Cochran allein ein Seminar über sozialen Wandel, und Spiller lehrte über das Verhältnis von Literatur und Gesellschaft mit Fragestellungen des Myth and Symbol-Ansatzes. Die ultimative Ironie, aus heutiger Sicht, liegt allerdings darin, daß die Gruppe der Wirtschaftshistoriker auch Werbetexten soziale Evidenz zuerkannte, während Spiller und seine Literaturwissenschaftler ihre Abscheu vor Forschung über Zahnpasta-Werbung ("advertisements of a brand of toothpaste") bekundeten und den in einem "erstklassigen" Roman ("a first-rate novel") angesprochenen Themen eine ungleich höhere Wertigkeit zumaßen, weil sie erbaulich ("uplifting") seien (18).

Am Ende seines Vortrags gab Spiller der DGfA den guten Rat, den Flirt zwischen Literatur- und Geschichtswissenschaft ("flirtation" war tatsächlich das Wort, das er gebrauchte) nicht dadurch in eine Trennung münden zu lassen, daß man die Vereinigung der beiden Disziplinen unbedingt in eine Einheit zu verwandeln trachtet: "With increased understanding of each other, differences rather than similarities become important in making or breaking a dynamic cooperation" (21). Mit anderen Worten: American Studies sollten Mediator sein zwischen Geschichte und Sozialwissenschaften einerseits und Literatur- und Kulturwissenschaft andererseits (24). Spiller sah American Studies in Deutschland in einer Art

Maklerfunktion, die sie aber nicht mehr würden ausüben können, falls sie sich zu einer synthetischen Wissenschaft entwickelten. Nun gehört Robert E. Spiller bekanntlich zu den Begründern der interdisziplinären American Studies. Darum glaube ich, daß er 1959 in Köln seinen Zuhörerinnen und Zuhörern einen guten Rat geben wollte, der speziell auf die Lage an den westdeutschen Universitäten gemünzt war.

Die Frage 'Wer sind wir wir?' die ich im Hinblick auf die DGfA stelle, wurde von Spiller zum ersten Mal während des Gründungsprozesses der American Studies Association aufgeworfen. Das Konzept von American Studies bestehe darin, so Spiller 1949, "to ask a single question, 'Who are we?,' [in order to discover] the configurations of thought and feeling with which we, both as individuals and as a nation, answer that question daily in our actions" (zit. nach Nye 291–92). "To answer that question daily in our actions": Heißt das nicht, daß für Spiller American Studies in den USA der Klärung perzipierter persönlicher und gesellschaftlicher Bedürfnisse dienen sollten? Aktionsforschung als handlungsorientierte Strategie zur sozialen Veränderung mag ihren Platz haben im Kanon sozialwissenschaftlicher Methoden. Aber ist sie auch für eine Kulturwissenschaft geeignet? Und was passiert, wenn die Forscherinnen und Forscher, die von außen, in diesem Fall aus Deutschland, kommen, nicht den Willen und schon gar nicht die Möglichkeit haben, ihren Forschungsgegenstand handlungsorientiert zu verändern?

Stehe ich allein da, wenn ich von mir sage, daß meine politischen Überzeugungen bei der Wahl des Studienfaches und in der Ausübung des Berufes keine nennenswerte Rolle spielten? Nun hat meine Meinung in Bezug auf diese oder jene Sache immer wieder einmal gewechselt, und es sind auch im Lauf der Jahrzehnte verschiedene Parteien gewesen, denen ich meine Stimme gab. Darum vermutlich verstehe ich Emory Elliott nicht, der in der Presidential Address auf der ASA-Jahrestagung von 2006 seine politischen Überzeugungen als treibende Kraft bei der Wahl des Studienfaches nannte, um dann, als gereifter Wissenschaftler, mit Noam Chomsky die USA einen "gescheiterten Staat" zu nennen, sein Entsetzen über Handlungen gesellschaftlicher Eliten und Regierungen in Vergangenheit und Gegenwart, jetzt unter Berufung auf Amy Kaplan, geradezu herauszuschreien und die American Studies Association, einen wissenschaftlichen Verband, aufzufordern, für eine radikale Änderung des dominanten Systems zu kämpfen— mit Worten zwar, aber immerhin (3–5).

"How can we, through our teaching and research, more effectively generate developments that will lead to thoughtful citizenship and to a more humane future?" lautete Elliotts Kernfrage (5-6), die dann in einen Appell für internationale Kooperation bei der Herbeiführung von politischen Zuständen in den USA, wie sie Elliott für wünschenswert hielt, einmündete. Udo Hebel hat darauf hingewiesen, daß solche Diskurse den US-amerikanischen American Studies inhärent sind: Der "mit dem umfassend kulturwissenschaftlichen und kulturhistorischen Ansatz verbundene gesellschaftspolitische Impetus" habe "oftmals zu einem aktivistischen Engagement außerhalb der akademisch-wissenschaftlichen Tätigkeit für eine angemessene Repräsentation der unterschiedlichen Gruppen und Interessen in der U.S. amerikanischen Geschichte und Gesellschaft" geführt (2). Aber sollen wir uns, können wir uns an diesem Engagement beteiligen und in diesem

Sinne American Studies betreiben, oder wäre es sinnvoll, zumindest dann, wenn wir uns unserer Muttersprache bedienen, konsequent von Amerikastudien zu sprechen, um zu verdeutlichen, daß die Beschäftigung mit Amerika in Deutschland aus einer anderen Perspektive erfolgt und von anderen Interessen geleitet ist als bei unseren US-amerikanischen Kolleginnen und Kollegen?

Die Hinwendung zu Transnational American Studies—die DGfA-Jahrestagung von 2011 war diesem Thema gewidmet—ist zumindest zum Teil dem angesprochenen Dilemma geschuldet. Sie sind auf einer pragmatischen Ebene in Deutschland und Europa, vermutlich auch in Asien, ein Instrument geworden, die Außenperspektiven mit den inneramerikanischen wissenschaftlichen Debatten zu verknüpfen. Aber wie 'transnational' sind unsere amerikanischen Kolleginnen und Kollegen, von denen dieser Impuls ausging? Marc Chénetier sieht im "transnational turn" einen "last-ditch attempt at reconducting still another version of American views of the field" und fährt fort: "Increasingly polemical centrifugal concentration on margins and peripheries, within and without, appear as a gesture to avoid facing the problems posed by an apparently unassailable center, compensate an increasingly felt powerlessness in front of an unchallenged economic system and mode of social development" (Abschnitt 4). In der polemischen Überspitzung steckt ein Stück Wahrheit, aber es wird mehr die Vergangenheit als die Gegenwart beschrieben. Schaut man auf die ASA-Präsidentinnen und Präsidenten der letzten Jahre, so findet man jedenfalls Wissenschaftlerinnen und Wissenschaftler, deren Œuvre nicht für Exzeptionalismus-Gläubigkeit oder periphere Interessen spricht. So hat zum Beispiel Vicky Lynn Ruiz, eine Historikerin, sowohl über Chicana/Latina History als auch über Women's History, Immigration History und Labor History gearbeitet.[16] Kevin Gaines, ASA-Präsident 2009/10 ist Autor, unter anderem, von *American Africans in Ghana: Black Expatriates and the Civil Rights Era*.[17] Und denken Sie an Matthew Frye Jacobson (Präsident 2012/13), der von der Literaturwissenschaft zur Geschichtswissenschaft "konvertierte," wie er es in einem "Why I Became a Historian" betitelten YouTube-Video geschildert hat, also kein Amalgam aus beiden Fächern vertritt.[18] Zu Jacobsons Werken gehören: *Barbarian Virtues: The United States Encounters Foreign Peoples at Home and Abroad, 1876–1917* und *Special Sorrows: The Diasporic Imagination of Irish, Polish, and Jewish Immigrants in the United States*.[19] In diesen Büchern wird ein transnationaler Anspruch nicht nur erhoben, sondern weitgehend eingelöst.

Als im Juni 2013 das fünfzigste Jubiläum des Kennedy-Instituts gefeiert wurde, hielten Heinz Ickstadt und Winfried Fluck einen Doppelvortrag zur Instituts-

---

[16] Vgl. z. B. *From Out of the Shadows: Mexican Women in Twentieth Century America* (New York: Oxford UP, 1998); *Western Women: Their Land, Their Lives* (Albuquerque: U of New Mexico P, 1988); Hg. mit Donna Gabaccia, *American Dreaming, Global Realities: Re-Thinking U.S. Immigration History* (Urbana: U of Illinois P, 2006); *Cannery Women, Cannery Lives: Mexican Women, Unionization, and the California Food Processing Industry, 1930–1950* (Albuquerque: U of New Mexico P, 1987)

[17] Chapel Hill: U of North Carolina Press, 2006.

[18] Das Video ist abrufbar unter http://histsociety.blogspot.de/2013/05/matthew-frye-jacobson-on-why-i-became.html, Web. 2 July 2014.

[19] New York: Hill and Wang, 2000; Cambridge, MA: Harvard UP, 1995.

geschichte. Ickstadt berichtete unter anderem von einem Memorandum, das John McCormick, 1954 bis 1959 Professor für amerikanische Literatur am Amerika-Institut, im November 1954 für die Universitätsleitung verfaßt hatte. Darin plädierte McCormick für eine Erweiterung des Instituts insofern, als neben literaturwissenschaftlicher Forschung auch "America Studies" betrieben werden sollten. Deren Inhalte beschrieb er so: "[T]he term 'America Studies' implies activity in the areas of history, philosophy and the social sciences (i.e. sociology, political science, economics and education) as well as theater, music and the arts."[20] Spontan dachte ich: Sollten wir, wenn wir uns der englischen Sprache bedienen, nicht auch von Americ*a* Studies statt von Americ*an* Studies sprechen? Man kann noch soviel von Transnationalen Studien oder auch von deutscher bzw. europäischer Sicht auf die USA reden: Das Adjektiv 'American' wird die Sache immer verengen und unsere Ziele an Definitionen koppeln, die zum Teil noch aus der Zeit des amerikanischen Exzeptionalismusdiskurses stammen. Und noch ein linguistisches Argument möchte ich anführen: Auf zahlreichen Tagungen, die ich in den letzten Jahren besuchte, konnte ich die Variante German Association *of* American Studies hören, analog auch European Association *of* American Studies. Der Wechsel der Präposition folgt dem sprachlichen Wandel in den USA. Es gibt aber aus meiner Sicht einen bedenkenswerten Unterschied zwischen 'for' und 'of.' 'For' deute ich so, daß die Gesellschaft sich der Aufgabe verschrieben hat, Amerikastudien zu fördern und zu betreiben. 'Of' würde anzeigen, daß sich die DGfA als Entität von Amerikastudien begreift und diese mit American Studies gleichsetzt. Für mich macht es durchaus einen Unterschied, ob ich Amerikastudien oder 'amerikanische Studien' betreibe. Sie könnten mir jetzt vorhalten, das seien Petitessen ohne tiefere semiotische Bedeutung. Vielleicht ist das so. Es geht mir vor allem darum, daß die DGfA autonom und gleichberechtigt am internationalen wissenschaftlichen Diskurs teilnimmt, diesen aber vielstimmig und multidisziplinär führt. Amerika bezeichnet unseren Forschungsgegenstand und nicht unsere Methode. Dessen sollten wir uns stets bewußt sein.

Daß die American Studies Association sich verändert hat, sagte ich schon. Daß sich die DGfA mittlerweile, um es mit dem Modewort auszudrücken, "auf Augenhöhe" mit der ASA befindet, zeigt unter anderem die Verleihung des Bode-Pearson Prize for Outstanding Contributions to American Studies an Alfred Hornung. Ein Indikator der Wertschätzung ist auch Udo Hebels Vorsitz im International Committee. Vielleicht kommt es zu einer doppelten Kongruenz—zwischen der ASA und der DGfA einerseits und zwischen den kulturwissenschaftlichen Amerikastudien und der Geschichtswissenschaft andererseits. Ich will aber nicht Dinge, die ich vorher als schwer vereinbar dargestellt habe, so mir nichts, dir nichts harmonisieren und weise deshalb vorsorglich darauf hin, daß sich kongruente Linien erst im Unendlichen treffen. Aber auch eine Annäherung hat ihren Wert. Jedenfalls bleibt noch viel Raum für die Fortführung des kooperativen Experiments.

Schon seit einigen Jahren können wir eine Entkrampfung des Verhältnisses zwischen Kulturwissenschaft und Geschichtswissenschaft in der DGfA beobach-

---

[20] Ich danke Heinz Ickstadt für die freundliche Überlassung seines Manuskripts. Das McCormick-Memorandum befindet sich im Archiv der Freien Universität Berlin.

ten. Die alten Kriegsbeile sind weitgehend begraben. Dazu hat ohne Zweifel der sogenannte 'cultural turn' beigetragen, der seit Mitte der 1990er Jahre in der Geschichtswissenschaft eine große Wirkung entfaltet hat (Depkat, "Cultural Turn"). Auf einer Tagung in Berlin am Kennedy-Institut im November 2011 zum Thema "American Studies Today" (Fluck et al.) habe ich mich übrigens dahingehend geäußert, daß ich 'Turns' grundsätzlich ablehne, weil ich den 'military turn'—Sie wissen schon: 'kehrt, marsch!'—seit meiner Bundeswehrzeit kenne und von abrupten oder gar totalen Richtungsänderungen in der Wissenschaft nichts halte. Zudem war die deutsche Geschichtswissenschaft immer viel besser als ihr Ruf bei manchen Literatur- und Kulturwissenschaftlern. Thomas Nipperdey zum Beispiel schrieb schon 1973 in seinem programmatischen Aufsatz "Die anthropologische Dimension der Geschichtswissenschaft," daß die "menschlich-historische Welt" als ein "Dreiecksverhältnis von Gesellschaft, Kultur und Person" begriffen werden müsse. Historiker dürften die Kulturgeschichte nicht zur Geistesgeschichte verkürzen (50 *et passim*). Auch persönliche Wahrnehmungen und Emotionen seien als historische Gegenstände zu erschließen. Ich könnte bis zu Karl Lamprecht zurückgehen, der an der Schwelle des 20. Jahrhunderts Geschichte als Kulturgeschichte und diese als Totalität sozialer, wirtschaftlicher, politischer und geistiger Erscheinungen begriff (Schorn-Schütte, 175), um Ihnen ähnliche Positionen vorzuführen.

Der Stand der Annäherung zwischen Kulturwissenschaft und Geschichte läßt sich sehr schön und auch persönlich anhand von Interviews nachzeichnen, die Astrid Eckert, eine Berliner Historikerin, die heute an der Emory University lehrt, im Herbst 2002 im Auftrag des Deutschen Historischen Instituts Washington führte. Es ging um die Lage der historischen Amerikastudien in Deutschland. Interviewt wurden Norbert Finzsch, Ursula Lehmkuhl, Detlev Junker und ich ("American History in Germany"). Die im Kontext dieses Vortrags interessanteste Frage lautete: "What are the themes of the twenty-first century? Where do you see the field going?" In den Antworten zeigen sich bemerkenswerte Unterschiede zwischen Finzsch und Lehmkuhl einerseits und Grabbe und Junker andererseits. Umweltgeschichte, so Norbert Finzsch, sei ein "heißes Thema" und postkoloniale Geschichte werde langfristig das wichtigste Paradigma sein—"the bringing together of race, class, gender, and culture into what you could label a 'cultural history of late capitalism'" (61). Frau Lehmkuhl erwähnte den "cultural turn" in der Diplomatiegeschichte, fand das "Borderlands"-Konzept fruchtbar und meinte, Historikerinnen und Historiker der USA in Deutschland würden sogar stärker als ihre amerikanischen Kolleginnen und Kollegen sozialwissenschaftliche sowie literatur- und kulturwissenschaftliche Ansätze für ihre Forschung nutzen (62–63).

Es ist wichtig zu wissen, daß wir einzeln und nicht als Gruppe interviewt wurden. Erst nachdem das *Bulletin* des DHI erschienen war, konnte ich nachlesen, was die anderen gesagt hatten. In meiner Antwort bekannte ich mich als politischer Historiker, der Fragen von Leben und Tod für die wichtigsten hielt, mit denen sich die Geschichtswissenschaft auch künftig würde befassen müssen. Herr Junker nannte Krieg und Frieden als zentrales Thema und befürchtete, daß die Fokussierung, insbesondere in den USA, auf "race, class, and gender" zur Selbstmarginalisierung der Disziplin führen könnte (62). Die Bewertung dieser Einschätzungen überlasse ich Ihnen. Mir ist es wichtig zu zeigen, daß ganz unterschiedliche Forschungsagenden verfolgt werden können und vermutlich auch künftig ihre Wirkung entfalten werden. Für alle muß die Deutsche Gesellschaft für Amerikastudien ein Forum bieten, was sie nur kann, wenn sie sich als multidisziplinär begreift.

Zum Ende meines Vortrags möchte ich einige Anmerkungen zum bisher Erreichten und noch zu Leistenden machen. Ich habe einen Vortrag über ein 1953 ausgerufenes Experiment gehalten. Dieses Experiment ist in vielen Fällen geglückt. In dem Brief von Martin Christadler, den ich eingangs zitierte, wies der Kollege stolz darauf hin, daß sein Institut für England- und Amerikastudien schon 1972 einen Fachfremden, nämlich den Historiker Willy Paul Adams, auf eine Professur berufen hatte. Das sei damals ein Unikum gewesen. So kann man es sagen; fünf Jahre später war dieses Unikum bereits Geschichte. Im *DGfA-Mitteilungsblatt* heißt es dazu lapidar: Die von Adams "geräumte und nach seinem Weggang [nach Berlin] gesperrte H3-Stelle (Amerikanische Geschichte) wurde vorläufig nicht wieder zur Besetzung freigegeben."[21] Parallel mit Adams war Klaus Schwabe 1972 ordentlicher Professor für Mittlere und Neuere Geschichte mit besonderer Berücksichtigung der anglo-amerikanischen Geschichte am Frankfurter Historischen Seminar geworden. Auch diese Stelle fiel weg, als Schwabe 1980 einen Ruf auf den Lehrstuhl für Neuere Geschichte an der RWTH Aachen annahm. Mit dessen Übernahme—hier sei noch einmal das *DGfA-Mitteilungsblatt* zitiert— "möchte Prof. Schwabe ein regelmäßiges, wenn auch begrenztes Angebot von Lehrveranstaltungen zur Geschichte der Vereinigten Staaten gewährleisten."[22] Dieses Versprechen hat Schwabe gehalten, und er ist auch in der Forschung einer der profiliertesten deutschen Amerikahistoriker geblieben. Institutionell allerdings waren die Verluste schmerzlich, und für das aufscheinende Muster, Stellen für historische Amerikastudien bei nächster Gelegenheit wieder einzukassieren, gibt es weitere Beispiele. In Frankfurt am Main sollten dreißig Jahre vergehen, bis mit Simon Wendt erneut ein Amerikahistoriker berufen werden konnte.

Aber in den letzten Jahren überwiegt das Positive: Die Regensburger Amerikanistik hat 2005 den Historiker Volker Depkat kooptiert. Am Institut für Amerikanistik in Leipzig lehrt nach dem Historiker Hartmut Keil der Politikwissenschaftler Crister Garrett, und in Augsburg ist Philipp Gassert mit seinem Lehrstuhl für die Geschichte des europäisch-transatlantischen Kulturraums (maßgeschneidert, wie mir scheint, für Transnational American Studies) so eng mit der Amerikanistik verbunden, daß die von ihm und seinen Mitarbeitern erbrachten Leistungen in das Forschungsrating Anglistik und Amerikanistik des Wissenschaftsrates zugunsten der Augsburger Amerikanistik einflossen.[23] Herrn Bergstraesser, da bin ich mir sicher, hätte das gefreut.

---

[21] 25 (1978): 47.
[22] 28 (1981): 17.
[23] Allerdings wurde Philipp Gassert im Februar 2014 auf eine Professur für die Geschichte des europäisch-transatlantischen Kulturraums an der Universität Mannheim berufen.

Erlauben Sie mir noch ein Wort zum Forschungsrating. Ich freue mich als Angehöriger einer ostdeutschen Universität besonders darüber, daß gleich fünf Universitäten in den neuen Bundesländern in den meisten Kategorien sehr gute oder bessere Noten erhalten haben. Ich denke, diese Ergebnisse sind Beweis genug, daß wir 1990 und den folgenden Jahren unter maßgeblicher Beteiligung zunächst von Heinz Ickstadt und Berndt Ostendorf und dann von Peter Freese und mir vieles richtig gemacht haben. Jedenfalls hat sich die DGfA, die über führende Mitglieder auch bei Berufungen mitsprach, große Verdienste beim Aufbau vitaler Amerikastudien in den neuen Bundesländern erworben. Aber es bleiben noch Aufgaben bestehen, nicht primär im Osten, sondern generell, und auch dafür liefert das 2012 abgeschlossene Forschungsrating des Wissenschaftsrats den Beweis (Wissenschaftsrat). Die sehr guten bis exzellenten Ergebnisse der Amerikanistik sind mit Recht gelobt worden. Aber das Rating läßt neben der Diagnose, daß es um Forschungsqualität, Nachwuchsförderung, Wissenstransfer und mithin auch um die Reputation sehr gut bestellt ist, noch eine andere Schlußfolgerung zu: Wenn ich richtig gezählt habe, gibt es unter den sechzig berücksichtigten Einrichtungen acht, überwiegend Pädagogische Hochschulen, die über keine Amerikanistik verfügen. Bei sechzehn weiteren Einrichtungen wurden die Ergebnisse nicht veröffentlicht. Aus datenschutzrechtlichen Gründen, wie es heißt, weil weniger als drei Wissenschaftlerinnen und Wissenschaftler gemeldet wurden. Man kann die Ergebnisse des Ratings also auch so lesen: Vierzig Prozent der untersuchten deutschen Hochschulen verfügen über keine hinreichend ausgebaute Amerikanistik oder haben schlicht keinen solchen Schwerpunkt. Weitere Universitäten, einige mit und einige ohne Amerikanistik, nahmen anscheinend nicht am Forschungsrating teil. Wir sollten uns, das wäre mein Fazit, darüber freuen, über Leuchttürme in der deutschen Forschungslandschaft zu verfügen, aber wir müssen darauf achten, daß wir an allen deutschen Universitäten mit Amerikastudien Flagge zeigen. Dieser und kommende Vorstände, da bin ich zuversichtlich, werden sich der Aufgabe stellen.

Lassen Sie mich mit 'famous last words' enden. Das Buch *The Machine in the Garden* von Leo Marx ist bekanntlich einer der Schlüsseltexte der frühen American Studies. Die Harvard-Dissertation von 1950 war noch "Hawthorne and Emerson: Studies in the Impact of the Machine Technology upon the American Writer" betitelt gewesen, und dieser Untertitel beschreibt meines Erachtens immer noch recht genau, wer in *The Machine in the Garden* im Mittelpunkt steht, nämlich "writers," also Romanciers, Poeten, Essayisten und deren Texte. Auch Shakespeare, Carlyle, Wordsworth und andere englische Autoren sind Teil der Untersuchung. Damit handelt es sich für mich im Kern um ein Produkt literaturwissenschaftlicher Forschung.[24] Ich weiß noch, daß ich das Buch als Student las, aber bald etwas ratlos beiseite legte. Bei der erneuten Beschäftigung, in

---

[24] In einer wohlwollend-kritischen Analyse von *The Machine in the Garden* aus der Feder des 2014 verstorbenen Wissenschaftshistorikers Thomas Hughes heißt es: "For all his genius and skill, Marx paid little heed to machines, technology or their creators in *The Machine in the Garden*. Indeed, the 'machine' and 'technology' appear more assertively in the book's title and subtitle than in his text" (Abschnitt 3).

Vorbereitung auf diesen Vortrag, fand ich den Schlüssel zu meinem damaligen Verhalten im letzten Satz. Er lautet: "The machine's sudden entrance into the garden presents a problem that ultimately belongs not to art but to politics" (Marx 365). Ich finde es tröstlich, daß auch nach Ansicht eines Mitbegründers der American Studies für die Geschichts- und Sozialwissenschaften noch einiges zu tun bleibt.

Works Cited

"American History in Germany: The View of the Practitioners. Norbert Finzsch, Hans-Jürgen Grabbe, Detlef Junker, and Ursula Lehmkuhl, Interviewed by Astrid M. Eckert." *Bulletin of the German Historical* Institute 32 (2003): 51-84. Print.

Bergstraesser, Arnold. "Amerikastudien als Problem der Forschung und Lehre." *Jahrbuch für Amerikastudien* 1 (1956): 8-14. Print.

Brumm, Ursula. "American Studies as We Found It." *America Seen from the Outside: Topics, Models, and Achievements of American Studies in the Federal Republic of Germany*. Ed. Brigitte Georgi-Findlay and Heinz Ickstadt. Berlin: John F. Kennedy-Institut für Nordamerikastudien, 1990. 8-17. Print.

Chénetier, Marc. "'New' 'American Studies': Exceptionalism redux?" *European Journal of American Studies* 3.3 (2008). Document 8. Web. 2 July 2014.

Christadler, Martin. "'Blindness and Fortune': Becoming an Americanist in Postwar Germany." *American Studies in Germany: European Contexts and Intercultural Relations*. Ed. Günter H. Lenz and Klaus Milich. Frankfurt/M.: Campus; New York: St. Martin's, 1995. 26-36. Print.

Depkat, Volker. "Literaturbericht: Geschichte der USA." *Geschichte in Wissenschaft und Unterricht* 61 (2010): 261-76, 358-75. Print.

---. "The 'Cultural Turn' in German and American Historiography." *Amerikastudien / American Studies* 54.3 (2009): 425-50. Print.

---, ed. "American History/ies in Germany: Assessments, Transformations, Perspectives." *Amerikastudien / American Studies* 54.3 (2009). Print.

Doerries, Reinhard R. "The Unknown Republic: American History at German Universities." *Amerikastudien / American Studies* 50.1/2 (2005): 99-125. Print.

Elliott, Emory. "Diversity in the United States and Abroad: What Does It Mean When American Studies Is Transnational?" *American Quarterly* 59.1 (2007): 1-22. Print.

Fischer, Walther. "Die Amerikanistik im gegenwärtigen Universitätslehrplan und in den Prüfungsordnungen der deutschen Länder." *Neuphilologische Zeitschrift* 3 (1951): 412-17. Print.

---. *Die englische Literatur der Vereinigten Staaten von Amerika*. Potsdam: Athenaion, 1929. Print.

Fluck, Winfried, et al., eds. *American Studies Today: New Research Agendas*. Heidelberg: Winter, 2014. Print.

Fluck, Winfried, and Thomas Claviez, eds. *Theories of American Culture, Theories of American Studies*. Tübingen: Narr, 2003. Print.

Grabbe, Hans-Jürgen. "50 Jahre Deutsche Gesellschaft für Amerikastudien." *Amerikastudien / American Studies* 48.2 (2003): 159-84. Print.
Hausmann, Frank-Rutger. *Anglistik und Amerikanistik im "Dritten Reich."* Frankfurt/M.: Klostermann, 2003. Print.
Hebel, Udo. *Einführung in die Amerikanistik/American Studies.* Stuttgart: Metzler, 2008. Print.
Huber, Ursula. "Von der Amerika-Kunde zum Amerika-Institut der Universität München." *Amerika-Institut 1949–1989: 40 Jahre Amerika-Studien an der Ludwig-Maximilians-Universität in München. Eine Institutsgeschichte.* München: Amerika-Institut, 1989. 1-56. Print.
Hughes, Thomas. "Garden or Wilderness?" *The American Interest.* The American Interest LLC 1 Dec. 2005. Web. 2 July 2014.
Jonas, Manfred. "American Studies: A Historian's View." *America Seen from the Outside: Topics, Models, and Achievements of American Studies in the Federal Republic of Germany.* Ed. Brigitte Georgi-Findlay and Heinz Ickstadt. Berlin: John F. Kennedy-Institut für Nordamerikastudien 1990. 76-84. Print.
Marx, Leo. *The Machine in the Garden: Technology and the Pastoral Ideal in America.* 1964. London: Oxford UP, 1967. Print.
Nipperdey, Thomas. "Die anthropologische Dimension der Geschichtswissenschaft." 1973. *Gesellschaft, Kultur, Theorie: Gesammelte Aufsätze zur neueren Geschichte.* Göttingen: Vandenhoeck & Ruprecht, 1976. 33-58. Print.
Nye, Russel B. "Robert E. Spiller and the ASA." *American Quarterly* 19.2 (1967): 291-92. Print.
Paulus, Stefan. *Vorbild USA? 'Amerikanisierung' von Universität und Wissenschaft in Westdeutschland 1945–1976.* München: Oldenbourg, 2010. Print.
"Professor Manfred Jonas Recalled as Distinguished Scholar and Exemplary Teacher." *Union College* 27 Aug. 2013. Web. 2 July 2014.
Schorn-Schütte, Luise. "Lamprecht, Karl Nathanael (1856–1915)." *Historikerlexikon: Von der Antike bis zum 20. Jahrhundert.* Ed. Rüdiger vom Bruch and Rainer A. Müller München: Beck, 1991. 175. Print.
Skard, Sigmund. *The American Myth and the European Mind: American Studies in Europe, 1776–1960.* Philadelphia: U of Pennsylvania Press, 1961. Print.
---. *American Studies in Europe: Their History and Present Organization.* 2 Vols. Philadelphia: U of Pennsylvania P, 1958. Print.
---. *Trans-Atlantica: Memoirs of a Norwegian Americanist.* Oslo: Universitetsforlaget, 1978. Print.
Spiller, Robert E. "Value and Method in American Studies: The Literary Versus the Social Approach." *Jahrbuch für Amerikastudien* 4 (1959): 11-24. Print.
Strunz, Gisela. *American Studies oder Amerikanistik? Die deutsche Amerikawissenschaft und die Hoffnung auf Erneuerung der Hochschulen und der politischen Kultur nach 1945.* Opladen: Leske + Budrich, 1999. Print.
Wissenschaftsrat. *Forschungsrating Anglistik und Amerikanistik: Einzelergebnisse der Einrichtungen.* 7 Dec. 2012. Web. 2 July 2004.

Usable Pasts, Possible Futures: The German Association for American Studies at Sixty

Udo J. Hebel, Carmen Birkle, Philipp Gassert, Introd. and Comp.

American Studies has always been concerned with its own history as a scholarly discipline and as an academic field of political and social negotiations. Revisions of research agendas, institutional politics, and teaching curricula in American Studies quite frequently were undertaken in view of the discipline's historical development and future interests. The idea of 'new American Studies,' which emerged repeatedly over time and most prominently in the early 1990s, presupposes the existence of an 'old' American Studies. The proliferation of 'posts' in American Studies similarly suggests precedents and precursors of various sorts, be they related to postmodernism, poststructuralism, postcolonialism, postfeminism, or posthumanism.

Despite this apparent interest in issues of disciplinary histories and lineages, the rise of new approaches, if not (sub-)disciplines such as Atlantic Studies, Hemispheric Studies, Pacific Studies, and Transnational American Studies, at times tends to blur the visibility of previous scholarship and past agents of change. Efforts to position our discipline and push it forward have often fueled the need to prove the field's uniqueness and newness. This sometimes has come at the prize of historical forgetfulness of earlier efforts to address some of the very same issues that we continue coming to grips with still today. Yet American Studies as a discipline has always been a self-reflexive endeavor. It has continuously asked questions about its own disciplinary prerequisites, its self-perception, and its own connections to the respective historical contexts. Innovation is, after all, one of the achievements of such self-reflection; we therefore find it useful to analyze and assess what has been explored and what has been achieved in order to understand where we would like to go in the future.

Revisiting the various pasts and envisioning the possible futures of American Studies seemed to be particularly appropriate on the occasion of the 60th anniversary of the German Association for American Studies, officially founded in June 1953 in Marburg as a truly inter- and multi-disciplinary enterprise. Walther Fischer, professor of English and American Studies at Philipps-Universität Marburg, was one of the founders of the Association and was elected as its first president. He initiated the Boppard Committee in 1951, which subsequently laid the groundwork for the foundation of the Association in 1953 in Marburg.[1]

---

[1] For more information on the foundation and the early years of the German Association for American Studies, see Hans-Jürgen Grabbe, "50 Jahre Deutsche Gesellschaft für Amerikastudien," *Amerikastudien / American Studies* 48.2 (2003): 159-84. For more recent information, see Hans-Jürgen Grabbe's contribution to the present issue.

How should we look at the pasts of our discipline, and how can we make them usable for our futures? In which specific ways has our contemporary practice of American Studies been shaped by past agendas and perspectives? Which past moments have triggered particular disciplinary and interdisciplinary developments? How far can reviewing the past go beyond mere nostalgia or rejection and rather become future-oriented and agenda-based? Which past experiences may help us to continue American Studies as an especially vibrant, intellectually stimulating, innovative, open-minded, and forward-looking venture that reaches beyond our individual academic and institutional fields and retains the capacity to ignite fruitful intellectual exchanges both within and beyond the humanities and social sciences? "Back to the Future" is another way of framing the intention of this conference: to pave the way for new directions in American Studies by self-critically assessing and reappropriating sixty years of American Studies in Germany.

In view of the openness and dynamics of the field of American Studies and its decided interest to reach out into various other disciplines and into cultural, social, and political debates, the conference brought together GAAS members of various (inter)disciplinary orientations and several generations as well as representatives of international (exchange) organizations such as the Fulbright Commission, and members of national or international research organizations such as the Deutsche Forschungsgemeinschaft. Also present were American Studies scholars in leading academic positions, such as presidents of German universities, and representatives of the various American Studies centers in Germany. Participants explored the futures of American Studies in its national and global networks of cooperation and webs of entanglements and raised pertinent disciplinary questions of the position of American Studies on and off academic platforms.

1. Interdisciplinarity: Frameworks, Issues, Perspectives

Panelists: Andreas Falke (Erlangen-Nürnberg), Hans-Jürgen Grabbe (Halle-Wittenberg), Frank Kelleter (Berlin)
Chair: Astrid Böger (Hamburg)

The panel took as its starting point the claim that American Studies has always been an interdisciplinary field of inquiry, which has proven both productive and challenging. In recent years, Americanists have forged links to the natural, social, and life sciences, among others. The panelists were asked to comment on the history, current state, and prospects of communication and collaboration among different disciplines and discuss the implications for the self-understanding of American Studies.

Frank Kelleter opened the discussion by pointing out that interdisciplinarity, though widely favored today, is a difficult concept, not least because it is used to describe the field of American Studies as a whole, while also being applied to actual scholarly practices. With an eye to the latter, he argued that multidisciplinary exchanges might appear to be particularly suited to the self-description of American Studies, but that truly interdisciplinary work tends to be fraught with problems. With reference to Bruno Latour, Kelleter argued that disciplinary boundaries should in fact be seen as demarcations between different modes of epistemological existence. In order to be successful, therefore, interdisciplinary practice should be based on what he termed 'diplomatic communication.'

In contrast, Andreas Falke described the relationship between American Studies and political science as a story of mutual estrangement. Indeed, in his account, political scientists (and possibly all social scientists) no longer feel at home within the field of American Studies. He primarily blamed the cultural turn for this development, as it seems rather incompatible with the empirical methods his discipline favors. Even worse, Falke argued, is that Americanists all too often focus on what he sees as trivial subjects at the expense of core issues central to American society. American Studies as an expanding cultural studies method is increasingly crowding out other disciplines, a development that Falke described as the 'latent imperial attitude' of American Studies scholars today. In a more self-critical vein, he conceded that there are too few political scientists within American Studies, and recommended that 'affirmative action' be used to increase productive, interdisciplinary exchanges.

As the final panelist to speak, Hans-Jürgen Grabbe looked back on his own career as a historian within American Studies and described his scholarly formation as a rocky road often slowed down by his forays into other disciplines, which is why he would not recommend such an approach to younger scholars today. To illustrate, he pointed out that methods from the natural or the life sciences cannot simply be adapted to one's own research. In contrast to the other speakers, Grabbe argued that American Studies is not a genuinely interdisciplinary field and recommended that scholars should consider the findings of other disciplines where suitable, but otherwise stay within their own, clearly demarcated areas of study.

The panelists' statements were followed by a lively discussion with each other as well as with members of the audience. Most of those who spoke up commented favorably on Kelleter's vision of 'diplomatic communication,' even though it will come as no surprise that no easy solutions to the problems raised by interdisciplinary scholarship were found.

Astrid Böger

2. Institutions, External Funding and American Studies

Panelists: Klaus Benesch (München), Jan Stievermann (Heidelberg), Thomas Wiemer (Bonn; DFG)
Chair: Antje Kley (Erlangen-Nürnberg)

Chaired by Antje Kley, this panel addressed prospects and challenges in the current institutional landscape of American Studies as well as funding opportunities, especially for young scholars. The panelists were Klaus Benesch (Director of the Bavarian American Academy), Jan Stievermann (Heidelberg Center for American Studies), and Thomas Wiemer (German Research Foundation [DFG], Program Director of the Humanities and Social Sciences).

The German Centers for American Studies differ considerably from each other in terms of their institutional structures. The Kennedy Institute for North

American Studies at the FU Berlin (founded in 1969) is genuinely interdisciplinary, as is the Heidelberg Center for American Studies (founded in 2003), a central university research facility financed through a unique public-private partnership that pools interdisciplinary research and teaching activities with a focus on the United States. Other interdisciplinary institutions include the Bavarian American Academy in Munich, which coordinates and facilitates American Studies research in Bavaria (founded in 1998 and funded through the state-endowed Bavarian Center for Transatlantic Relations); inter-departmental programs like the Center for North American Research (ZENAF, founded in 1979) at the Goethe University in Frankfurt; and the more recent Bayreuth Institute for American Studies (BIFAS, founded in 2011). There are also independent American Studies Institutes in Munich and Leipzig. These American Studies centers—even those consisting of rather loose networks within individual universities—provide coordinated course offerings, guest lectures, conferences, summer schools, and support in securing research fellowships. Such offerings help strengthen young researchers' efforts to build professional identities and pursue successful careers. Wiemer encouraged conference participants to make greater use of these various co-operations in applications to the DFG for interdisciplinary projects focused on the United States.

American Studies is itself a genuinely interdisciplinary field, but the field's inner- interdisciplinarity (in terms of research questions and methodologies) does not translate easily into the outer-interdisciplinarity demanded by collaborative or integrated research projects. Benesch voiced concern over the fact that while German American Studies scholars are involved in a number of collaborative projects, they rarely set the agendas for those projects. He argued that this may lead to a paradoxical redisciplinarization within collaborative research projects in which American Studies scholars are in charge of sub-projects as historians, political scientists, literary scholars, or cultural studies experts. Thus, American Studies tends not to be adequately visible within these projects, and the field is less able to dynamically develop its own agenda. The field of American Studies may be instrumental in securing prestigious third-party funds (e.g., for the Rachel Carson Center in Munich, founded in 2009), but the projects generated so far have not always made subjects pertaining to American Studies their main research interest.

Panelists agreed that the effect of third-party funding is enormously strong, still rising, and decidedly ambivalent in its consequences. It does provide positive incentives, but it also has problematic repercussions. From his experience as a dean, Benesch reported that the acquisition of large amounts of third-party funding has by and large become the only criterion of scholarly prestige. Since collaborative research generates return cash flows to the institution, institutional acknowledgement mainly goes to those researchers who succeed in securing funding for large integrated projects. Successful individual research does not generate funds for the university and the faculty and therefore does not receive adequate credit. Here, Benesch maintained, one can observe a tendency toward a culture of funding and acknowledgement that allows economic criteria to interfere with intrinsically academic criteria.

Wiemer confirmed this evaluation from the perspective of the DFG. On the one hand, external funding has developed a long-term stimulating effect on research programs. The incentives set by DFG programs have contributed to the development of a more structured and more reliable organization of postgraduate education and the articulation of rules of good scientific practice. Furthermore, external assessment within the scope of the "Excellence Initiative" clarified that incentives have to be created to prompt German universities to make more notable progress in the field of gender equality. On the other hand, the DFG is concerned about the institutional fixation on third-party funding, which may be a consequence of the structural underfunding of German universities. Structural underfunding pushes the DFG into the position of providing basic rather than additional and specifically focused funding for research (see also the Foundation's dossier "Von Drittmitel-Druck, Antragsflut und sekundärer Währung" online, dating from October 2013). The DFG is therefore faced with tasks and responsibilities that the institution, as a promoter of excellent research by *additional* means, is not equipped to bear. Increasingly, even academically convincing applications have to be turned down. Also, not all research questions can be successfully addressed within a project phase of a limited number of years. There has been an alarming increase of precarious employment conditions within German universities because of their structural dependence on third-party funding. Driven by agreements about research goals, the trend toward a concentration on collaborative research projects also compensates for basic funding deficits and often reflects economic need rather than genuine research questions. The result can be a leveling of research formats and the imposition of standards from one disciplinary culture on others. Wiemer added that the DFG has tried to respond to these developments, and to other problems related to the 'mass' university and the juridification and management of research, by creating the format of the research group and making it possible for professors to apply for costs of replacement, in an attempt to secure the necessary time and space for research within the humanities and the social sciences.

Antje Kley

3. Teaching American Studies

Panelists: Peter Freese (Paderborn), Nancy Grimm (Jena), Martina Kohl (U.S. Embassy, Berlin), Sylvia Mayer (Bayreuth), Peter Schneck (Osnabrück)
Chair: Catrin Gersdorf (Würzburg)

The discussions of this panel centered on the teaching of American Studies at the university as part of teacher training programs and at schools as part of foreign-language education. In their contributions to the panel, Nancy Grimm and Peter Freese agreed on two central points: 1. The cooperation between schools and universities must be improved; and 2. The standards for the "Common European Framework of Reference for Languages" (CEFR) have led to a deplorable shift in emphasis "from concrete educational content to abstract learning objectives, from knowledge to competence, and from reading representative texts to the successful negotiation of everyday communication situations" (Freese). In this context, Freese regretted that in English-as-a-foreign-language curricula, American literature is now merely deemed "inert knowledge" and is no longer an important means of accessing knowledge about other cultures, in this case American culture. The term "inert knowledge" also played a role in Grimm's statements. Topics like "the correlation between myths and nation-building, space and identity, gender and ethnic differences, postcolonial and postmodern literary theory," while "incredibly fascinating," do not really play an important role for prospective teachers, neither in the practical phase of their training nor later in their work as English teachers. With this provocatively worded perspective on research and didactic content in the field of American Studies (as well as English literature), Grimm emphasized her demand for a stronger integration of English didactics into seminars and lectures in literary and cultural studies, triggering a lively and controversial discussion among the panelists and the audience. An important result of this discussion was the agreement that new theories and issues concerning cultural studies provide a valuable contribution toward the development of educators who are able to think critically. "If I am able to find my own position [on issues such as gender and racial identity], if I am aware of these issues, then it will influence my teaching, even if I do not address them directly," summarized one teacher who participated in the discussion.

In her contribution, Martina Kohl commented on the request, also aired by Grimm and Freese, for the ongoing training of teachers. The U.S. embassy considers it their responsibility, together with representatives of American Studies from universities, to offer "substantial and high-quality advanced training." At the same time, it is well understood that the United States can only be one of many topics in English classes. Therefore, Kohl strongly argued for connecting knowledge concerning America with teaching topics such as 'Science and Technology,' 'The Individual and Society,' and 'The Media.'

Drawing on her experience of teaching at Bayreuth, Sylvia Mayer expanded these important observations on the education and further training of English teachers, but emphasized the importance of American Studies as a discipline taught in B.A. and M.A. programs. Faced with the Bologna goal of internationalization, these programs in particular are confronted with unique challenges. Students who did not obtain their bachelor's degrees at a German university, or in American Studies, often do not meet the language and disciplinary requirements necessary for successfully pursuing an M.A. degree in American Studies. One option for alleviating that problem would be to offer more propaedeutic courses. But that, Mayer warned, would result in a smaller number of specialized American Studies seminars and lectures. Later in the discussion, Udo Hebel referred to Mayer's contribution and insisted that M.A. programs should be the reference point for determining the disciplinary content of American Studies modules in B.A. and teacher training programs.

In his contribution, Peter Schneck brought many of the previous speakers' topics to a point. He elaborated on Kohl's suggestion, drawing attention to the fact that knowledge about *America* is not only conveyed in English classes, but also in history, geography, and social studies. A further important aspect pertains to the organization of the university curriculum. The demand for a more practice-oriented degree program for teachers is valid and important. However, at the same time one must not overlook the fact that there are other factors that influence the way in which American Studies will be taught at universities in the future. One problem is that the interests of students in teacher's training, B.A., and M.A. programs must be met and balanced in the same classrooms—not always an easy task in the face of different curricular demands. Another challenge is to develop good working relationships with colleagues in English Literature and Linguistics because most of the faculty in American Studies is institutionally integrated in English departments and does not enjoy the luxury of being organized in American Studies departments.

Catrin Gersdorf

4. Women's Caucus

Panelists: Birgit M. Bauridl (Regensburg), Carmen Birkle (Marburg), Eva Boesenberg (Berlin), Anne Koenen (Leipzig)
Chair: Miriam Strube (Paderborn)

The Women's Caucus has come of age. Unofficially active since the 1976 annual GAAS conference in Tutzing, it was officially institutionalized as a committee at the annual conference in 1990. Therefore, the panel discussion primarily addressed questions of whether and how the Women's Caucus can still be seen as important and necessary.

The panel's speakers agreed that the Women's Caucus has been (at least largely) successful in promoting representation, visibility, and equal rights for women. However, another conclusion of the panel's discussion was the notion that the Women's Caucus should undergo a critical and thorough self-reflection. In order to achieve a revised or renewed self-image, the Women's Caucus would have to lead a debate on its own mechanisms of inclusion and exclusion (which would include questioning the very name of the Women's Caucus); it would have to establish potential cooperations as well as discuss openly structures of (mis-)communication. In this context, concrete suggestions for the Women's Caucus's activities were made: mentoring programs; the promotion of female doctoral and post-doctoral candidates; international networking and coalition building or, as in the ASA, a women's breakfast/brunch as well as special workshops or shop talks. The hope is that such concrete forms of support and promotion would complement or amend symbolic acts (for instance, on the level of discourse) that currently comprise the main focus of attention.

The panel presentations likewise highlighted that the Women's Caucus should not exclusively have the formal and administrative function that it appears to embody at the moment. Thus, a recommendation for the Women's Caucus's future was to include more content-based work in order to supplement political-institutional commitment. This agenda should entail focusing on gender (more clearly) as an intersectional category, which in turn would lead to a changed perception or understanding of the processes of knowledge production, the institutional politics of knowledge, and academic organizations.

There was less concensus when the discussion turned to the issue of the growing underrepresentation of male students in American Studies classrooms, and whether or how this phenomenon should be dealt with. While some saw this development as unproblematic, others called for designing courses that would be more appealing to men so that more would choose to get a degree in American Studies.

So what can be retained as the panel's conclusion? What is to be done with the Women's Caucus? The vast majority of the actively participating members of the panel discussion voiced or stressed the need for its continued existence and significance. But the times and conditions have changed (at least to a certain extent), so that the call for a revision, critical self-analysis, and a modified self-conception seemed just as vocal and harmonious.

Miriam Strube

5. Young Scholars and Postgraduate Forum

Panelists: Florian Bast (Leipzig), Cedric Essi (Erlangen-Nürnberg), Johanna Heil (Marburg), Susanne Leikam (Regensburg), Ulfried Reichardt (Mannheim), Anna Thiemann (Münster)
Chair: Sabine Sielke (Bonn)

Celebrating the German Association for American Studies (GAAS) at 60 in 2013 was also an occasion to celebrate the Postgraduate Forum (PGF) at 25. Initiated in 1988 by four (then) young scholars at the John F. Kennedy Institute—Hannah Möckel, Ulfried Reichardt, Hans-Joachim Rieke, and Sabine Sielke—the PGF evolved as a forum for the debate of current theory and for collaborations between young scholars at different German universities in a time before the internet. As such, the PGF not only inspired colleagues from other European associations of American Studies to organize themselves in similar ways, it also changed considerably the age structure of the constituency of our Association and transformed the ways in which scholars and teachers of American Studies in Germany cooperate. As a consequence, academic hierarchies within our field became more porous: in the late 1980s, publishing one's work (or even a book review) in *Amerikastudien / American Studies* required a Ph.D. degree. Young scholars now drive and dominate the agenda of our annual conferences and publish in various media formats, including their own journal founded in 1999, *COPAS: Current Objectives in Postgraduate American Studies*.

The panel, moderated by Sabine Sielke, featured Florian Bast, Cedric Essi, Johanna Heil, Susanne Leikam, Anna Thiemann, and founding member Ulfried Reichardt. All participants (have) actively engaged in the PGF for a number of years, organizing PGF workshops and conferences, editing *COPAS*, and testing new ways of collaboration between the PGF and the board of the GAAS. The debate highlighted the impact of such commitment on younger scholars in our field as well as the transformations the cooperative enterprise of the PGF has undergone recently. The discussants shared having experienced the PGF as a forum for initiatives, self-organization, and networking where exchanges between Ph.D. students and post-docs take place in a mutually supportive, non-competitive, relaxed-but-dynamic environment. They consider plurality, communality, and loyalty as important as the common endeavor of putting current theory into analytical practice, of sharing work-in-progress, and of gaining considerable professional experience through collaboration. Such cooperative commitment is particularly relevant in the light of the fundamental changes that have affected the German university system and its funding policies in recent years.

Maintaining the interdisciplinary agenda of American Studies in Germany remains an ongoing challenge for the PGF as for all of us working in the field. Due in part to the ongoing generous support that the PGF has received from the board of the GAAS and from senior colleagues from Heinz Ickstadt to Udo Hebel, the PGF at 25 is alive and kicking—as it should be. After all, the future of American Studies in Germany builds on the continuous, sustainable engagement of young scholars. Long live the PGF!

Sabine Sielke

6. Diversity

Panelists: Mita Banerjee (Mainz), Karsten Fitz (Passau), Gabriele Pisarz-Ramirez (Leipzig)
Chair: Eva Boesenberg (Berlin)

In order to avoid confusion, I would like to note that the panel was not equivalent to a "Diversity Round Table" held in the context of a GAAS/DGfA annual conference. Rather, it was a roundtable of experts working on topics of 'race' and ethnicity in North American literature and culture.

Karsten Fitz spoke about the significance of Native American Studies and its relevance for an understanding of diversity in U.S.-American history and culture, emphasizing the importance of the multi-faceted contributions to this topic by members of the GAAS. Gabriele Pisarz-Ramirez, an expert in Chicano/a literature, elaborated on the commodification of 'race' in the framework of "thin diversity," considering, for example, the exploitation of diversity as a resource for advertising purposes by businesses and institutions. In contradistinction, she argued for a democratization of knowledge production and a critique of epistemology that considers the researcher's own position in hierarchical power relations.

The final speaker, Mita Banerjee, head of the Center for Comparative Native and Indigenous Studies in Mainz and specialist for the literature and culture of the South Asian diaspora in North America, emphasized connections between social positions and research agendas. Ideally, Americanist insights into the topic of diversity might result in a critical reconsideration of our own institutional framework and *Habitus*. To give a concrete example, Banerjee asked why the conference dinner was going to take place in the restaurant "Sonne" instead of a local Indian restaurant.

To structure the discussion following the panelists' statements, I suggested that we consider steps against racism, heterosexism, and cis-sexism in the German university landscape and measures that might further promote diversity in the GAAS. In our discussion, Gabriele Pisarz-Ramirez explained that the term cis-sexism is analogous to concepts such as sexism and heterosexism and refers to the discrimination of trans people. The lively debate primarily continued the panelists' ideas and the overall significance of diversity in North American Studies in Germany as well as in the politics of the GAAS as an academic institution. I look forward to the continuation of our talks in North American Studies and the GAAS, as this topic will doubtlessly continue to engage us.

Eva Boesenberg

7. Publications, Visibility, Research Transfer

Panelists: Udo Hebel (Regensburg), Alfred Hornung (Mainz), Holger Kersten (Magdeburg), Oliver Scheiding (Mainz)
Chair: Carmen Birkle (Marburg)

In the wider context of current increasing internationalization, the four panelists, Udo Hebel (President of the GAAS), Alfred Hornung (Managing Editor of American Studies: A Monograph Series), Holger Kersten (online publications and open access), and Oliver Scheiding (General Editor of *Amerikastudien / American Studies*) addressed the particular relevance of the Association's own publications in the worldwide transfer of research and knowledge. The need for visibility and, thus, the possibility of a fruitful international research transfer can only be managed through platforms that are considered international players by an American Studies market that does not shy away from local *and* global politics.

The publications of the German Association for American Studies have always been inextricably connected to discussions about the development and directions in American Studies in Germany and worldwide. Walther Fischer (Marburg), the Association's first president (1956-74), initiated the Yearbook (*Jahrbuch für Amerikastudien* that in 1974 became the quarterly *Amerikastudien / American Studies*), the so-called *Beihefte zum Jahrbuch für Amerikastudien* (1957, which were later transformed into the series American Studies: A Monograph Series), and the *Mitteilungsblatt* (1954), the annual newsletter with information on American Studies in Germany, Switzerland, and Austria. From their very inception, these publications were geared toward both German and international readerships even though German was the main language of the contributions for a number of years but has, by now, largely been replaced by English. Areas of discussion among members and editors over the years have included not only debates regarding the language of publication but also financial issues, the choice of publisher, and, more recently, an online presence in order to maintain visibility in an international context.

As both Hornung and Scheiding pointed out, the Association's journal and monograph series have become highly visible on the international market through cooperation with American publishers and the inclusion of Winter Verlag's books and journals in Amazon sales platforms and in databases such as JSTOR, rendering the Association's publications accessible even in places where print copies are not or have never been available. Recent developments have shown that the monograph series has become a preferred site of publication particularly (but not exclusively so) for young scholars seeking publishers for their first-class dissertations and habilitations. Similarly, American Studies scholars from all over the world now choose *Amerikastudien / American Studies* for publication due to its reputation as an internationally peer-reviewed and widely distributed journal—far exceeding the 1,000 Association members' subscriptions—that draws the attention of scholars from around the globe. Furthermore, as argued by both Hornung and Scheiding, the series and the journal offer inter- and cross-generational readings since their widespread availability makes research transfer—and thus potential cooperations with scholars from multiple locations and generations—not only possible, but a fact.

Close cooperation with the European Association for American Studies (EAAS) and, especially in recent years, with the American Studies Association (ASA), as Udo Hebel showed, have resulted in a network of relationships that have led, for example, to a European issue of *Amerikastudien / American Studies* (47.1 [2002]), joint reactions to 9/11, and most visible—participation of members of the GAAS in both the EAAS and ASA biannual and annual conferences. GAAS members represent the Association on the board of the EAAS as well as in various committees of the ASA, such as the ASA International Committee and the ASA Women's Committee, and at the regular venue of the Journal Editors' Meeting. The ASA has expressed its recognition of the work done by German American Studies scholars through the Bode-Pearson Prize for Outstanding Contributions to American Studies (Lifetime Achievement Award) awarded to two members of the GAAS: Günter H. Lenz in 1999 and Alfred Hornung in 2013.

While visibility on the international academic marketplace is a necessary priority for American Studies scholars today, the path leading to such a prominent presence is immediately connected to each member's tasks as scholars and teachers. Our teaching in B.A. and M.A. programs, as well as in teachers' training programs, offers the unique opportunity to reach a young audience who, in turn, will eventually become multiplication factors themselves on local, national, and international levels. Future high school teachers will have to be aware of the inter- and transnational relevance of American Studies scholarship and, thus, the knowledge of the history, culture, literature, and politics of the United States in order to prepare their own students for the ever-increasing entanglements in the global world. Last but not least, our own public-relations activities, such as writing articles for local, regional, or national newspapers and journals, commenting on public events related to U.S. politics and events, and reaching out to the outer-university world, thus claiming the authority to explain American Studies-related phenomena, have become important aspects of American Studies scholars' lives. This ultimately also means that visibility can be a question of terminology, that is, a question like the one Janice Radway posed in her 1998 inaugural presidential address to the American Studies Association: "What's in a Name?" This question is most relevant in the terminology chosen for new study programs, in the wake of the introduction of B.A. and M.A. programs, in the denomination of Ph.D. programs, and in hiring committees.

As Holger Kersten pointed out, this visibility and the exchange with international scholars has more recently led to a consideration of new publication media such as online journals and open-access material that makes access to each other's research easier and more widely available. Although the democratization of academia is a possible result, a number of important questions still need to be discussed and solutions must be found. The financial survival problems faced by traditional publishers should be addressed as well as the ephemerality of online publications within a vast array of information that can no longer be separated into serious and hard-won scholarly insights on the one hand, and less qualified and (perhaps) unreliable information on the other. Massive Open Online Courses (MOOCs) pose similar problems as well as advantages, so pros and cons must be weighed carefully and specific needs addressed. The "Electronic Publishing and Digital Scholarship Initiative" within the GAAS discusses these issues on a regular basis within the context of the Digital Humanities. Open-access journals also exist within the GAAS (*aspeers*; *COPAS*; *Fiar*; *American Studies Journal*). All journals are listed online in *American Studies Journals: A Directory of Worldwide Resources*. But the appearance on the internet and on the Association's website still needs significant improvement. Consequently, visibility, as this panel concluded, is an important factor in and for our discipline on the levels of research transfer and academic work, the general public and the press, and at institutions as well as in all digital media. This will be possible only with a strong vision of a digital GAAS and a website that allows insights into the members' scholarly expertise.

Carmen Birkle

8. Internationalization and International Outreach

Panelists: Rolf Hoffmann (Fulbright, Berlin), Alfred Hornung (Mainz), Thomas Miller (U.S. Embassy, Berlin)
Chair: Udo Hebel (Regensburg)

In the wider context of the ongoing internationalization of German universities, the three panelists, Rolf Hoffmann (German American Fulbright Commission), Alfred Hornung (former President of the GAAS and winner of the 2013 ASA Carl Bode – Norman Holmes Pearson Prize), and Thomas Miller (Minister Counselor for Public Affairs, Embassy of the United States), addressed the overriding significance of internationalism and internationalization for the GAAS and for American Studies in Germany and worldwide.

Rolf Hoffmann provided a topical survey of international academic relations and exchange programs, emphasizing the specific role of American Studies and the United States in and for programs of internationalization. Despite statistical fluctuations and the further diversification of international academic mobility, U.S.-American universities and colleges remain a desired target for international students. At the same time, Germany has become the second most attractive international option for U.S.-American students and researchers. With its English-language programs and American cultural studies agenda, American Studies plays a key role in both transatlantic and global student mobility. The future development of international programs and the increase of academic mobility will, Rolf Hoffmann argued, depend to a considerable extent on recruitment efforts, more short-term options, more split grants, adequate responses to demographic changes, more dual degrees, more transcultural teaching models, the availability of English-language programs (especially at the master's level), and internationalization at home.

Thomas Miller took his cues from the traditions of State Department support for international American Studies and an understanding of American Studies as an interdisciplinary platform for institutional and political reorientation and reform. American Studies approaches, methods, and materials have endorsed and should continue to advocate the democratization of the classroom and of the distribution and availability of knowledge. The need to remain focused on the United States notwithstanding, Miller maintained, recent trends in American Studies serve well to challenge notions of national borders and to stress intellectual openness and the chance for individual and collective reinvention. Specific American Studies agendas of social outreach and political responsibility may well be a suitable frame of reference for other disciplines in the humanities and social sciences.

Alfred Hornung argued for the present and future relevance of transnational American Studies in his sketch of the history of (German) American Studies from the 1950s until today as a trajectory toward internationalization and transnational agendas in scholarly exchange and academic transfer. As an interdisciplinary and transcultural movement, American Studies is to concern itself, Hornung postulated, with 'America' and with the United States wherever and whenever the mobility and impact of conceptualizations of 'America' and the United States as a political, social, economic, and cultural force may be traceable. The GAAS, its membership, and its publications and conference venues should continue to enact its defining role in the internationalization of American Studies worldwide.

The discussion part of the session bore further witness to the centrality of internationalization for American Studies in all its promises and pitfalls. The increasing political and institutional pressure to implement internationalism and interdisciplinarity puts a heavy strain on smaller American Studies units that may be faced with the erosion of their core American Studies agenda. In a similar vein, the obvious advantages of e-learning, and especially of blended learning, for innovative teaching environments and transcultural education should be seen against the equally evident implications of an unlimited expansion of MOOCs. Short-term mobility was seen as a possible threat to genuine transcultural experiences for the sake of superficial professionalization and budgetary savings. However, the further internationalization of American Studies and the possibilities of transcultural learning were generally endorsed as fruitful perspectives and promising options for American Studies as a transnational turntable in global academia.

Udo J. Hebel

9. Futures of German American Studies

Panelists: Udo Hebel (Regensburg), Alfred Hornung (Mainz), Elke Lütkemeier (WR), Heike Paul (Erlangen-Nürnberg), Nicole Waller (Potsdam), Simon Wendt (Frankfurt/Main)
Chair: Philipp Gassert (Mannheim)

After two days of an intellectually stimulating stock-taking exercise, the concluding session focused on some of the forces that will be shaping the future(s) of American Studies in Germany. As Philipp Gassert (Mannheim) pointed out in his introductory remarks, the very real challenges facing both the Association and our craft relate to institutional developments and to questions of what we study when we do American Studies. Institutional challenges include the questions of where and how (as part of which disciplines, in which departments, in which academic programs, and on which academic levels) American Studies are being taught at German universities, who is teaching and studying American Studies (with respect to their class, gender, and ethnicity as well as their disciplinary and methodological backgrounds), how we relate to the larger community (particularly with regard to the presence of American issues in the media), and how we relate to American Studies outside Germany and Europe. Content-wise we need to ask ourselves where the "cooperative experiment" has gone, sixty years after the Association was founded in 1953. What was quite revolutionary in the context of postwar German academia has since gone mainstream. Interdisciplinarity continues to be a particularly sticky issue as is the question of how we relate what we know about American society, culture, and politics to our students and general audiences. As scholars we face a paradox: we have rightly become skeptical of canons within a field that has grown so successfully. Yet by pushing back the boundaries of what legitimately counts as scholarship, we have seen increasing specialization and a turn to what sometimes appears arcane or seemingly mundane. For the world outside the scholarly community but also for our students, generalization often is in greater demand than intricate differentiation.

Elke Lütkemeier of the German Council of Sciences and Humanities (*Wissenschaftsrat*) explained the aims of the rating process and which procedures and guidelines influence the work of the *Wissenschaftsrat* in applying its evaluation tools beyond the natural and social sciences. Lütkemeier explained that the results of the highly successful rating process of English and American Studies in Germany do not represent a mandatory recommendation (*Empfehlung*) of the Council, but rather provide a basis for further discussion (*Diskussionsgrundlage*) among the members of a particular scholarly community. The rating should also help participants assess their strengths and weaknesses within their given field while providing relevant information to university departments and administrations when making strategic development decisions. The pioneering humanities evaluation of English and American Studies has shown that the rating process produces valuable results not only in the natural sciences, but also in our disciplines. Lütkemeier also highlighted the fact that individuals and institutes can partake in more than one rating, which is important for historians and political scientists, who usually teach outside English and American Studies departments, but must be evaluated as part of their own disciplines.

The latter point was further underscored by Alfred Hornung (Mainz), who had been a member of the English and American Studies Rating Committee of the *Wissenschaftsrat*. Arguably, American Studies in Germany has been one of the great winners of the recent rating, which has much to do with the interdisciplinary nature of American Studies. Interdisciplinarity turned out to be a real asset for American Studies and gave it an edge within the larger field. Although interdisciplinarity is hard to achieve, the interdisciplinary founding impulse of the 1950s and 1960s turned out to be right on target. It is something to be proud of and to build on for the future. On the occasion of the 60th anniversary of the GAAS, we seem to have come back to the future. Because of its particular strength as a "cooperative experiment," American Studies offers a unique platform for larger research agendas and has the potential for research clusters that bring the approaches of the humanities together with those of the social and natural sciences.

The following contributions focused on the practice of American Studies within the present university context. Heike Paul (Erlangen-Nürnberg) dwelt on the question of how usable the past really is and the possible paths to the future that a look back to the past will help us to chart. Quoting Theodor Adorno, Paul reminded us of the "messy beginnings" of our field. Obviously, American Studies in Germany did not emerge as a tabula rasa; the founding fathers of 1953 were very aware of the problematic precedents that had been set in the decades before 1945. Paul encouraged today's representatives of American Studies to take the future in our own hands and to avoid too much "prospective nostalgia" (Christopher Bigsby). The sheer growth of what nowadays legitimately goes for American Studies presents a challenge and a promise of an almost "Cosmic American Studies" (Jared Hickman). Nicole Waller (Potsdam) began her contribution with observations on the very real connections between scholarly debates and institutional developments, especially when we look at the impact on young academics. Here, we have seen a successive deterioration of the basic conditions under which most members of the next generation of scholars are starting their professional careers. Work contracts in Germany have become shorter and less secure, teaching loads are rising, fewer postdoc positions are being advertised, and American Studies has been struggling to not be subsumed by English Studies in English Departments. Simon Wendt (Frankfurt/Main) also pointed out that competition seems to have become stronger. Department and university administration seem to expect the impossible from many young scholars (especially the 'junior professors'). They need to prove themselves by finishing a second book while at the same time busily churning out grant applications, learning the ropes of interdisciplinary interaction, and constantly engaging in networking exercises. He recommended that the GAAS should devote more space to the junior scholars both on its homepage and as part of its conference agenda.

GAAS president Udo Hebel (Regensburg) summed up several of the findings of the meeting. As far as multidisciplinarity goes, Hebel first stressed the fact that American history or American politics are often not represented within the respective scholarly association (like the German Historians' Association). Therefore, the GAAS is well-advised to continue seeing itself as the organization that strives to represent all scholars in Germany who work on U.S. topics within a transnational context. Second, it has been the particular strength of the GAAS that it provides resources and an institutional network to junior scholars (particularly through the Postgraduate Forum, or PGF). In recent years young scholars have applied for GAAS membership in record numbers. Third, M.A. programs in American Studies are central to the field's identity and its existence; they allow us to bring teaching and researching American Studies together. Fourth, we need to be better aware of what opportunities we have, and to bring our knowledge and expertise to society at large. Fifth, American Studies is uniquely international. The GAAS has a strong foothold in the ASA (the American Studies Association), which should be our central focus outside Germany. Sixth, the GAAS has always been striving to have various regions as well as both large and small institutes represented among its elected officers and board members. Seventh, American Studies is a platform that offers a degree of transnational and multi-disciplinary interaction that is unique not only in Germany, but in the humanities in general.

To conclude: American Studies in Germany, which started with a small group of pioneers sixty years ago, has grown into a thriving academic venture. It continues to live up to its potential by inspiring members of its own field and by affecting scholarly debates in the humanities. We are optimistic that this will stay so for many years to come.

Philipp Gassert

Reviews

The following reviews are freely available at www.dgfa.de and
www.winter-verlag.de/de/programm/zeitschriften/amerikastudien/

KLAUS SCHMIDT	Review Essay: Edward Watts and David J. Carlson, eds., *John Neal and Nineteenth-Century American Literature and Culture* (2012)
TIBOR FABINY	Reiner Smolinski and Jan Stievermann, eds., *Cotton Mather and Biblia Americana – America's First Bible Commentary: Essays in Reappraisal* (2010)
PHILIPP SCHWEIGHAUSER	Philip F. Gura, *Truth's Ragged Edge: The Rise of the American Novel* (2013)
JOHANNES VOELZ	François Specq, Laura Dassow Walls, and Michel Granger, eds., *Thoreauvian Modernities: Transatlantic Conversations on an American Icon* (2013)
MARTIN KLEPPER	Susanne Rohr and Miriam Strube, eds., *Revisiting Pragmatism: William James in the New Millennium* (2012)
NICOLE J. CAMASTRA	Miriam B. Mandel, ed., *Hemingway and Africa* (2011)
BIRGIT DÄWES	Kathryn Hume, *Aggressive Fiction: Reading the Contemporary American Novel* (2012)
MICHAEL BUTTER	Sebastian M. Herrmann, Carolin Alice Hofmann, Katja Kanzler, and Frank Usbeck, eds., *Participating Audiences, Imagined Public Spheres: The Cultural Work of Contemporary American(ized) Narratives* (2012)
SIGRUN MEINIG	Ulfried Reichardt, *Globalisierung: Literaturen und Kulturen des Globalen* (2010)
MICHAEL BASSELER	Christof Mauch and Sylvia Mayer, eds., *American Environments: Climate—Cultures—Catastrophes* (2012)

Publications in American Studies from German-Speaking Countries, 2013

Laura Caprioara and Damien Schlarb

This bibliography contains books and articles published in 2013 (with some supplementary entries from previous years) by Americanists from German-speaking countries. It lists those publications compiled by the American Studies departments of Germany, Switzerland, and Austria, and publications reported by individual DGfA members to the editorial office of *Amerikastudien / American Studies*.

The subdivision is meant to facilitate orientation. The short titles used in some entries refer to the anthologies and *Festschriften* assembled in the first section, which are listed alphabetically by title.

1. General Studies, Bibliographies, Collections of Articles, Dictionaries, Festschriften

1. *"1968" – Eine Wahrnehmungsrevolution? Horizont-Verschiebungen des Politischen in den 1960er und 1970 Jahren*. Ed. Ingrid Gilcher-Holtey. München: Oldenbourg, 2013. Print.
2. *AAA – Arbeiten aus Anglistik und Amerikanistik* 38.2 (2013). Ed. Walter Grünzweig, Walter Hölbling, Allan James, Andreas Mahler, Christian Mair, Annemarie Peltzer-Karpf, Werner Wolf, and Alwin Fill. Print.
3. *A Companion to Woodrow Wilson*. Ed. Ross Kennedy. New York: John Wiley's Sons, 2013. Print.
4. *Abschied von 9/11: Distanznahmen zur Katastrophe*. Ed. Ursula Hennigfeld and Stefan Packard. Berlin: Frank & Timme, 2013. Print.
5. *The Ages of Life: Living and Aging in Conflict?* Ed. Ulla Kriebernegg and Roberta Maierhofer. Bielefeld: Transcript, 2013. Print.
6. *Agents of Transculturation: Border Crossers, Mediators, Go-Betweens*. Ed. Sebastian Jobs and Gesa Mackenthun. Münster: Waxmann, 2013. Print.
7. *Anglia. Zeitschrift für Englische Philologie* 131.1 and 131.4 (2013). Ed. Gabriele Rippl, et al. Print.
8. *A Peculiar Mixture: German-Language Culture and Identities in Eighteenth Century North America*. Ed. Jan Stievermann and Oliver Scheiding. University Park: Pennsylvania State UP, 2013. Print.
9. *Abraham David – Jüdische Auswanderung im Neunzehnten Jahrhundert*. Ed. Gabriele Hannah and Hans-Dieter Graf. Hamm/R: Kehl, 2013. Print.
10. *Abschied von 9/11: Distanznahmen zur Katastrophe*. Ed. Ursula Hennigfeld and Stefan Packard. Berlin: Frank & Timme, 2013. Print.

11. *American Studies Journal* 57 (2013). Ed. Hans-Jürgen Grabbe, Alfred Hornung, Martina Kohl, and Carsten Hummel. Web.
12. *American Studies: A Monograph Series*. Ed. Alfred Hornung, Heike Paul, and Anke Ortlepp. Heidelberg: Winter, 2013. Vols. 203, 215, 230, 231, 232, 233, 234, 235, 236, 237, 238, 239, 240, 241, 242. Print.
13. *American Lives*. Ed. Alfred Hornung et al. Heidelberg: Winter, 2013. Print.
14. *Die amerikanischen Präsidenten: 44 historische Portraits von George Washington bis Barack Obama*. 6th ed. Ed. Christof Mauch. München: Beck, 2013. Print.
15. *Amerikastudien / American Studies* 58 (2013). Edited for the German Association for American Studies by Oliver Scheiding, Christa Buschendorf, Andreas Falke, Hans-Jürgen Grabbe, Alfred Hornung, and Sabine Sielke. Print.
16. *American Studies Today: Recent Developments and New Perspectives*. Ed. Hubert Zapf, Erik Redling, Sabine Sielke, and Winfried Fluck. Heidelberg: Winter, 2013. Print.
17. *ANGLIA: Journal of English Philology / Zeitschrift für Englische Philologie* 131.1-4 (2012). Ed. Gabriele Rippl, et al. Berlin: de Gruyter, 2013. Print.
18. *Anglophone Literaturdidaktik: Zukunftsperspektiven für den Englischunterricht*. Ed. Julia Hammer, Maria Eisenmann, and Rüdiger Ahrens. Heidelberg: Winter, 2012. Print.
19. *Archetypen, Artefakte: Komparatistische Beiträge zur kulturellen und literarischen Repräsentation von Tieren*. Ed. Alena Diedrich, Julia Hoffmann, and Niels Penke. Frankfurt/M: Lang, 2013. Print.
20. *Arriving in the Future: Stories of Home and Exile*. Ed. Asoka Esuruoso and Philipp Khabo Koepsell. Münster: Edition Assemblage, 2013. Print.
21. *aspeers: emerging voices in american studies* 6 (2013). Ed. Florian Bast, Ewa Adamkiewicz, Richard Bachmann, Elisabeth Böhme, Eric W. Fraunholz, Katharina Gensch, Alexandra, Máté Vince Horvath, Wiebke Kartheus, Theresia Lakomy, Erica L. Larson, Martin N. Opitz, Sören Schoppmeier, and Tyrone T. White Jr. Web.
22. *Augsburg und Amerika: Aneignungen und globale Verflechtungen in einer Stadt*. Ed. Philipp Gassert, Günther Kronenbitter, Stefan Paulus, and Wolfgang E.J. Weber. Augsburg: Wiesner, 2013. Print.
23. *Autobiographie: Eine interdisziplinäre Gattung zwischen klassischer Tradition & (post-)moderner Variation*. Göttingen: V & R UP and Bonn: Bonn UP, 2013. Print.
24. *Beyond 9/11: Transdisciplinary Perspectives on Twenty-First Century U.S. American Culture*. Ed. Christian Kloeckner, Simone Knewitz, and Sabine Sielke. Frankfurt/M: Lang, 2013. Print.
25. *Bildung – Kompetenz – Literalität. Fremdsprachenunterricht zwischen Standardisierung und Bildungsanspruch*. Ed. Andreas Grünewald, Jochen Plikat, and Katharina Wieland. Seelze: Klett, 2013. Print.
26. *Black Intersectionalities: A Critique for the 21st Century*. Ed. Monica Michelin and Jean-Paul Rocchi. Liverpool: Liverpool UP, 2013. Print. FORECAAST – Forum for European Contributions to African American Studies 23.

27. *Breaking up Time: Negotiating the Borders between Present, Past and Future.* Ed. Chris Lorenz and Berber Bervernage: Göttingen: Vandenhoeck & Ruprecht, 2013. Print.
28. *Celebrity: The Idiom of a Modern Era.* Ed. Bärbel Czennia. New York: AMS, 2013. Print. AMS Studies in the 18th Century 70.
29. *Colonialism and Beyond – Race and Migration from a Postcolonial Perspective.* Ed. Eva Bischoff and Elisabeth Engel. Münster: LIT, 2013. Print.
30. *Communicating Disease: Cultural Representations of American Medicine.* Ed. Carmen Birkle and Johanna Heil. Heidelberg: Winter, 2013. Print.
31. *Conceptions of Collectivity in Contemporary American Literature.* Special Issue *Amerikastudien/American Studies* 57 (2). Ed. Philipp Löffler and Clemens Spahr. Heidelberg: Winter, 2013. Print.
32. *The Conditions of Hospitality: Ethics, Politics, and Aesthetics on the Threshold of the Possible.* Ed. Thomas Claviez. New York: Fordham UP, 2013. Print.
33. *ConFiguring America: Iconic Figures, Visuality, and American Culture.* Ed. Klaus Rieser, Michael Fuchs, and Michael Phillips. Bristol: Intellect Books, 2013. Print.
34. *Coverstrategien in the Popularmusik nach 1960.* Ed. Joachim Brügge. Freiburg/B: Rombach, 2013. Print.
35. *COPAS: Current Objectives in Postgraduate American Studies* 14.1, 2 (2013). Ed. Janina Rojek, Britta Bein, Johanna Heil, and Silke Schmidt. Web.
36. *Cultural Circulation: Dialogues between Canada and the American South.* Ed. Waldemar Zacharasiewicz, and Christoph Irmscher. Wien: Verlag der Österreichischen Akademie der Wissenschaften, 2013. Print.
37. *The Cultural Career of Coolness: Discourses and Practices of Affect Contol in European Antiquity, the United States, and Japan.* Ed. Ulla Haselstein, Irmela Hijiya-Kischnereit, Catrin Gersdorf, and Elena Giannoulis. Lanham, MD: Lexington, 2013. Print.
38. *The Cultural Dynamics of Generic Change in Contemporary Fiction: Theoretical Frameworks, Genres and Model Interpretations.* Ed. Michael Basseler, Ansgar Nünning, and Christine Schwanecke. Trier: WVT, 2013. Print.
39. *Cultural Representations of (American) Medicine: A Study in Interdisciplinarity.* Ed. Carmen Birkle and Johanna Heil. Heidelberg: Winter, 2013. Print.
40. *Cultures in Conflict / Conflicting Cultures.* Ed. Mario Klarer and Christina Ljungberg. Tübingen: Narr, 2013. Print. SPELL 29.
41. *Deconstructing Terrorism: 9/11, 7/7, and Contemporary Culture.* Ed. Jürgen Kamm, Jürgen Kramer, and Bernd Lenz. Passau: Stutz, 2013. Print.
42. *Ecology and Life Writing.* Ed. Alfred Hornung and Zaho Baisheng. Heidelberg: Winter, 2013. Print.
43. *Encyclopedia of American Indian Issues Today.* Ed. Russell M. Lawson. Santa Barbara, CA: Greenwood, 2013. Print.
44. *Encyclopedia of American Immigration.* 2nd ed. Ed. James Ciment and John Radzilowski. New York: M.E. Sharpe, 2013. Print.
45. *Europe and America in the 1980s: Old Barriers, New Openings.* Ed. Kiran Klaus Patel and Kenneth Weisbrode. New York: Cambridge UP, 2013. Print.

46. *Europe - Canada: Transcultural Perspectives / Perspectives Transculturelles.* Ed. Klaus-Dieter Ertler, Martin Löschnigg, and Yvonne Völkl. Frankfurt/M: Lang, 2013. Print.
47. *Eyes Deep with Unfathomable Histories: The Poetics and Politics of Magic Realism Today and in the Past.* Ed. Liliana Sikorska and Agnieszka Rzepa. Frankfurt/M: Lang, 2012. Print.
48. *Fake Identity? The Impostor Narrative in North American Culture.* Ed. Caroline Rosenthal and Stefanie Schäfer. Frankfurt/M: Campus, 2013. Print.
49. *Familientraditionen und Familienkulturen: Theoretische Konzeptionen, historische und aktuelle Analysen.* Ed. Meike Sophia Baader, Petra Götte, and Carola Groppe. Wiesbaden: Springer, 2013. Print.
50. *F(e)asting Fitness? Cultural Images, Social Practices, and Histories of Food and Health.* Ed. Annekatrin Metz, Markus M. Müller, and Lutz Schowalter. Trier: WVT, 2013. Print.
51. *Films, Graphic Novels and Visuals: Developing Multiliteracies in Foreign Language Education-An Interdisciplinary Approach.* Ed. Daniela Elsner, Sissy Helff, and Britta Vierbrock. Münster: LIT, 2013. Print.
52. *Flugblätter – Plakate – Propaganda: Die Arbeit mit appelativen Bild-Text-Dokumenten im Geschichtsunterricht.* Ed. Michael Wobring, Susanne Popp, Daniel Probst, and Claudius Springkart. St. Ingbert: Röhrig UP, 2013. Print.
53. *Friedrich Gerstäcker: Mississippi-Bilder.* Ed. Wolfgang Hochbruck and Thomas Ostwald. Braunschweig: Gerstäcker Gesellschaft, 2013. Print.
54. *From Comic Strips to Graphic Novels: Contributions to the Theory and History of Graphic Narrative.* Ed. Daniel Stein and Jan-Noël Thon. Berlin: de Gruyter, 2013. Print.
55. *Germany and the Black Diaspora, 1450-1914.* Ed. Mischa Honeck, Martin Klimke, and Anne Kuhlmann-Smirnov. New Milford, CT: Berghahn Books, 2013. Print.
56. *Gewalt: Ein interdisziplinäres Handbuch.* Ed. Christian Gudehus, Michaela Christ, and Harald Welzer. Stuttgart: J.B. Metzler, 2013. Print.
57. *Global Communication Electric: Business, News and Politics in the World of Telegraphy.* Ed. Michaela Hampf and Simone Müller-Pohl. Frankfurt/M: Campus, 2013. Print.
58. *Handbuch Kanon und Wertung*: *Theorien, Instanzen, Geschichte.* Ed. Gabriele Rippl and Simone Winko. Stuttgart: Metzler, 2013. Print.
59. *Haunted Narratives: Life Writing in an Age of Trauma.* Ed. Gabriele Rippl, Philipp Schweighauser, Margit Sutrop, Therese Steffen, and Tiina Kirss. Toronto: Toronto UP, 2013. Print.
60. Healthy and Liveable Cities: Selected Papers from the Essen Conference / Gesunde und lebenswerte Städte: Ausgewählte Beiträge der Essener Tagung. Ed. Stefanie Caeners, Michael Eisinger, Jens-Martin Gurr, and J. Alexander Schmidt. Ludwigsburg: av edition, 2013. Print.
61. *Heilige Texte: Literarisierung von Religion und Sakralisierung von Literatur im modernen Roman.* Ed. Klaus Antoni, Matthias Bauer, Jan Stievermann, Birgit Weyel, and Angelika Zirker. Münster: LIT, 2013. Print.

62. *Hemispheric Indigenous Studies.* Ed. Heidrun Mörtl and Antonio Barrenechea. Spec. issue of *Comparative American Studies: An International Journal* 11.2 (2013): 109-209. Print.
63. *Hip-Hop in Europe: Cultural Identities and Transnational Flows.* Ed. Sina A. Nitzsche and Walter Grünzweig. Münster: LIT, 2013. Print.
64. *Iconographies of the Calamitous in American Visual Culture.* Ed. Ingrid Gessner and Susanne Leikam. Spec. issue of *Amerikastudien / American Studies* 58.4 (2013). Heidelberg: Winter, 2013. Print.
65. *The Imaginary and Its Worlds: American Studies after the Transnational Turn.* Ed. Laura Bieger, Ramón Saldívar, and Johannes Völz. Hanover, NH: Dartmouth College P/UP of New England, 2013. Print.
66. *Indigenous North American Drama: A Multivocal History.* Ed. Birgit Däwes. Albany: SUNY P, 2013. Print.
67. *Intellectual Authority and Literary Culture in the US, 1790-1900.* Ed. Günter Leypoldt. Heidelberg: Winter, 2013. Print.
68. *Interculturalism in North America: Canada, the United States, Mexico, and Beyond.* Ed. Josef Raab and Alexander Greiffenstern. Trier: WVT and Tempe, AZ: Bilingual, 2013. Print. Inter-American Studies/Estudios interamericanos 8.
69. *Interpiktorialität: Theorie und Geschichte der Bild-Bild-Bezüge.* Ed. Guido Isekenmeier. Bielefeld: Transcript, 2013. Print.
70. *Is It 'Cause It's Cool: Affective Encounters with American Culture.* Ed. Astrid M. Fellner, Klaus Heissenberger, Susanne Hamscha, and Jennifer Moos. Wien: LIT, 2013. Print.
71. *Journal of Transnational American Studies* 5.1 (2013). Ed. Thomas Bender, Shelley Fisher Fishkin, Alfred Hornung, Greg Robinson, Shirley Geok-Lin Lim, Nina Morgan, and Takayuki Tatsumi. Web.
72. *Kindlers Literatur Lexikon.* 3rd ed. (Online Supplement). Ed. Heinz Ludwig. Stuttgart: Metzler, 2013. Web.
73. *Literaturwissenschaftliches Jahrbuch* 53 (2013). Ed. Volker Kapp, Kurt Müller, Klaus Ridder, Ruprecht Wimmer, and Jutta Zimmermann. Berlin: Duncker & Humbolt. Print.
74. *The Living Cano:. Theory and Pedagogy in Contemporary African American Literature.* Ed. Lovalerie King and Shirley C. Moody. Bloomington: Indiana UP, 2013. Print.
75. *Locating Postcolonial Narrative Genres.* Ed. Walter Goebel and Saskia Schabio. New York: Routledge 2013. Print.
76. *Medialisierungsformen des (Auto)Biografischen.* Ed. Carsten Heinze and Alfred Hornung. München: UVK, 2013. Print.
77. *The Methuen Drama Guide to Contemporary American Playwrights.* Ed. Martin Middeke, Christopher Innes, Peter Paul Schnierer, and Matthew Roudané. London: Methuen, 2013. Print.
78. *Mobile Narratives: Travel, Migration, and Transculturation.* Ed. Eleftheria Arapoglou, Mónika Fodor, and Jopi Nyman. New York: Routledge, 2013. Print.
79. *Modernism and the Orient.* Ed. Zhaoming Qian. New Orleans: U of New Orleans P, 2013. Print.

80. *Modern American Poetry: Points of Access.* Ed. Kornelia Freitag and Brian Reed. Heidelberg: Winter, 2013. Print.
81. *Mosaic: Studien und Texte zur amerikanischen Kultur und Geschichte.* Ed. Bernd Engler, Michael Hochgeschwender, Jörg Nagler, Udo Sautter, and Oliver Scheiding. Trier: WVT, 2013. Vols. 45-49. Print.
82. *Multicultural America: A Multimedia Encyclopedia.* Ed. Carlos E. Cortés. Thousand Oaks, CA: SAGE Reference, 2013. Pint.
83. *Music, Longing and Belonging: Articulations of the Self and the Other in the Musical Realm.* Ed. Magdalena Waligorska. London: Cambridge Scholars, 2013. Print.
84. *New Approaches to Narrative: Cognition - Culture - History.* Ed. Vera Nünning. Trier: WVT, 2013. Print.
85. *New Theories, Models and Methods in Literary and Cultural Studies: Theory into Practice.* Ed. Ansgar Nünning and Greta Olson. Trier: WVT, 2013. Print.
86. *The Oxford Handbook on the Cold War.* Ed. Richard H. Immermann and Petra Goedde. Oxford: Oxford UP, 2013. Print.
87. *Perspectives on Mobility.* Ed. Ingo Berensmeyer and Christoph Ehland. Amsterdam: Rodopi, 2013. Print.
88. *Placing America: American Culture and Its Spaces.* Ed. Michael Fuchs and Maria-Theresia Holub. Bielefeld: Transcript, 2013. Print.
89. *The Politics of Passion: Reframing Affect and Emotion in Global Modernity.* Ed. Dirk Wiemann and Lars Eckstein. Frankfurt/M: Lang, 2013. Print.
90. *Postcolonial Studies across the Disciplines.* Ed. Jana Gohrisch and Ellen Grünkemeier. Amsterdam: Rodopi, 2013. Print.
91. *Postcolonial Translocations.* Ed. Marga Munkelt, Markus Schmitz, Mark Stein, and Silke Stroh. Amsterdam: Rodopi, 2013. Print.
92. *Post-World War II Masculinities in British and American Literature and Culture - Towards Comparative Masculinity Studies.* Ed. Stefan Horlacher and Kevin Floyd. Surrey, UK: Ashgate, 2013. Print.
93. *Präsenz und implizites Wissen: Zur Interdependenz zweier Schlüsselbegriffe der Kultur- und Sozialwissenschaften.* Ed. Heike Paul and Christoph Ernst. Bielefeld: transcript, 2013. Print.
94. *Realisms in Contemporary Culture: Theories, Politics, and Medial Configurations.* Ed. Dorothee Birke and Stella Butter. Berlin: de Gruyter, 2013. Print.
95. *Religion and Politics in Europe and the United States: Transnational Historical Approaches.* Ed. Volker Depkat and Jürgen Martschukat. Baltimore: Johns Hopkins UP, 2013. Print.
96. *Rethinking Narrative Identity: Persona and Perspective.* Ed. Claudia Holler and Martin Klepper. Amsterdam: John Benjamins, 2013. Print.
97. *Rethinking the American City: An International Dialogue.* Ed. Klaus Benesch and Miles Orvell. Philadelphia, PA: U of Pennsylvania P, 2013. Print
98. *Revisiting the Sixties: Interdisciplinary Perspectives on America's Longest Decade.* Ed. Laura Bieger and Christian Lammert. Frankfurt/M: Campus, 2013. Print.
99. *Ritual and Narrative: Theoretical Explorations and Historical Case Studies.* Ed.Vera Nünning, Jan Rupp, and Gregor Ahn. Bielefeld: Transcript, 2013. Print.

100. *Road Movies and Other Travel Narratives.* Ed. Graciela Martínez-Zalce Sánchez and Wilfried Raussert. Trier: WVT and Tempe, AZ: Bilingual, 2013. Print.
101. *Spielkulturen: Funktionen und Bedeutungen des Phänomens Spiel in der Gegenwartskultur und im Alltagsdiskurs.* Ed. Jochen Koubek, Michael Mosel, and Stefan Werning. Glückstadt: Hülsbusch, 2013. Print.
102. *Stilepochen des Films: Classical Hollywood.* Ed. Elisabeth Bronfen and Norbert Grob. Leipzig: Reclam, 2013. Print.
103. *Tasks Revisited.* Ed. Wolfgang Hallet and Michael K. Legutke. Spec. issue of *Fremdsprachenlernen und -lehren* 42.2 (2013). Print.
104. *Teaching Contemporary Literature and Culture: Film Part I.* Ed. Susanne Peters, Klaus Stierstorfer, Dirk Vanderbeke, and Laurenz Volkmann. Trier: WVT, 2013. Print.
105. *Teaching Contemporary Literature and Culture: Film Part II.* Ed. Susanne Peters, Klaus Stierstorfer, Dirk Vanderbeke, and Laurenz Volkmann. Trier: WVT, 2013. Print.
106. *Teaching Contemporary Literature and Culture: Film Part III.* Ed. Susanne Peters, Klaus Stierstorfer, Laurenz Volkmann, and Dirk Vanderbeke. Trier: WVT, 2013. Print.
107. *Television and the Self: Knowledge, Identity and Media Representation.* Ed. Deborah Macey and Kathleen M. Ryan. Lanham: Lexington, 2013. Print.
108. *Text or Context: Reflections on Literary and Cultural Criticism.* Ed. Rüdiger Kunow and Stephan Mussil. Würzburg: Königshausen & Neumann, 2013. Print. ZAA Monograph Series, 15.
109. *Thoreauvian Modernities: Transatlantic Conversations on an American Icon.* Ed. François Specq, Laura Dassow Walls, and Michel Granger. Athens, GA: U of Georgia P, 2013. Print.
110. *Tocqueville's Legacy: Towards a Cultural History of Recognition in American Studies.* Ed. Winfried Fluck. Spec. issue of *American Studies / Amerikastudien* 57.4 (2012). Hedeilberg: Winter, 2012. Print.
111. *The Transatlantic Sixties: Europe and the United States in the Counterculture Decade.* Ed. Britta Waldschmidt-Nelson, Clara Juncker, Grzesiek Kosc, and Sharon Monteith. Bielefeld: Transcript, 2013. Print.
112. *The Transatlantic World of Heinrich Melchior Mühlenberg in the Eighteenth Century.* Ed. Hermann Wellenreuther, Thomas Müller-Bahlke, and A. Gregg Roeber. Halle: Verlag der Franckeschen Stiftungen, 2013. Print.
113. *Transmediality and Transculturality.* Ed. Gabriele Pisarz-Ramirez and Nadja Gernalzick. Heidelberg: Winter, 2013. Print. American Studies Monograph Series.
114. *Transnational Americas: Envisioning Inter-American Area Studies in Globalization Processes.* Ed. Olaf Kaltmeier. Trier: WVT and Tempe, AZ: Bilingual, 2013. Print. Inter-American Studies / Estudios interamericanos 7.
115. *Transnational American Studies.* Ed. Udo Hebel. Heidelberg: Winter, 2012. Print.
116. *Transnational Perspectives on Graphic Narratives: Comics at the Crossroads.* Ed. Shane Denson, Christina Meyer, and Daniel Stein. London: Bloomsbury, 2013. Print.

117. *The Writing Cure: Literature and Medicine in Context.* Ed. Alexandra Lembert and Jarmila Mildorf. Münster: LIT, 2013. Print.
118. *Unter dem roten Wunderschirm: Lesarten klassischer Kinder- und Jugendliteratur.* Ed. Christoph Breuer and Wolfgang Wangerin. Göttingen: Wallstein, 2013. Print.
119. *USA-Lexikon: Schlüsselbegriffe zu Politik, Wirtschaft, Gesellschaft, Kultur, Geschichte und zu den deutsch-amerikanischen Beziehunge.* Ed. Christof Mauch and Rüdiger B. Wersic. Berlin: Schmidt, 2013. Print and Web.
120. *The U. S. South and Europe. Transatlantic Relations in the Nineteenth and Twentieth Centuries. New Directions in Southern History.* Ed. Cornelis A. Van Minnen and Manfred Berg. Lexington, KY: UP of Kentucky, 2013. Print.
121. *Violence and Visibility in Modern History.* Ed. Jürgen Martschukat and Silvan Niedermeier. New York: Palgrave, 2013. Print.
122. *ZAA—Zeitschrift für Anglistik und Amerikanistik: A Quarterly of Language, Literature and Culture* 61 (2013). Ed. Lars Eckstein, Joachim Frenk, Brigitte Georgi-Findlay, Thomas Herbst, Barbara Korte, Günter Leypoldt, Gesa Mackenthun, Christian Mair, and Christoph Reinfandt. Print.

2. Literature and Culture

123. Achilles, Jochen, and Ina Bergmann. "Richard Greenberg." *The Methuen Guide to Contemporary American Drama.* Ed. Christopher Innes, Martin Middeke, Peter Paul Schnierer, and Matthew Roudané. London: Methuen, 2013. 39-57. Print.
124. Achilles, Jochen. "Transnational Ireland and Elizabeth Kuti's Drama." *Anglistentag 2012 Potsdam: Proceedings.* Ed. Katrin Röder and Ilse Wischer. Trier: WVT, 2013. 21-33. Print.
125. Aho, Tanja. "Juno for Real: Negotiating Teenage Sexuality, Pregnancy, and Love in MTV's *16 and Pregnant/Teen Mom.*" *Television and the Self: Knowledge, Identity and Media Representation* 205-23.
126. Assmann, Aleida. Afterword. *Emergenz. Von Wolfgang Iser.* Konstanz: Konstanz UP, 2013. 309-20. Print.
127. Assmann, Aleida. "Civilizing Societies: Recognition and Respect in a Global World." *New Literary History* 44.1 (2013): 69-91. Print.
128. Assmann, Aleida. *Ist die Zeit aus den Fugen? Aufstieg und Fall des Zeitregimes der Moderne.* München: Hanser, 2013. Print.
129. Assmann, Aleida. "Theorien des kulturellen Gedächtnisses." *Handbuch Kanon und Wertung: Theorien, Instanzen, Geschichte* 76-85.
130. Assmann, Aleida. "Transformations of the Modern Time Regime." *Breaking up Time: Negotiating the Borders between Present, Past and Future* 39-56.
131. Balestrini, Nassim. "Hass, Robert." *Kindlers Literatur Lexikon.* 3rd ed. (Online Supplement). n.pag. Web.
132. Balestrini, Nassim. "Hass, Time and Materials." *Kindlers Literatur Lexikon.* 3rd ed. (Online Supplement). n. pag. Web.

133. Balestrini, Nassim. "Photography as Online Life Writing: Miranda July's and Harrell Fletcher's *Learning to Love You More* (2002–09)." *American Lives* 341–53.
134. Banerjee, Mita. *Color Me White: Naturalism/Naturalization in American Literature*. Heidelberg: Winter, 2013. Print.
135. Banerjee, Mita. "Life Sciences and Life Writing." "Forum: Life Writing and Life Sciences." *American Lives* 537-40.
136. Banerjee, Mita, Thomas Efferth, and Alfred Hornung. "Therapeutic Intervention of Posttraumatic Stress Disorder by Chinese Medicine: Perspectives for Trans-disciplinary Cooperation between Life Sciences and Humanities." *Medicine Studies: An International Journal for History, Philosophy, and Ethics of Medicine & Allied Sciences* 3.4 (Nov. 2012): 1-21. Print.
137. Banerjee, Mita, Norbert Paul, and Susanne Michl. "Captious Certainties: Making, Meanings and Misreadings of Consumer-Oriented Genetic Testing." *Community Genetics* 5.1 (2014): 81-87. Print.
138. Basseler, Michael. "Close Reading." *Über die Praxis des kulturwissenschaftlichen Arbeitens: Ein Handwörterbuch*. Ed. Ute Frietsch and Jörg Rogge. Bielefeld: Transcript, 2013. 84-89. Print.
139. Basseler, Michael, Ansgar Nünning, and Christine Schwanecke. "The Cultural Dynamics of Generic Change: Surveying Kinds and Problems of Literary History and Accounting for the Development of Genres." *The Cultural Dynamics of Generic Change in Contemporary Fiction: Theoretical Frameworks, Genres, and Model Interpretations* 1-44.
140. Basseler, Michael, and Ansgar Nünning. "Literary Studies as a Form of 'Life Science': The Knowledge of Literature." *New Theories, Models and Methods in Literary and Cultural Studies: Theory into Practice* 189-212.
141. Basseler, Michael. "Tradition, Innovation and Defamiliarization in the Evolution of Genres: Explanations of Generic Change from Russian Formalism to the Renaissance of Genre Theory in the 21st century." *The Cultural Dynamics of Generic Change in Contemporary Fiction: Theoretical Frameworks, Genres, and Model Interpretations* 45-66.
142. Bast, Florian, and Anne Koenen. Foreword. *aspeers: emerging voices in american studies* 6 (2013): 3-5. Print.
143. Bast, Florian, et al. Introduction. *aspeers: emerging voices in american studies* 6 (2013): 7-21.Print.
144. Bauridl, Birgit M. *Betwixt, between, or beyond? Negotiating Transformations from the Liminal Sphere of Contemporary Black Performance Poetry*. Heidelberg: Winter, 2013. Print.
145. Bauridl, Birgit M. "'Deep-Mapping' the Diversity of New York Lives." *American Lives* 355-68.
146. Bauridl, Birgit M. "Rowing for Palestine, Performing the Crossroads, Living Multiple Consciousness: Mark Gerban and Suheir Hammad." *Arab American Literature and Culture*. Ed. Alfred Hornung and Martina Kohl. Heidelberg: Winter, 2012. 221-42. Rpt. in *Journal of Transnational American Studies* 5.1 (2013). Web.

147. Beck, Günter. "Slapstick Humor: Physical Comedy in Vonnegut's Fiction." *Studies in American Humor* 3.26 (2012): 59-72. Print.
148. Benesch, Klaus. "Adrienne Kennedy." *The Methuen Drama Guide to Contemporary American Playwrights* 95-110.
149. Benesch, Klaus. "Cultural Immobility: Thoreau, Heidegger, and the Modern Politics of Place." *Amerikastudien / American Studies* 57.3 (2012): 403-18. Print.
150. Benesch, Klaus, and Miles Orvell. Introduction. *Rethinking the American City: An International Dialogue* xi-xvi.
151. Benesch, Klaus. "Mobility." *Rethinking the American City: An International Dialogue* 143–66.
152. Benesch, Klaus. "Places of Beginning: Topography and Renewal in Thoreau's Walden and Douglass's Narrative." *Perspectives on Mobility* 77-88.
153. Berensmeyer, Ingo, and Christoph Ehland. "Movement and Mobility. An Introduction." *Perspectives on Mobility* 11-28.
154. Berning, Nora. "Graphic Narrative Theory Meets Genre Theory: A Model Interpretations of Joe Sacco's *Safe Area Goražde*." *The Cultural Dynamics of Generic Change in Contemporary Fiction: Theoretical Frameworks, Genres and Model Interpretations* 315-28.
155. Bieger, Laura. "Freedom, Equality, Beauty for Everyone. Notes on Fantasizing the Modern Body." *American Studies / Amerikastudien* 57.4 (2012): 663-88. Print.
156. Bieger, Laura, Ramón Saldívar, and Johannes Völz. Introduction. *The Imaginary and Its World: American Literature after the Transnational Turn* vii-xxviii.
157. Bieger, Laura, and Christian Lammert. "Preface." *Revisiting the Sixties. Interdisciplinary Perspectives on America's Longest Decade* 7-11.
158. Bieger, Laura. "Architectures of Immersion: The Material Fictions of the 'New' Las Vegas." *Aesthetic Illusion in Literature and Other Media Aesthetic Illusion in Literature and Other Media*. Ed. Werner Wolf, Walter Bernhart, and Andreas Mahler. Amsterdam: Rodopi, 2013. 315-38. Print.
159. Birkle, Carmen. "Communicating Disease: An Introduction." *Communicating Disease: Cultural Representations of American Medicine* ix-xxxiv.
160. Böger, Astrid, Dirk Vanderbeke, and Sebastian Domsch. "Comics and Graphic Novels: Introduction." *Proceeding of the Conference of the German Association of University Teachers of English: Anglistentag*. Ed. Katrin Röder and Ilse Wischer. Trier: WVT, 2013. 233-36. Print.
161. Böger, Astrid. "On-Site Disaster: Exposing Calamity in Twentieth-Century Art Photography." *Iconographies of the Calamitous in American Visual Culture* 607-24.
162. Boesenberg, Eva. "Family Business: Death in Alison Bechdel's *Fun Home*." *American Lives* 327-38.
163. Boesenberg, Eva. "Productive Investments: Masculinities and Economies in Fisher's *The Walls of Jericho*." *Black Intersectionalities: A Critique for the 21st Century* 51-67.

164. Brinker, Felix. "Contemporary American Prime-Time Serials and the Logics of Conspiracy." *Media Res Theme Week: Conspiracies and Surveillance.* April, 2013. Media Commons. Web.
165. Broeck, Sabine. "The Challenge of Black Feminist Desire: Abolish Property." *Black Intersectionalities: A Critique for the 21st Century* 211–24.
166. Broeck, Sabine. "In the Presence of Racism." *American Studies Today: Recent Developments and New Perspectives* 291-97.
167. Broeck, Sabine. "The Legacy of Slavery: White Humanities and its Subject. A Manifesto." *Human Rights from a Third World Perspective: Critique, History and International Law.* Ed. Jose Barreto. Cambridge: Cambridge Scholars, 2013. 102–16. Print.
168. Broeck, Sabine. "Lessons for A-Disciplinarity: Some Notes on What Happens To an Americanist When She Takes Slavery Seriously." *Postcolonial Studies across the Disciplines?* 349–57.
169. Broeck, Sabine. "Die Lust an der Nicht-Beziehung: Versklavung und weiße Macht." *Erogene Gefahrenzonen. Aktuelle Produktionen des (infantilen) Sexuellen.* Ed. Insa Haertel. Berlin: Kadmos, 2013. 139–53. Print.
170. Broeck, Sabine. "One More Trip to the Quarters: Uncle Tom's Cabin Revisited with Toni Morrison." *Philological Sciences* 2 (2013): 94-103. Web.
171. Broeck, Sabine. "Versklavung, Schwarze Feministische Kritik und die Epistemologie der Gender Studies." *Wanderungen, Migrationen und Transformationen aus geschlechterwissenschaftlichen Perspektiven.* Ed. Annika McPherson, Barbara Paul, Sylvia Pritsch, Melanie Unseld, and Silke Wenk. Bielfeld: Transcript, 2013. 51–71. Print.
172. Brunner, Eva. "Confessional Poetry: A Poetic Perspective on Narrative Identity." *Rethinking Narrative Identity: Persona and Perspective* 187-202.
173. Buchenau, Barbara. "The Captive's Crucible: Haudenosaunee Violence in Early North American Narratives of Christian and Cultural Conversion." *Interculturalism in North America: Canada, the United States, Mexico, and Beyond* 27-56.
174. Buchenau, Barbara. "Erdichtetes Wissen über das präkoloniale Amerika: Junge Märkte und Ideen im Bann des *Song of Hiawatha* (1855)." *Von Käfern, Märkten und Menschen: Kolonialismus und Wissen in der Moderne.* Ed. Rebekka Habermas and Alexandra Przyrembel. Göttingen: Vandenhoeck & Ruprecht, 2013. 221-32. Print.
175. Buchenau, Barbara, and Zohra Hassan. "Lewis Carroll, *Alice's Adventures in Wonderland.*" *Unter dem roten Wunderschirm: Lesarten klassischer Kinder- und Jugendliteratur* 347-61.
176. Buschendorf, Christa. "A Figure of Our Times.' An Interview with Cornel West on W.E.B. Du Bois." *Du Bois Review* 10.1 (2013): 261-78. Print.
177. Buschendorf, Christa. "Properly speaking there are in the world no such men as self-made men': Frederick Douglass's Exceptional Position in the Field of Slavery." *Intellectual Authority and Literary Culture in the US, 1790-1900* 159-84.
178. Buschendorf, Christa. "The Shaping of We-Group Identities in the African American Community: A Perspective of Figurational Sociology on the Cul-

tural Imaginary." *The Imaginary and Its Worlds: American Studies after the Transnational Turn* 84-106.
179. Butler, Martin. "Representations and Implications of (Touring on) the Road in Bruce McDonald's Hard Core Logo." *Road Movies and Other Travel Narratives* 55-65.
180. Butler, Martin, and Jens-Martin Gurr. "On the 'Cultural Dimension of Sustainability' in Urban Systems: Urban Cultures as Ecological 'Force-Fields' in Processes of Sustainable Development." *Healthy and Liveable Cities / Gesunde und lebenswerte Städte* 138-51.
181. Butter, Michael. "Konspirationismus in den USA. " *Konspiration: Soziologie des Verschwörungsdenkens*. Ed. Andreas Anton, et al. Wiesbaden: Springer, 2013. Print. 259-76.
182. Caupert, Christina. "Kanongeschichte USA." *Handbuch Kanon und Wertung: Theorien, Instanzen, Geschichte* 296-300.
183. Claviez, Thomas. "Done and Over With –Finally? Otherness, Metonymy, and the Ethics of Comparison." *PMLA* 128.3 (2013): 69-80. Print.
184. Claviez, Thomas. "Introduction: 'Taking Place' – Conditional/Unconditional Hospitality." *The Conditions of Hospitality: Ethics, Politics, and Aesthetics on the Threshold of the Possible* 1-11.
185. Claviez, Thomas. "Jamming What Exactly? Some Notes on the 'Anthropological Machine' and Ethics in Derrida, Agamben, Calaro and Latour." *Literature, Ecology, Ethics: Recent Tends in Ecocriticism*. Ed. Timo Müller and Michael Sauter. Heidelberg: Winter, 2012. 69-80.
186. Claviez, Thomas. "Transcendifferance, or: Limping Toward a Radical Hospitality." *The Conditions of Hospitality: Ethics, Politics, and Aesthetics on the Threshold of the Possible* 24-41.
187. Däwes, Birgit. "Life Science and Life Writing: Notes for Discussion." *American Lives* 542-45.
188. Däwes, Birgit. "Haunted Fiction: The Ghosts of Ground Zero." *Beyond 9/11: Transdisciplinary Perspectives on Twenty-First Century U.S. American Culture* 341-58.
189. Däwes, Birgit. "'I don't write Native stories, I write universal stories': An Interview with Tomson Highway." *Indigenous North American Drama: A Multivocal History* 141-55.
190. Däwes, Birgit. "Of Homelands and Islands: Notes on Taiwanese American Studies." 英美文学评论: *Review of English and American Literature* [in Chinese] 23 (2013): 145-59. Print.
191. Däwes, Birgit. "Performing Memory, Transforming Time: History and Indigenous North American Drama." *Indigenous North American Drama: A Multivocal History* 1-15.
192. Däwes, Birgit. "Traumorama? The Pathological Landscapes of Richard Powers's The Echo Maker." *Communicating Disease: Cultural Representations of American Medicine* 413-30.
193. Däwes, Birgit. "'What happens when the vanishing race doesn't vanish?' Scenes of Native North American Historio/Biography." *American Lives* 77-110.

194. Däwes, Birgit. "William S. Yellow Robe, Jr." *The Methuen Drama Guide to Contemporary American Playwrights* 447-66.
195. Dallmann, Antje. "'Doctors Are Never Mistaken': Doctor Romances and Re-Negotiations of the Nature of Marriage in Late Nineteenth-Century America." *Cultural Representations of (American) Medicine: A Study in Interdisciplinarity* 119-44.
196. Dallmann, Antje. "Nathalie Mispagel: New York in der europäischen Dichtung des 20. Jahrhundert." *Archiv für das Studium der Neueren Sprachen und Literaturen* 250.165 (2013): 175-77. Print.
197. Denson, Shane, and Andreas Jahn-Sudmann. "Digital Seriality: On the Serial Aesthetics and Practice of Digital Games." *Eludamos: Journal for Computer Game Culture* 7.1 (2013): 1-32. Web.
198. Denson, Shane. "Framing, Unframing, Reframing: Retconning the Transnational Work of Comics." *Transnational Perspectives on Graphic Narratives: Comics at the Crossroads* 271-84.
199. Denson, Shane, Christina Meyer, and Daniel Stein. "Introducing Transnational Perspectives on Graphic Narratives: Comics at the Crossroads." *Transnational Perspectives on Graphic Narratives: Comics at the Crossroads* 1-12.
200. Detmers, Ines. "Männlichkeit im Zeichen der Schönheit und der neo-dekadente Roman: Bret Easton Ellis' *American Psycho.*" *Von Hexen Politik und schönen Männern – Geschlecht in Wissenschaft, Kultur und Alltag.* Ed. Kathleen Starck. Münster: LIT, 2013. 83-92. Print.
201. Dickel, Simon. "Between Mumblecore and Post-Black Aesthetics: Barry Jenkins's *Medicine for Melancholy.*" *Understanding Blackness through Performance: Contemporary Arts and the Representation of Identity.* Ed. Anne Crémieux, Xavier Lemoine, and Jean-Paul Rocchi. Basingstoke: Palgrave, 2013. 109-23. Print.
202. Dietrich, René. *Revising and Remembering (after) the End: American Post-American Poetry since 1945 from Ginsberg to Forché.* Trier: WVT, 2013. Print.
203. Dietrich, René. "The Inclusive Exclusion of Native Americans: Indigenous Life Writing and the Threat to US-Nationhood in Leslie Marmon Silko's *Storyteller.*" *Transnational American Studies* 305-22.
204. Dietrich, René. "The Dead shall inherit the Dead: After Life and Beyond Catastrophe in Mark Strand's Post-Apocalyptic Poetry." *The Cultural Life of Catastrophes and Crisis.* Ed. Carsten Meiner and Kristin Veel. Berlin: de Gruyter, 2012. 203-12. Print.
205. Domsch, Sebastian. "Halftone Reality: Iconicity and Symbolism in Graphic Narrative." *Symbolism* 12 (2013): 321-35. Print.
206. Domsch, Sebastian. "Signal to Noise: Engaging the Information Society from Pope to Year Zero." *Anglistik* 24:1 (2013): 165-76. Print.
207. Domsch, Sebastian. *Storyplaying: Agency and Narrative in Video Games.* Berlin: de Gruyter, 2013. Print.
208. Dorson, James. "The Aesthetics of Mastery: American Literary Naturalism and the Cultural Foundations of Bureaucracy." *CAS Studies Working Paper Series* 1 (2013): 3-50. Print.

209. Dorson, James. "Demystifying the Judge: Law and Mythical Violence in Cormac McCarthy's *Blood Meridian*." *Journal of Modern Literature* 36.2 (2013): 105-21. Print.
210. Drennig, Georg. "Eminem Rejects Ruin Porn: Imported from Detroit as a Construction of Motor City 'Cool.'" *Is It 'Cause It's Cool: Affective Encounters with American Culture* 161-79.
211. Drennig, Georg. "Fallujah Manhattan Transfer: The Sectarian Dystopia of DMZ." *Placing America: American Culture and Its Spaces* 75–89.
212. Drennig, Georg. "Taking a Hike and Hucking the Stout: The Troublesome Legacy of the Sublime in Outdoor Recreation." *Culture Unbound* 5 (2013): 551-68. Print.
213. Dunkel, Mario. "The Conceptualization of Race, Masculinity, and Authenticity in Early Jazz Historiography." *Gender and Notions of Authenticity in Jazz: Proceedings of the 10th Nordic Jazz Conference*. Ed. Alf Arvidsson and Roger Bergner. Stockholm: Center for Swedish Folk Music and Jazz Research, 2013. 25-34. Print.
214. Dunkel, Mario. "Duke Ellington, Charles Mingus and the Aesthetics of Pan-Africanism." *Music, Longing and Belonging: Articulations of the Self and Other in the Musical Realm* 64-81.
215. Ernst, Jutta. "'Beyond the Bayou': Sociocultural Spaces in Kate Chopin's Louisiana Short Stories." *Cultural Circulation: Dialogues between Canada and the American South* 51-66.
216. Ernst, Jutta. "De/marcations: Border Discourse in Jane Urquhart's *The Underpainter*." *Streifzüge durch die Welt der Sprachen und Kulturen: Festschrift für Dieter Huber zum 65. Geburtstag* Ed. Melanie Arnold, Silvia Hansen-Schirra, and Michael Poerner. Frankfurt/M: Lang, 2013. 259-75. Print.
217. Ernst, Jutta. "Joan Didion, Das Prosawerk." Kindlers Literatur Lexikon 3rd ed. (Online Supplement). n. pag. Web.
218. Esch-van Kan, Anneka. "Perfomance (Studies): Contemporary American Theater between Entertainment and Efficacy." *New Theories, Models and Methods in Literary and Cultural Studies* 99-122.
219. Essi, Cedric. "Transnational Affiliations in the Mixed Race Memoir: Barack Obama's Dreams from My Father." *American Lives* 261-81.
220. Etter, Lukas. "On the Drawing Board: The Many Autobiographical 'Wedges' of Alison Bechdel." *American Lives* 313-26.
221. Etter, Lukas. "The 'Big Picture' as a Multitude of Fragments: Jason Lutes's Depiction of Weimar Republic Berlin." *Transnational Perspectives on Graphic Narratives: Comics at the Crossroads* 229-41.
222. Faisst, Julia. "Rebuilding the Neighborhood: Race, Property, and Urban Renewal in *Tremé*." *American Lives* 443-63.
223. Faisst, Julia. "Sites of Slavery: Imperial Narratives, Plantation Architecture, and the Ideology of the Romance of the South." *Imagining Spaces and Places*. Ed. Saija Isomaa, Pirjo Lyytikäinen, Kirsi Saarikangas, and Renja Suominen-Kokkonen. Newcastle upon Tyne: Cambridge Scholars, 2013. 185-97. Print.
224. Fehrle, Johannes. "*Django Unchained* and the Neo-Blaxploitation Western." *Iperstoria: Testi Letterature Linguaggi* 2 (2013): n. pag. Web.

225. Fehrle, Johannes. "'We Have No Leaders, Holy Men or Gurus': The Carnivalesque as an Egalitarian Alternative in Ishmael Reed's Yellow Back Radio Broke-Down." *On the Aesthetic Legacy of Ishmael Reed: Contemporary Reassessments*. Ed. Sämi Ludwig. Huntington Beach, CA: World Parade, 2013. 26-55. Print.
226. Fehrle, Johannes, and Philipp Fidler. "'What's happened to the American Dream?' Transnationalism and Intertexts in Alan Moore and Dave Gibbons's *Watchmen.*" *International Journal of Comic Art* 15.2 (2013): 495-527. Print.
227. Fellner, Astrid M. "The Flavors of Multi-Ethnic North American Literatures: Language, Ethnicity and Culinary Nostalgia." *Culinary Linguistics: The Chef's Special*. Ed. Maximiliane Frobenius, Cornelia Gerhardt, and Susanne Ley. Amsterdam: John Benjamins, 2013. 241-60. Print.
228. Fellner, Astrid M. "Mondschein und Magnolien: Südstaatenklassiker von Margaret Mitchell, William Faulkner und Toni Morrison." *Klassiker Neu-Lektüren*. Ed. Ralf Bogner and Manfred Leber. Saarbrücken: Universaar, 2013. 211-28. Print.
229. Fick, Annabella. "Conrad Hilton, Be My Guest and American Popular Culture." *European Journal of Life Writing* 2 (2013): 18-34. Web.
230. Fluck, Winfried. "Fiction and the Struggle for Recognition." *Amerikastudien / American Studies* 57.4 (2012): 689-709. Print.
231. Fluck, Winfried. "The Free University and the John F. Kennedy-Institute in the Sixties." *Revisiting the Sixties: Interdisciplinary Perspectives on America's Longest Decade* 111-27.
232. Fluck, Winfried. "The Imaginary and the Second Narrative: Reading as Transfer." *The Imaginary and Its Worlds: American Studies After the Transnational Turn* 237-64.
233. Fluck, Winfried. "Reading for Recognition." *New Literary History* 44.1 (2013): 45-67. Print.
234. Fluck, Winfried. "Thomas Eakins: Superiority and Inferiority as Sources of Symbolic Capital." *Intellectual Authoriy and Literary Culture in the US, 1790-1900* 289-327.
235. Flügge, Anna. "Ryan Bingham and Capitalism in Jason Reitman's *Up in the Air.*" *Interfaces: Expanding Adaptations* 34 (2012-2013): 131-7. Print.
236. Freitag, Florian. *The Farm Novel in North America: Genre and Nation in the United States, English Canada, and French Canada, 1845-1945*. Rochester, NY: Camden House, 2013. Print.
237. Freudenberg, Maren. "Self and Other in Chinese Canadian Literature: Identity and Belonging in Larissa Lai's 'When Fox is A Thousand.'" *Interculturalism in North America, Canada, the United States, Mexico, and Beyond* 119-132.
238. Friedl, Herwig. "Out of Bounds: American Visions of the Thinker and of Thinking." *Intellectual Authority and Literary Culture in the US, 1790-1900* 205-17.
239. Friedl, Herwig. "William James versus Charles Taylor: Philosophy of Religion and the Confines of the Social and Cultural Imaginaries." *The Imaginary and Its Worlds: American Studies After the Transnational Turn* 67-83.

240. Frotscher, Mirjam M. "Gendered and Racialized: Reclaiming Chinese American Masculinities since the 1970s." *Post-World War II Masculinities in British and American Literature and Culture – Towards Comparative Masculinity Studies* 159-74.
241. Furlanetto, Elena. "The Rumi Phenomenon between Orientalism and Cosmopolitanism: The Case of Elif Shafak's *The Forty Rules of Love*." *European Journal of English Studies* 17.2 (2013): 201-13. Web.
242. Georgi-Findlay, Brigitte. "Does Region Matter? The West in American Women's Detective Novels." *Detective Fiction and Popular Visual Culture*. Ed. Cecile Sandten, Gunter Süß, and Melanie Graichen. Trier: WVT, 2013. 17-28. Print.
243. Gersdorf, Catrin. "Early American Cool: Benjamin Franklin, Thomas Jefferson, and the Affective Foundation of Republican Government." *Cosmopolitanism in the Age of Thomas Jefferson*. Ed. Peter Nicolaisen and Hannah Spahn. Heidelberg: Winter, 2013. 195-224. Print.
244. Gersdorf, Catrin. "Kinds of Cool: Emotions and the Rhetoric of Nineteenth-Century American Abolitionism." *The Cultural Career of Coolness: Discourses and Practices of Affect Contol in European Antiquity, the United States, and Japan* 81-108.
245. Gersdorf, Catrin. "Flânerie as Ecocritical Practice: Thoreau, Benjamin, Sandilands." *Ecology and Life Writing* 27-53.
246. Gerund, Katharina. "'Alle Menschen werden Schwestern'? Präsenz, implizites Wissen und feministische Solidarität." *Präsenz und implizites Wissen: Zur Interdependenz zweier Schlüsselbegriffe der Kultur- und Sozialwissenschaften*. Ed. Heike Paul and Christoph Ernst. Bielefeld: transcript, 2013. 185-209. Print.
247. Gerund, Katharina. Transatlantic Cultural Exchange: African American Women's Art and Activism in West Germany. Bielefeld: transcript, 2013. Print. American Studies 5.
248. Gessner, Ingrid. "Contagion, Crisis, and Control: Tracing Yellow Fever in Nineteenth-Century American Literature and Culture." *Communicating Disease: Cultural Representations of American Medicine* 219-42.
249. Goebel, Walter, and Saskia Schabio. "Towards a Postcolonial Narrative Aesthetics." Introduction. *Locating Postcolonial Narrative Genres* 1-10.
250. Goebel, Walter. "V. S. Naipaul's Heterobiographical Fictions or Postcolonial Melancholia Reinterpreted." *Locating Postcolonial Narrative* 108-24.
251. Golimowska, Karolina. "Cricket as a Cure: Post-911 Urban Trauma and Displacement in Joseph O'Neill's Novel *Netherland*." *The Journal of American Culture* 36.3 (2013): 230–39. Print.
252. Graaff, Kristina. "Street Literature and the Mode of Spectacular Writing. Popular Fiction between Sensationalism, Education, Politics and Entertainment." *The Living Canon: Theory and Pedagogy in Contemporary African American Literature* 113-34.
253. Grabes, Herbert. "On the Function and Value of Theory." *New Theories, Models and Methods in Literary and Cultural Studies*.
254. Grabes, Herbert. "Sequentiality." *The Living Handbook of Narratology*. Ed. Peter Hühn, et al. Hamburg: Hamburg UP, 2013. Web.

255. Grabher, Gudrun. "A Mother's Loss of Her Daughter's Face: Ethical Issues of Facial Disfigurement in Natalie Kusz's Memoir Road Song." *Disjointed Perspectives on Motherhood*. Ed. Catalina Florina Florescu. Lanham, MD: Lexington, 2013. 1-20. Print.
256. Greiffenstern, Alexander. "Ballad of the Big Man: The Soundtrack of *The Autobiography of a Brown Buffalo*." *Interculturalism in North America: Canada, the United States, Mexico, and Beyond* 203-13.
257. Greiffenstern, Alexander, and Josef Raab. "Introduction: Interculturalism and Difference." *Interculturalism in North America: Canada, the United States, Mexico, and Beyond* 1-23.
258. Groß, Florian. "Lost in Translation: Narratives of Transnational Displacement in the Wordless Graphic Novel." *Transnational Perspectives to Graphic Narratives: Comics at the Crossroads* 197-210.
259. Gurr, Jens-Martin. "Sofia Coppola: Lost in Translation." *Teaching Contemporary Literature and Culture: Film* 463-79.
260. Gurr, Jens-Martin. "Without contraries is no progression": Emplotted Figures of Thought in Negotiating Oppositions, Funktionsgeschichte and Literature as 'Cultural Diagnosis.'" *Text or Context: Reflections on Literary and Cultural Criticism* 59-77.
261. Gurr, Jens-Martin, and Olaf Kaltmeier. "Conflicting Constructions of Cross-Border Regional Identities in the Cascadia Region (Seattle/Vancouver)." *Transnational Americas: Envisioning Inter-American Area Studies in Globalization Processes* 35-53.
262. Gygax, Franziska. "Theoretically ill: Autobiographer, patient, theorist." *The Writing Cure: Literature and Medicine in Context*. Ed. A. Lembert-Heidenreich and Jarmila Mildorf. Münster: LIT, 2013. 173-190. Print. Kultur- und Naturwissenschaften im Dialog/Natural Sciences and Humanities in Dialogue 2.
263. Haas, Astrid. "Between Monroe Doctrine and Manifest Destiny: Spanish American Travel Narratives of Jacksonian America." *Mobile Narratives: Travel, Migration, and Transculturation* 30-42.
264. Haas, Astrid. "Remedial Laughter: American Stage Comedy about AIDS." *Communicating Disease: Cultural Representations of American Medicine* 243-64. Print.
265. Haas, Astrid. "Worte als Waffe, Theater als Therapie: Der Beitrag der Literatur zur Wahrnehmung von AIDS." *Gesellschaft braucht Wissenschaft— Wissenschaft braucht Gesellschaft: Mobilität, Kommunikation, Interaktion*. Ed. Ludwig Schultz, et al. Stuttgart: Thieme, 2013. 171-86. Print. Verhandlungen der Gesellschaft Deutscher Naturforscher und Ärzte 127.
266. Haas, Astrid, and Alexia Schemien. "Revisiting the Ancestral Past, Envisioning Chicana Lives: An Interview with Santa Barraza, Artist of the Borderlands." *Interculturalism in North America: Canada, the United States, Mexico, and Beyond* 259-74.
267. Hamscha, Susanne. "Coolness Has a Number: The Americana Cool of Beverly Hills, 90210." *Is It 'Cause It's Cool? Affective Encounters with American Culture* 95-116.

268. Hamscha, Susanne. "Thirty Are Better Than One: Marilyn Monroe and the Performance of Americanness." *ConFiguring America: Iconic Figures, Visuality, and American Culture* 115-32.
269. Haselstein, Ulla. "Cool: Vom Dandy des 19. zum Hipster des 21. Jahrhunderts." *Archithese* 2 (2013): 33-37. Print.
270. Haselstein, Ulla. "The Cultural Career of Coolness." *The Cultural Career of Coolness: Discourses and Practices of Affect Contol in European Antiquity, the United States, and Japan* 47-64.
271. Hebel, Udo J. "Interpiktoriale Dialoge in der amerikanischen Malerei und Fotografie: Beobachtungen zu einem Arbeitsfeld der American Studies nach dem Iconic Turn." *Bilder sehen: Perspektiven der Bildwissenschaft.* Ed. Marc Greenlee et al. Regensburg: Schnell & Steiner, 2013. 155-72. Print.
272. Heide, Markus. "Cosmopolitics in Border Film: *Amores Perros* and *Sleep Dealer.*" *Comparative American Studies* 11.1 (2013): 89-113. Print.
273. Heide, Markus. "José Martí, Cuban Cultural Theory, and Inter-American Studies." *Transmediality and Transculturality* 141-157.
274. Heil, Johanna. "Embedding Richard Powers's *The Echo Maker* in Narrative Medicine: Narrativity, Delusions, and the (De-)Construction of Unified Minds." *Communicating Disease: Cultural Representations of American Medicine* 387-411.
275. Heinze, Rüdiger. "Gattaca." *Teaching Contemporary Literature and Culture Vol. 3: Film* 321-35.
276. Heinze, Rüdiger. "Gazpacho & Tomato Soup: What We Talk About When We Talk About (Post)Multicultural U.S.-American Literature." *Transnational Americas: Envisioning Inter-American Area Studies in Globalization Processes* 255-64.
277. Heinze, Rüdiger. "Strange Perspectives = Strange (Narrative?) Identities?" *Rethinking Narrative Identity: Persona and Perspective* 117-127.
278. Heinze, Rüdiger. "The Whirligig of Time: Towards a Poetics of Unnatural Temporality." *A Poetics of Unnatural Narrative.* Ed. Jan Alber, Henrik Skov Nielsen, and Brian Richardson. Columbus, OH: Ohio State UP, 2013. 31-44. Print.
279. Henderson, Marius. "Soft Berry Metal – Eine 'häretische' Annäherung an Black Metal Theory." *testcard: Beiträge zur Popgeschichte* 23 (2013). n. pag. Mainz: Ventil. Print.
280. Herzog, Alexandra. "The Power of AH, E/B, Very OOC: Agency in Fanfiction Jargon." *COPAS: Current Objectives of American Studies* 14 (2013): 1-23. Web.
281. Herzogenrath, Bernd. "Bluebeard." *Stilepochen des Films: Classical Hollywood* 273-78.
282. Herzogenrath, Bernd. "On the Lost Highway: An Encounter." *Films, Graphic Novels and Visuals: Developing Multiliteracies in Foreign Language Education - An Inter-disciplinary Approach* 185-200.
283. Hirmer, Karin. "Female Empowerment: Buffy and Her Heiresses in Control." *Images of the Modern Vampire. The Hip and the Atavistic.* Ed. Barbara Brodman and James E. Doan. Madison: Farleigh Dickinson UP, 2013. 71-84. Print.

284. Hirmer, Karin. "*Smallville*'s Lois Lane: From New Woman to Female Hero." *Examining Lois Lane: The Scoop on Superman's Sweetheart*. Ed. Nadine Farghaly. Lanham: Scarecrow, 2013. 235-59. Print.
285. Hollm, Jan. "The Development of Environmental Awareness: From the Past to the Future." *Englisch betrifft uns* 3 (2013): 1-6. Print.
286. Hollm, Jan. "Utopian or Dystopian Communities in North America?" *Englisch betrifft uns* 5 (2013): 1-6. Print.
287. Holtz, Martin. "The Pathological Protagonist in Recent Films by Martin Scorsese." *American Lives* 507-20.
288. Holtz, Martin. "The Proposition (2005)." *Teaching Contemporary Literature and Culture: Film Part II* 527-41.
289. Horn, Mirjam. "'Through no Badness or Villainy of His Own:' Generic Change from Law to Literature in Vanessa Place's Statements of Facts." *The Cultural Dynamics of Generic Change in Contemporary Fiction: Theoretical Frameworks, Genres and Model Interpretations* 381-96.
290. Hornung, Alfred. "Chinese Garden Culture and Ecological Life Writing." *Ecology and Life Writing* 209-307.
291. Hornung, Alfred. "Ecology and Life Writing." Preface. *Ecology and Life Writing* ix-xix.
292. Hornung, Alfred. "Editor's Note." *Journal of Transnational American Studies*, 5.1 (2013): 1-5. Print.
293. Hornung, Alfred. "Literature." *USA-Lexikon* 635-47.
294. Hornung, Alfred. "American Lives: Preface." Preface. *American Lives* ix-xvii.
295. Hornung, Alfred. "The Mediation of Public Lives: The Performance of Barack Obama's Self." *Medialisierungsformen des(Auto-)Biografischen*. 203-14.
296. Höttges, Bärbel. "'Am Anfang war...' Religion, Intertextualität und Identität im Romanwerk Toni Morrisons." *Heilige Texte: Literarisierung von Religion und Sakralisierung von Literatur im modernen Roman*. Ed. Klaus Antoni et al. Berlin: LIT, 2013. 149-67. Print.
297. Isekenmeier, Guido. "In Richtung einer Theorie der Interpiktorialität." *Interpiktorialität: Theorie und Geschichte der Bild-Bild-Bezüge* 11-86.
298. Isekenmeier, Guido. "Visual Event Realism." *Realisms in Contemporary Culture: Theories, Politics, and Medial Configurations* 214-26; 228-29.
299. Junker, Carsten. "Benjamin Franklin's Ethnic Drag – Notes on Abolition, Satire, and Affect." *Black Intersectionalities: A Critique for the 21st Century* 84–97.
300. Junker, Carsten. "Narrating Family Lives: Religion and Enslavement in Samuel West's Memoirs (1807)." *American Lives* 158–71.
301. Junker, Carsten. "Writing Anti-Slavery: Abolition as Boundary Object in Transatlantic Enlightenment." *Language. Philology. Culture*. 2-3 (2013): 32–49. Web.
302. Kaltmeier, Olaf, and Jens-Martin Gurr. "Conflicting Constructions of Cross-Border Regional Identities in the Cascadia Region (Seattle/Vancouver)." *Transnational Americas. Envisioning Inter-American Area Studies in Globalization Processes* 35-54.

303. Kaltmeier, Olaf. "Transnational Americas. Envisioning Inter-American Area Studies in Globalization Processes." *Transnational Americas. Envisioning Inter-American Area Studies in Globalization Processes* 1-16.
304. Kanzler, Katja. "Adaptation and Self-Expression in *Julia/Julia*." *American Lives* 369-80.
305. Keck, Michaela. "Complicating the Reading of Nineteenth-Century American Landscape Painting: Albert Bierstadt's Western Visions, Aesthetics, and Sociology." *Concentric: Literary and Cultural Studies* 39.2 (2013): 139-61. Print.
306. Kelleter, Frank. "Commitment and Competition: A Religious Enlightenment in Revolutionary America?" *Religion and Politics in Europe and the United States: Transnational Historical Approaches* 15-44.
307. Kelleter, Frank. "Kultur." *Handbuch Komparatistik: Theorien, Arbeitsfelder, Wissenspraxis*. Ed. Rüdiger Zymner and Achim Hölter. Stuttgart: Metzler, 2013. 110-14. Print.
308. Kelleter, Frank. "L. Frank Baums *The Wonderful Wizard of Oz*: Immigranten und Sonderlinge im wunderbaren Land." *Unter dem roten Wunderschirm: Lesarten klassischer Kinder- und Jugendliteratur* 167-80.
309. Kindellan, Michael. "Responsibility in Verse: William Wordsworth and J. H. Prynne." *Ethics of Alterity: Confrontation and Responsibility in 19th-21st Century British Literature*. Ed. Christine Reynier and Jean-Michel Ganteau. Montpellier: PULM, 2013. 231-50. Print.
310. Klarer, Mario. *An Introduction to Literary Studies*. 3rd ed. London: Routledge, 2013. Print.
311. Klarer, Mario. *Literaturgeschichte der USA*. München: Beck, 2013. Print.
312. Klecker, Cornelia. "'Are You Watching Closely?' The Conflict of Mind-Tricking Narratives in Recent Hollywood Film." *Cultures in Conflict / Conflicting Cultures* 65-78.
313. Klepper, Martin: "Experiential Approaches to Narrative: 'Discordant Concordance' in Dave Eggers's A Heartbreaking Work of Staggering Genius." *New Approaches to Narrative: Cognition – Culture – History* 31-42.
314. Kley, Antje. "Literatur als Präsentifikation impliziten Wissens: Kulturkontakt in Mary Rowlandsons captivity narrative (1682) und Toni Morrisons Kurzgeschichte 'Recitatif' (1983)." *Präsenz und implizites Wissen: Schlüsselbegriffe der Kultur- und Sozialwissenschaften* 211-37.
315. Kley, Antje. "Narratives of Recognition in Contemporary American Fiction: Edward P. Jones's *The Known World* and Richard Powers's *The Echo Maker*." *Tocqueville's Legacy: Towards a Cultural History of Recognition in American Studies* 643-61.
316. Kloeckner, Christian, and Christoph Faulhaber. "9/11 as 'Unbild': A Conversation." *Beyond 9/11: Transdisciplinary Perspectives on Twenty-First Century U. S. American Culture* 383-407.
317. Kloeckner, Christian."'Double Games': Das Spiel der (Auto)Biografie in Paul Austers *Leviathan*." *Autobiographie: Eine interdisziplinäre Gattung zwischen klassischer Tradition und (post-)moderner Variation* 433-49.

318. Kloeckner, Christian, Simone Knewitz, and Sabine Sielke. Introduction. *Beyond 9/11: Transdisciplinary Perspectives on Twenty-First Century U.S. American Culture* 13-25.
319. Kloeckner, Christian. "Mapping 9/11: A Review of Recent German Scholarship." *Archiv für das Studium der neueren Sprachen und Literaturen* 250.2 (2013): 371-79. Print.
320. Kloeckner, Christian. "On Hallowed Ground: The Sacred Space of Ground Zero and the Consecration of Global Business." *Beyond 9/11: Transdisciplinary Perspectives on Twenty-First Century U.S. American Culture* 245-62.
321. Kloeckner, Christian. "Re-Orienting Impersonality: T.S. Eliot and the Self of the Far East." *Modernism and the Orient* 163-84.
322. Klopfer, Nadine. *Die Balkone von New Orleans: Städtischer Raum und lokale Identität um 1900*. Bielefeld: Transcript, 2013. Print.
323. Knopf, Kerstin. "Birdwatchers." *Directory of World Cinema: Brazil*. Ed. Natalia Pinazza and Louis Bayman. Bristol: intellect, 2013. 156-58. Print.
324. Knopf, Kerstin. "Chris Eyre, Smoke Signals (1998)." *Teaching Contemporary Literature and Culture: Film Part II* 611-32.
325. Knopf, Kerstin. "'The exquisite horror of their reality': Native and 'White' Cannibals in American and Canadian Historiography and Literature." *F(e)asting Fitness? Cultural Images, Social Practices, and Histories of Food and Health* 19-46.
326. Knopf, Kerstin. "Kangaroos, Petrol, Joints, and Sacred Stones: Australian Cinema Decolonized." *Decolonizing Screens*. Ed. Felicity Collins and Jane Landman. Special issue of *Studies in Australasian Cinema* 7.2 (2013): 189-200. Print.
327. Knopf, Kerstin. "Zacharias Kunuk, Atanarjuat: *The Fast Runner* (2001)." *Teaching Contemporary Literature and Culture: Film Part I* 47-67.
328. Knox, Melissa. "Protean Identity: Religion and Contemporary American Autobiography." *Forum for Inter-American Research* 6.1 (2013): n. pag. Web.
329. Köhler, Angelika. "Constructions of Masculinity in Philip Roth's *Portnoy's Complaint*, Frank Chin's *The Chickencoop Chinaman*, and Ishmael Reed's *Flight to Canada*." *Post-World War II Masculinities in British and American Literature: Towards Comparative Masculinity Studies* 143-58.
330. Köhler, Angelika. "Religious Syncretism, Iconography, and Transethnic Subjectivity Construction: The Role of the Virgin of Guadalupe in María Cristina Meena's and Cherríe Moraga's Literary Work." *Mobile Narratives: Travel, Migration, and Transculturation* 124-35.
331. Koenen, Anne. "Color line." *USA-Lexikon: Schlüsselbegriffe zu Politik, Wirtschaft, Gesellschaft, Kultur, Geschichte und zu den deutsch-amerikanischen Beziehunge* 247-48.
332. Koenen, Anne. "Race relations." *USA-Lexikon: Schlüsselbegriffe zu Politik, Wirtschaft, Gesellschaft, Kultur, Geschichte und zu den deutsch-amerikanischen Beziehunge* 917-19.
333. Kovach, Elizabeth. "Cataclysmic Events as Genre Shapers? A Case Study of the Fantastic in Jonathan Safran Foer's *Extremely Loud and Incredibly*

Close." *The Cultural Dynamics of Generic Change in Contemporary Fiction: Theoretical Frameworks, Genres and Model Interpretations* 301-14.
334. Kozyrakis, Yulia. "Reading Fiction under False Assumptions? Emma Dunham Kelley-Hawkins and her Posthumous Passing for Black." *Fake Identity? The Impostor Narrative in North American Culture* 113-27.
335. Kriebernegg, Ulla, and Roberta Maierhofer. "The Ages of Live: Living and Aging in Conflict? *The Ages of Live: Living and Aging in Conflict?* 9-17.
336. Kriebernegg, Ulla. "Ending Aging in the Shteyngart of Eden: Biogerontological Discourse in a *Super Sad True Love Story*." *Journal of Aging Studies* 27.1 (2013): 60-71. Print.
337. Kriebernegg, Ulla. "'It'll remain a shock for a while': Resisting Socialization into Long-Term Care in Joan Barfoot's Exit Lines." *Methoden der Alter(n)sforschung: Disziplinäre Positionen und transdisziplinäre Perspektiven*. Ed. Andrea von Hülsen-Esch, Miriam Seidler, and Christian Tagsold. Bielefeld: Transcript, 2013. 189-208. Print.
338. Kriebernegg, Ulla. "Locating Life: Intersections of Old Age, Space and Place in Contemporary Canadian Nursing Home Narratives." *Space and Place: Exploring Critical Issues*. Ed. Rob Fisher. Oxford: Oxford UP, 2013. n. pag. Web.
339. Kuester, Martin. "Canadian Studies in Europe: Understanding Canada No More?" *Europe – Canada: Transcultural Perspectives / Perspectives Transculturelles* 15-21.
340. Kuester, Martin. "Cunning Man and/or Shaman? Robertson Davies's Dr. Hullah." *Communicating Disease: Cultural Representations of American Medicine* 61-70.
341. Kuester, Martin. "'It does a man good to take a few pills every day': Robertson Davies and Samuel Marchbanks on Health, Food and Fitness." *F(e)asting Fitness? Cultural Images, Social Practices, and Histories of Food and Health: A Fe(a)stschrift in Honor of Wolfgang Klooß* 181-89.
342. Kuester, Martin, and Julia Michael. "Narrativizing Migration – The Mennonite Case: Collective vs. Individual Memories." *Cultural Challenges of Migration in Canada/Les défis culturels de la migration au Canada*. Ed. Klaus-Dieter Ertler and Patrick Imbert. Frankfurt/M: Lang, 2013. 283-95. Print.
343. Kunow, Rüdiger. "The Biology of Community: Contagious Diseases, Old Age, Biotech, ad Cultural Studies." *Communicating Disease: Cultural Representations of American Medicine* 265-87.
344. Kunow, Rüdiger. "Going Native with God on the Side: Mission as Travelling Culture." *fiar - forum for interamerican research*. 6.1 (2013): n. pag. Web.
345. Kunow, Rüdiger. "The Pain of Representation." *Text or Context: Reflections on Literary and Cultural Criticism* 79-93.
346. Kunow, Rüdiger. "Postscript: Cultural Critique as Redemptive Fantasy?" *Text or Context: Reflections on Literary and Cultural Criticism* 167-72.
347. Kunow, Rüdiger. "'Watching one another out of fear': Affective Communities and Medical Emergencies in the United States." *The Politics of Passion: Reframing Affect and Emotion in Global Modernity* 51-68.

348. Kuroszczyk, Miriam. *Poetic Brokers: Robert Hayden, Melvin B. Tolson, and International Modernism in African American Poetry*. Trier: WVT, 2013. Print.
349. Laemmerhirt, Iris-Aya. *Embracing Differences: Transnational Cultural Flows between Japan and the United States*. Bielefeld: Transcript, 2013. Print.
350. Laemmerhirt, Iris-Aya. "Trying to Recapture the Front: A Transnational Perspective of Hawaii in R. Kikuo Johnson's *Night Fisher*." *Transnational Perspectives on Comics and Graphic Narratives. Comics at the Crossroad* 83-94.
351. Laemmerhirt, Iris-Aya. "Anata o Rikai Shite Hoshii Nara, Mazu Kikukoto Kara Hajime Mashō: Transnational Eika to Shite no *Babel ni Kanshite*." ["If You Want to Be Undestood, Listen: Reading *Babel* as a Transnational Movie."] Trans. Yoneyuki Sugita. *Amerika o Shiru Tame no 18 Shō [18 Chapters to Understand America]*. Ed. Yoneyuki Sugita. Tokyo: Daigaku Kyōiku Shuppan, 2013. 32-45. Print.
352. Lanzendörfer, Tim. *The Professionalization of the American Magazine: Periodicals, Biography, and Nationalism in the Early Republic*. Paderborn: Schöningh, 2013. Print.
353. Lanzendörfer, Tim. "Collective Life: E. O. Wilson's "Trailhead" and Insect-Life Writing." *Ecology and Life Writing* 287-95.
354. Lanzendörfer, Tim. "The Marvelous History of the Dominican Republic in Junot Díaz's *The Brief Wondrous Life of Oscar Wao*." *MELUS: Multiethnic Literature of the U. S.* 38.2 (2013). 127-42. Print.
355. Laschinger, Verena. "The Reluctant Orientalist: Critical Reflections on How to Look At Istanbul – A Photoessay." *Cityscapes: World Cities and Their Cultural Industries*. Ed. Asunción Lopez-Varela Azcárate. Champaign, IL: Common Ground, 2013. 343-57. Print.
356. Lerg, Charlotte, and Dorothea Schwarzhaupt-Scholz. *Blues on the Road: Jazz and Images of the South—Photographien von Axel Küstner*. München: Lasky Center for Transatlantic Studies, 2013. Print.
357. Leuchtenmüller, Thomas. "Kosmopolit und Puzzlespieler: Zum 70. Geburtstag des kanadischen Schriftstellers Michael Ondaatje." *Neue Zürcher Zeitung* 12 September 2013: 20. Print.
358. Leuchtenmüller, Thomas. "Von der betörenden Magie des Alltags: Literaturnobelpreis für die Kanadierin Alice Munro. " *Neue Zürcher Zeitung* 11 Oktober 2013: 23. Print.
359. Leypoldt, Günter. "Introduction: Intellectual Authority and Literary Culture." *Intellectual Authority and Literary Culture in the US, 1790-1900* 1-25.
360. Leypoldt, Günter. "Specters of Feminization in Nineteenth-Century Literary Culture." *Intellectual Authority and Literary Culture in the US, 1790-1900* 141-58.
361. Löffler, Philipp, and Clemens Spahr. "Introduction: Conceptions of Collectivity in Contemporary American Literature." *Conceptions of Collectivity in Contemporary American Literature* 161-76.
362. Lösch, Klaus, and Heike Paul. "Präsenz, implizites Wissen und Fremdheit aus kulturwissenschaftlicher Perspektive." *Präsenz und implizites Wissen:*

Zur Interdependenz zweier Schlüsselbegriffe der Kultur- und Sozialwissenschaften 151-83.
363. Loock, Kathleen. "Jonathan Franzen: *Freedom.*" *Kindlers Neues Literatur Lexikon* (Online Supplement). Web.
364. Loock, Kathleen. "Laughing at the Greenhorn: Humor in Immigrant Autobiographies." *American Lives* 207-23.
365. Lüthe, Martin. "Infinite Deaths: The Death of and by the Media in David Foster Wallace's *Infinite Jest.*" *Life without Media.* Ed. Klaus Zilles, Eva Comas, and Juan Cuenca. Frankfurt/M: Lang, 2013. 151-68. Print.
366. Lüthe, Martin. "Remembering Motown: Baby Boomers, Blackness, and the Sixties in Pop-Cultural Memory." *Revisiting the Sixties: Interdisciplinary Perspectives on America's Longest Decade* 301-16.
367. Lüthe, Martin. "(Re-) producing the Body: Motion Capture and the Meaning of Physicality in DigitalSoccer Games." *Build,'Em Up, Shoot 'Em Down: Körperlichkeit in Digitalen Spielen.* Ed. Rudolf Inderst and Peter Just. Boizenburg: Hülsbusch, 2013. 25-41. Print.
368. Lutz, Hartmut. "Sagas of Northern contacts and magic realism: From historical conflict to fictional conciliations." *Eyes Deep with Unfathomable Histories: The Poetics and Politics of Magic Realism Today and in the Past* 33-48.
369. Lutz, Hartmut. "'Whom Do We Eat? – Thoughts on the Columbian Exchange, and 'How Food Was Given.'" *F(e)asting Fitness: Cultural Images, Social Practices, and Histories of Food and Health* 137-48.
370. Mahlknecht, Johannes. "'Based on Entirely Coincidental Resemblances': The Legal Disclaimer in Hollywood Cinema." *Cultures in Conflict / Conflicting Cultures* 109-22.
371. Maierhofer, Roberta. "Auf den Schultern des 'Scheinriesen'. Das Plagiat als Simulacrum." *Plagiat, Fälschung, Urheberrecht im interdisziplinären Blickfeld.* Ed. Dietmar Goltschnigg, Charlotte Grolleg-Edler, Patrizia Gruber. Berlin: Erich Schmidt, 2013. 113-18. Print.
372. Maierhofer, Roberta. "Das Selbst im Kontext des Lebens. Überlegungen zur Darstellung des Lebensverlaufs." *Erinnern und Erzählen: Theologische, geistes-, human- und kulturwissenschaftliche Perspektiven.* Ed. Konstantin Lindner, Andrea Kabus, Ralph Bergold, and Harald Schwillus. Münster: LIT, 2013. 15-23. Print.
373. Matter-Seibel, Sabina. *"Contending Forces": Romantraditionen amerikanischer Schriftstellerinnen, 1850-1900.* Frankfurt/M: Lang, 2013. Print.
374. McSherry, Siofra. "Joseph Cornell's Subversive Materialism." *Comparative American Studies* 11.4 (2013): 374-86. Print.
375. Meindel, Dieter. "Canada/American South in the Short Story: Flannery O'Connor – Jack Hodgins – Leon Rooke." *Cultural Circulation: Dialogues between Canada and the American South* 291-306.
376. Meinel, Dietmar. "'Space: The Final Fun-tier' – Returning Home to the Frontier in Pixar's *WALL-E.*" *Animation Studies Online Journal* 8 (2013). n. pag. Web.

377. Meyer, Christina, and Jens Bonk. "'Serializing 'Gravitational Distortions': Techniques of Refutation, Digression and Interruption in *The Unwritten*." *International Journal of Comic Art* 15.2 (2013): 682-701. Print.
378. Meyer, Christina. "Patriotic Laughter? World War I in British and American Newspaper and Magazine Comics." *Heroisches Elend/Misères de l'héroisme/Heroic Memory: Der Erste Weltkrieg im intellektuellen, literarischen und bildnerischen Gedächtnis der europäischen Kulturen / La Première Guerre mondiale dans la mémoire intellectuelle, littéraire et artistique des cultures européennes / The First World War in the Intellectual, Literary and Artistic Memory of the European Cultures*. 2 Vols. Ed. Thomas Stauder and Gislinde Seybert. Frankfurt/M: Lang, 2013. 1525-52. Print.
379. Meyer, Christina. "Un/taming the Beast, or Graphic Novels (Re)-Considered." *From Comic Strips to Graphic Novels: Contributions to the Theory and History of Graphic Narrative* 271-99.
380. Meyer, Evelyn P. "'Romanized Gauls': The Significance of the United States and the Canada-U.S. Border for Canadian National Identity Construction." *Placing America: American Culture and Its Spaces* 145-57.
381. Meyer, Sabine N., and Peter Schneck. "*American Beauty* (1999), Sam Mendes (dir.)." *Teaching Contemporary Literature and Culture 3* 21-46.
382. Meyer, Sabine N. "Decentering Man's Place in the Universe: Yakari and Its Visual Representation of Native Americans." *Zmkb / online Zeitschrift Kunst Medien Bildung* 20 July 2013: n. pag. Web.
383. Meyer, Sabine N. "'If you're an Indian, why don't you write nature poetry?' The Environment in Selected Works of Sherman Alexie." *Ecology and Life Writing* 143-60.
384. Meyer, Sabine N. "German Americans." *Multicultural America: A Multimedia Encyclopedia* 954-59.
385. Meyer, Sabine N. "Worcester v. Georgia." *Multicultural America: A Multimedia Encyclopedia* 2184-85.
386. Meyer, Sabine N. "The World Was Not Made for Men: Representations of Native Americans in Yakari." *Ethnoscripts* 15.1 (2013): 86-100. Print.
387. Mischke, Dennis. "Othering Otherness: Fictocriticism and the Cosmopolitan Vision." *Postcolonial Studies across the Disciplines* 323-41.
388. Mischke, Dennis. "'Unexpected Item in the Bagging Area'? Der berechenbare Prosument, Datenbanken und die Kontrollgesellschaft." *The Road to Surveillance Society? Hard-Ti*mes 92 (2012): 40-47. Print.
389. Mohr, Hans-Ulrich. "Horace Walpole - Six Dimensions of an Eighteenth Century Celebrity." *Celebrity: The Idiom of a Modern Era* 47-63.
390. Mörtl, Heidrun, and Antonio Barrenechea. Introduction. *Hemispheric Indigenous Studies* 109-23. Print.
391. Moos, Jennifer. "Boy Bands, Drag Kings, and the Performance of (Queer) Masculinities." *Transposition: Musique et sciences sociales* 3 (2013): n. pag. Web.
392. Mosel, Michael. "Game Noir: Einfluss des Film noirs im Computerspiel." *Spielkulturen: Funktionen und Bedeutungen des Phänomens Spiel in der Gegenwartskultur und im Alltagsdiskurs* 93-110.

393. Müller, Kurt. "Allegorische Seelenreise in das politische Unbewußte der 'Jacksonian Era': Edgar Allan Poes *The Narrative of Arthur Gordon Pym.*" *Archiv für das Studium der neueren Sprachen und Literaturen* 250 (2013): 66-84. Print.
394. Müller, Kurt. "Der Kindheits- und Jugendkult in der amerikanischen Erzählliteratur am Beispiel Mark Twains." *Kinder, Kinder! Vergangene, gegenwärtige und ideelle Kindheitsbilder Kinder, Kinder! Vergangene, gegenwärtige und ideelle Kindheitsbilder.* Ed. Dominik Becher and Elmar Schenkel. Frankfurt/M: Lang, 2013. 25-43. Print.
395. Müller, Kurt. "Ernest Hemingway's Shifting Positions within the Literary Field: A Reconsideration." *Comparative Studies in Anglophone Literatures: (Trans)National, (Post)Colonial, and (Auto)Thematic (Re)Considerations and (Re)Visions.* Ed. Grzegorz Koneczniak. Torun: Wydawnictwo Naukowe Universytetu Mikollaja Korpernika, 2012. 251-70. Print.
396. Müller, Kurt. "The Virtue of Temperance: Food, Drink and Health in Benjamin Franklin's Conception of the Good Life." *F(e)asting Fitness? Cultural Images, Social Practices, and Histories of Food and Health* 99-111.
397. Müller, Monika. "'I Have Seen the Future and It Is Mongrel': Time Travel, Race and Music in Richard Powers's *The Time of Our Singing.*" *Mobile Narratives: Travel, Migration, and Transculturation* 199-209.
398. Müller, Stefanie. "Corporate Power and the Public Good in Sloan Wilson's *The Man in the Gray Flannel Suit.*" *COPAS: Current Objectives of American Studies* 14 (2013): n. pag. Web.
399. Müller, Stefanie. *The Presence of the Past in the Novels of Toni Morrison.* Heidelberg: Winter, 2013. Print.
400. Mulvihill, Bryan, and Alexander Greiffenstern. "Interculturalism: Vancouver and the World Tea Party." *Interculturalism in North America: Canada, the United States, Mexico, and Beyond* 275-96.
401. Munkelt, Marga. "Myths of Rebellion: Translocation and (Cultural) Innovation in Mexican-American Literature." *Postcolonial Translocations: Cultural Representation and Critical Spatial Thinking* 181-99.
402. Nischik, Reingard M. "Two Nations, One Genre? The Beginnings of the Modernist Short Story in the United States and Canada." *Cultural Circulation: Dialogues between Canada and the American South* 277-89.
403. Nitz, Julia. "History, a Literary Artifact? – The Travelling Concept of Narrative in/on Historiographic Discourse." *Interdisciplinary Literary Studies* 15.1 (2013): 69-85. Print.
404. Nitzsche, Sina. "Hip-Hop in Europe as a Transnational Phenomenon: An Introduction." Hip-Hop in Europe: Cultural Identities and Transnational Flows 3-34.
405. Nünning, Ansgar, and Christine Schwanecke. "Crossing Generic Borders: Hybridisation as a Catalyst of Genre Development." *The Cultural Dynamics of Generic Change in Contemporary Fiction: Theoretical Frameworks, Genres and Model Interpretations* 115-46.
406. Nünning, Ansgar, and Jan Rupp. "Media and Medialisation as Catalysts of Generic Change: Theoretical Frameworks, Analytical Concepts and a Se-

lective Overview of Varieties of Intermedial Narration in British Fiction." *The Cultural Dynamics of Generic Change in Contemporary Fiction: Theoretical Frameworks, Genres and Model Interpretations* 201-36.
407. Nünning, Ansgar. "Meta-Autobiographien: Gattungstypologische, narratologische und funktionsgeschichtliche Überlegungen zur Poetik und zum Wissen innovativer Autobiographien." *Autobiographie: Eine interdisziplinäre Gattung zwischen klassischer Tradition und (post-) moderner Variation* 27-81.
408. Nünning, Ansgar. *Metzler Lexikon Literatur- und Kulturtheorie: Ansätze – Personen – Grundbegriffe.* Stuttgart: Metzler, 2013. Print.
409. Nünning, Ansgar. "New Narratologies: Recent Developments and New Directions." *Germanisch-Romanische Monatsschrift* 63.1 (2013): 47-67. Print.
410. Nünning, Ansgar. "No Contextualization without Literary Theory and Concepts: Problems, Kinds and Criteria of Contextualizing Literary History." *(Re)Contextualizing Literary and Cultural History: The Representation of the Past in Literary and Material Culture.* Ed. Elisabeth Wåghäll Nivre, Beate Schirrmacher, and Claudia Egerer. Stockholm: Stockholm University, 2013. 13-47. Print.
411. Nünning, Ansgar, and Vera Nünning. "On the Narrativity of Rituals: Interfaces between Narratives and Rituals and their Potential for Ritual Studies." *Ritual and Narrative: Theoretical Explorations and Historical Case Studies* 51-75.
412. Nünning, Ansgar. "Renaissance und Neue Forschungsrichtungen der Narratologie: Ansätze, Grenzüberschreitungen und Impulse für die Literaturwissenschaften." *New Narratologies: Recent Developments and New Directions.* Ed. Ansgar Nünning. Spec. issue of *Germanisch-Romanische Monatsschrift* 63.1 (2013): 1-29. Print.
413. Nünning, Ansgar. "Wie Erzählungen Kulturen erzeugen: Prämissen, Konzepte und Perspektiven für eine kulturwissenschaftliche Narratologie." *Kultur – Wissen – Narration: Perspektiven transdisziplinärer Erzählforschung für die Kulturwissenschaften.* Ed. Alexandra Strohmaier. Bielefeld: Transcript, 2013. 15-53. Print.
414. Nünning, Ansgar. "Zwischen Gedächtnisbildung, Gedächtnisreflexion und Gedächtniskritik: Funktionen und Wert von Literatur." *Literatur als Gedächtnisbildung und Gedächtnisreflexion.* Ed. Thomas Eder. Linz: Stifter Haus, 2013. 9-25. Print.
415. Odabas, Janna. "Do Ghosts Grow Up? Ghostliness in Maxine Hong Kingston's The Woman Warrior and China Men." *On the Legacy of Maxine Hong Kingston: The Mulhouse Book.* Ed. Sämi Ludwig and Nicoleta Alexoae-Zagni. Berlin: LIT, 2013. 147-60. Print.
416. Odabas, Janna. "Ghostly Presences in *The Gangster We Are All Looking For* by Lê Thi Diem Thuy." *Migration and Exile: Charting New Literary and Artistic Territories.* Ed. Ada Savin. Newcastle upon Tyne: Cambridge Scholars, 2013. 103-12. Print.
417. Olson, Greta. *Criminals as Animals from Shakespeare to Lombroso.* Berlin: De Gruyter, 2013. Print. Law and Literature Series 8.

418. Olson, Greta. "Intersections of Gender and Legal Culture in Two Women Judge Shows: Judge Judy and Richterin Barbara Salesch." *Contemporary Gender Relations and Changes in Legal Culture*. Ed. Hanne Petersen, José M. Villaverde, and Ingrid Lund-Andersen. Copenhagen: DJØF, 2013. 29-58. Print.
419. Olson, Greta, and Ansgar Nünning. "Introduction: Approaches to Literature and Culture in the Post-Theory Era." *New Theories, Models and Methods in Literary and Cultural Studies* 1-18.
420. Olson, Greta. "Reading 9/11 Texts through the Lens of Critical Media Studies." *New Theories, Models and Methods in Literary and Cultural Studies: Theory into Practice* 161-85.
421. Olson, Greta. "Recovering from the Men We Loved to Hate: Barack Obama as a Representative of Post-Post September 11 White House Masculinity." *Beyond 9/11: Transdisciplinary Perspectives on Twenty-First Century U.S. American Culture* 93-119.
422. Ortlepp, Anke. "Air transport", "Los Angeles." *USA-Lexikon: Schlüsselbegriffe zu Politik, Wirtschaft, Gesellschaft, Kultur, Geschichte und zu den deutsch-amerikanischen Beziehunge*. n. pag. Web.
423. Ortlepp, Anke, and Berndt Ostendorf. "Design." *USA-Lexikon: Schlüsselbegriffe zu Politik, Wirtschaft, Gesellschaft, Kultur, Geschichte und zu den deutsch-amerikanischen Beziehunge*. n. pag. Web.
424. Ostendorf, Berndt. "Et in Acadia ego: Some Versions of the Pastoral in the Cajun Renaissance since 1964." *Cultural Circulation: Dialogues between Canada and the American South* 37-50.
425. Ostendorf, Berndt."Leitkultur oder Multikulturalismus: Nationale Identität in den USA und Frankreich im Vergleich." *Reassessing History from Two Continents*. Ed. Martin Eichtinger, Stefan Karner, Mark Kramer, and Peter Ruggenthaler. Innsbruck: Innsbruck UP, 2013. 343-62. Print. Festschrift Günter Bischof.
426. Ostendorf, Berndt. "Multiculturalism," "Minstrelsy/Minstrel Show," "Blues," "Folksong," "Popular Culture," and "Jazz." *USA-Lexikon: Schlüsselbegriffe zu Politik, Wirtschaft, Gesellschaft, Kultur, Geschichte und zu den deutsch-amerikanischen Beziehunge*. n. pag. Web.
427. Ostendorf, Berndt. *New Orleans, Creolization and all that Jazz*. Innsbruck: Studienverlag, 2013. Print.
428. Palladini, Giulia, and Nicholas Ridout. "Berceuses et Révolution." Trans. David Bernagout. *La Vie Manifeste* 6 Jan. 2013: n. pag. Web.
429. Parker, Joshua. "Absence as Presence, Presence as Absence: Museological Storytelling in Berlin." *Narrative Works* 3.1 (2013): n. pag. Web.
430. Parker, Joshua. "Emerging Vectors of Narratology: Towards Consolidation or Diversification? A Response." *Enthymema* 9 (2013): 154-56. Print.
431. Parker, Joshua. "'This is our Armageddon': Berlin in Postwar American Fiction." *Amaltea: Journal of Myth Criticism* 5 (2013): n. pag. Web.
432. Paul, Heike. "The German Reception of Black Writing and Black Authorship in the 18th and 19th Century." *Germany and the Black Diaspora, 1450-1914* 115-33.

433. Paul, Heike, and Christoph Ernst. Introduction. *Präsenz und implizites Wissen: Zur Interdependenz zweier Schlüsselbegriffe der Kultur- und Sozialwissenschaften* 9-32.
434. Pfeiler, Martina. "Hunting Moby Dick: Melville in the Global Context of the American Studies Classroom." *Leviathan: A Journal of Melville Studies* 15.3 (2013): 81-89. Print.
435. Pfeiler, Martina. "Teaching and Learning from Slam Poetry." *Modern American Poetry: Points of Access* 195-210.
436. Poole, Ralph. "Das Dilemma des Schweigens oder: Zum epistemologischen Enigma von Melvilles 'Bartleby.'" *Tatort Kultur: Atelier Gespräche II*. Ed. Sabine Coelsch-Foisner. Salzburg: Anton Pustet, 2013. 124-33. Print.
437. Poole, Ralph. "'Everybody Loves a Muscle Boi': Homos, Heroes, and Foes in Post-9/11 Spoofs of the 300 Spartans." *Ancient Worlds in Film and Television: Gender and Politics*. Ed. Almut-Barbara Renger and Jon Solomon. Leiden: Brill, 2013. 95-122. Print.
438. Poole, Ralph. "'It's Called Hazing, Asshole': Locker-Room Dramas of Sexual Violence against Males." *Spell: Swiss Papers in English Language and Literature* 29 (2013): 177-98. Print.
439. Poole, Ralph. "(Kein) Cover in der Literatur? Literarische Cover-Strategien der Postmoderne." *Coverstrategien in der Popularmusik nach 1960* 103-28.
440. Priewe, Marc. "Staging Final Illnesses: Religion and Medicine in Experience Mayhew's Indian Converts (1727)." *Communicating Disease: Cultural Representations of American Medicine* 3-20.
441. Priewe, Marc. "'Too Many My Diseases to Cite': Anne Bradstreet's Illness Poetry." *The Writing Cure: Literature and Medicine in Context* 115-34. Print.
442. Prutsch, Ursula. "Aufbrüche und Grenzüberschreitungen: Brasilien im 21. Jahrhundert." *Literatur + Kritik*. Ed. Karl-Markus Gau. Salzburg: Müller, 2013. 71-78. Print.
443. Prutsch, Ursula, and Enrique Rodrigues-Moura. *Brasilien: Eine Kulturgeschichte*. Bielefeld: Transcript, 2013. Print.
444. Prutsch, Ursula. "Rückzug und Rampenlicht – Leopold von Andrian und Paul Frischauer im brasilianischen Exil." *Zwischenwelt: Literatur/Widerstand/Exil* 30.3-4 (2013): 42-45. Print.
445. Puff, Simone. "Colors in Conflict: Light vs. Dark Reloaded; or, the Commodification of (Black) Beauty." *Cultures in Conflict / Conflicting Cultures* 159-76.
446. Puff, Simone. "Modern Acts of Passing: How Stereotypes Make African American Women Yearn for 'Lightness' in the Twenty-First Century." *Theories and Practice: Proceedings of the Fourth International Conference on English and American Studies*. Ed. Roman Trušník, Katarína Nemčoková, and Gregory Jason Bell. Zlín: Tomas Bata UP, 2013. 187-98. Print.
447. Quendler, Christian. "A Series of Dated Traces: Diaries and Film." *Biography: An Interdisciplinary Quarterly* 36.2 (2013): 339-58. Print.
448. Raab, Josef. "Bearing Witness to Mexican America: A Conversation with Ana Castillo." *Interculturalism in North America: Canada, the United States, Mexico, and Beyond* 239-50.

449. Raussert, Wilfried. "Border, Heterotopia, and Translocal Communities: Courtney Hunt's Frozen River." *Cine y Frontera, Film and Border*. Ed. Juan Carlos Vargas, et al. Guadalajara, MX: UdeG, DF Unam, 2013. 45-61. Print.
450. Raussert, Wilfried, and Heinrich Schäfer. "Religion in the Americas." *fiar* 6.1 (2013): n. pag. Web.
451. Raussert, Wilfried, and Claudius Clairborne. *Transcultural Mobility: A Celebration of African American Cultural Production*. Houston, TX: CB, 2013. Print.
452. Ravizza, Eleonora. "'We don't want life to look difficult, do we?' Representations of the Fifties and Self-Reflexive Nostalgia in *Mad Men*." *COPAS: Current Objectives of American Studies* 14.1 (2013): 1-14. Print.
453. Rechtsteiner, Stefanie. *Das Konzept des Continued Growth im Leben und Werk von Margaret Fuller*. Frankfurt/M: Lang, 2013. Print. Mainzer Studien zur Amerikanistik 63.
454. Redling, Erik. "Spectacular Drama: The Black Crook and American Show Business in the 19th Century." *Melodrama: Zwischen Populärkultur und "Moralisch-Okkultem"?* Ed. Marion Schmaus. Heidelberg: Winter, 2013. 141-55. Print.
455. Redling, Erik. "'When I Tree Myself': Paratextual Elements in the Canadian-Asian Fred Wah's Poetic Life Writings." *Ecology and Life Writing* 241-56.
456. Ridvan, Askin. "Fantastic Aesthetics: A Report on the International Conference 'Aesthetics in the 21st Century.'" *Dichtung Digital: Journal für Kunst und Kultur digitaler Medien* (2013): n. pag. Web.
457. Rippl, Gabriele. Introduction. *Handbuch Kanon und Wertung*: *Theorien, Instanzen, Geschichte* 1-5.
458. Rippl, Gabriele, Philipp Schweighauser, and Therese Steffen. "Introduction: Live Writing in an Age of Trauma." *Haunted Narratives: Life Writing in an Age of Trauma* 3-18.
459. Rippl, Gabriele. Introduction. *Towards a New Monumentalism?* Spec. issue of *Anglia: Zeitschrift für Englische Philologie* 131.2 + 3 (2013): 207-17. Print.
460. Rippl, Gabriele. "John Updikes Seek My Face (2002) zwischen kunstgeschichtlicher Anekdote und fiktionaler (Meta-)Biographie." *Anekdote – Biographie – Nakon: Zur Geschichtsschreibung der schönen Künste*. Köln: Böhlau, 2013. 293-314. Print.
461. Rippl, Gabriele. "'Why hath this Lady writ Her own Life' – Frühneuzeitliche Lebensbeschreibungen englischer Frauen zwischen klassischer (männlicher) lettere e virtù-Tradition und neuen Formen autobiographischen Schreibens." *Autobiographie: Eine interdisziplinäre Gattung zwischen klassischer Tradition & (post-)moderner Variation* 151-74.
462. Rippl, Gabriele, and Lukas Etter. "'Don't laugh – this ain't the funny pages': Comics und Bildende Kunst (Alain Séchas, Raymond Pettibon)." *Interpiktorialität: Theorie und Geschichte der Bild-Bild-Bezüge* 261-79.
463. Rippl, Gabriele, and Lukas Etter. "Intermediality, Transmediality, and Graphic Narrative." *From Comic Strips to Graphic Novels: Contributions to the Theory and History of Graphic Narrative* 191-217.

464. Rippl, Gabriele, and Julia Straub. "Zentrum und Peripherie: Kanon und Macht (Gender, Race, Postcolonialism)." *Handbuch Kanon und Wertung* 110-18.
465. Rohr, Susanne. "On Being in Love with the World: Getrude Stein's *Tender Buttons*." *Anglistik und Englischunterricht* 79 (2013): 59-77. Print.
466. Rosenthal, Caroline. "Culinary Roots/Routes: Local and Global Foodways in North American Writing." *Cultural Circulation: Canadian Writers and Authors from the American South: A Dialogue* 351-63.
467. Rosenthal, Caroline. "Fortschritt versus Nachhaltigkeit: Kulturelle Essordnungen in Rudy Wiebes *A Discovery of Strangers*." *Literaturwissenschaftliches Jahrbuch* 54 (2013): 311-22. Print.
468. Rosenthal, Caroline. "Sean Penn's *Into the Wild*." *Teaching Contemporary Literature and Culture 3* 69-386.
469. Roth, Julia. "'A legible face' auf Facebook?: Politiken von Gender und De/ Kolonialität im Netz." *Kollektivität nach der Subjektkritik: Geschlechtertheoretische Positionen*. Ed. Gabriele Jähnert, Karin Aleksander, and Marianne Kriszio. Bielefeld: Transcript, 2013: 335–55. Print. Gender Codes.
470. Roth, Julia. "Entangled Inequalities as Intersectionalities: Towards an Epistemic Sensibilization." *desiguALdades.net: Research Network on Interdependent Inequalities in Latin America* (2013): 1-41. Web. desiguALdades. net Working Paper Series 43.
471. Saal, Ilka. "Suzan-Lori Parks." *Methuen Drama Guide to Contemporary American Playwrights* 243-60.
472. Säckel, Sarah. "What Exactly Is It about Wooster's Voice? A Response to Lawrence Dugan." *Connotations* 22.2 (2013): 279-97. Print.
473. Sarkowsky, Katja."'Is this my own?' – Zugehörigkeit, Citizenship und Literatur." *Theorien der Literatur VI. Grundlagen und Perspektiven*. Ed. Günter Butzer and Hubert Zapf. Tübingen: Francke, 2013. 217-31. Print.
474. Sarkowsky, Katja. "Kanada." *Handbuch Kanon und Wertung: Theorien, Instanzen, Geschichte* 301-04.
475. Sarkowsky, Katja. "Transcultural Autobiography and the Staging of (Mis) Recognition in Edward Said's 'Out of Place' and Gerald Vizenor's 'Interior Landscapes: Autobiographical Myths and Metaphors.'" *Tocqueville's Legacy: Towards a Cultural History of Recognition in American Studies* 627-42.
476. Sarkowsky, Katja. "Urbane Modernen: New Yorks Immigrantenviertel in Jacob Riis' How the Other Half Lives (1890) und Anzia Yezierskas Salome of the Tenements (1923)" *Stadt der Moderne*. Ed. Christoph Fassbender and Cecile Sandten. Trier: WVT, 2013. 93-106. Print.
477. Sattler, Julia, and Walter Grünzweig. *Abschiedskuss für Gott—Gedichte*. Bonn: Weidle, 2013. Print.
478. Sattler, Julia. "I am she who will be free—June Jordan's transnational feminist poetics." *Journal of American Studies of Turkey* 38 (2013): 65-82. Print.
479. Schabio, Saskia. "'... At the Edge of Writing and Speech': Shifting Genre, Relocating the Aesthetic." *Locating Postcolonial Narrative Genres* 44-57.
480. Schäfer, Heike. "The Parodic Play with Realist Aesthetics and Authenticity Claims in Cheryl Dunye's Black Queer Mockumentary The Watermelon

Woman." *Realisms in Contemporary Culture: Theories, Politics, and Medial Configurations* 195-213.
481. Schäfer, Stefanie. "Paul Haggis: *Crash.*" *Teaching Contemporary Literature and Culture 3* 179-98.
482. Schäfer, Stefanie. "'Recognition Is a Form of Agreement:' The Workings of Self-Narration in *The Catcher in the Rye* and *Invisible Man*." *Tocqueville's Legacy: Towards a Cultural History of Recognition in American Studies* 603-26.
483. Schemien, Alexia. "Hybrid Spiritualites in Ana Castillo's *The Guardians*." *Forum for Inter-American Research* 6.1 (2013): n. pag. Web.
484. Scherr, Alexander. "Discursive Hybrids between Literature and Science: Self-Reflexivity as a Catalyst for Generic Change in Jeffrey Eugenides' *The Marriage Plot*." *The Cultural Dynamics of Generic Change in Contemporary Fiction: Theoretical Frameworks, Genres and Model Interpretations* 285-300.
485. Scherr, Nadine. *Die Übersetzung amerikanischerTexte in deutschen Printmedien: Eine Analyse der Textsorten "Nachricht" und "Reportage" vor dem Hintergrund der deutsch-amerikanischen Beziehungen*. Frankfurt/M: Lang, 2013. Print. Mainzer Studien zur Amerikanistik 62.
486. Schlarb, Damien. "Publications in American Studies from German-Speaking Countries, 2012." *Amerikastudien / American Studies* 58.2 (2013): 325-82. Print.
487. Schleusener, Simon. "The Cinema of Insanity: Psychiatry, Popular Culture, and the Flexibilization of Normality." *Revisiting the Sixties: Interdisciplinary Perspectives on America's Longest Decade* 237-60.
488. Schloss, Dietmar. "Shifting Positions: The Literary Intellectual in Charles Brockden Brown's 'Walstein's School of History' and *Arthur Mervyn*." *Intellectual Authority and Literary Culture in the US, 1790-1900* 58-81.
489. Schmidt, Jochen. "Gut planen und organisieren mit minimalem Zeitaufwand." *Klexer 11*. Berlin: Cornelsen, 2013. 1-6. Print.
490. Schmidt, Jochen. "Neill Blomkamp: *District 9.*" *Teaching Contemporary Literature and Culture 3* 241-58.
491. Schmidt, Jochen. *Rituale für den Schulalltag: Das Komplettpaket*. Buxtehude: Persen, 2013. Print.
492. Schmidt, Kerstin. "Donald Margulies." *The Methuen Drama Guide to Contemporary American Playwrights* 168-186.
493. Schmieder, Katja. "'Do Not Cross' – TV Women Doctors Trespassing on Male Territory."*Communicating Disease: Cultural Representations of American Medicine* 175-98.
494. Schneck, Peter. "Finding Words for (Not) Losing One's Mind: Alice James, Charlotte Perkins Gillman, and the Sense of Self in Narratives of Mental Illness." *Cultural Representations of American Medicine* 309-43.
495. Schneck, Peter, and Alexander Bergs. "Kognitive Poetik." *Handbuch Kognitionswissenschaften*. Ed. Achim Stephan and Sven Walter. Stuttgart: Metzler, 2013. 518-22. Print.
496. Schneider, Edgar. "Regional profile: North America." *The Mouton World Atlas of Variation in English*. Ed. Bernd Kortmann and Kerstin Lunkenheimer. Berlin: de Gruyter, 2013. 734-62. Print.

497. Scholz, Anne-Marie. *From Fidelity to History: Film Adaptations as Cultural Events in the Twentieth Century.* New York: Berghahn, 2013. Print. Transatlantic Perspectives 3.
498. Schubert, Stefan. "'Lose Yourself': Narrative Instability and Unstable Identities in Black Swan." *COPAS: Current Objectives of American Studies* 14.1 (2013): 1-17. Print.
499. Schultz, Dieter. "Nature, Knowledge, and the Method of Thoreau's Excursions." *Thoreauvian Modernities: Transatlantic Conversations on an American Icon* 173-86.
500. Schweighauser, Philipp. "Sympathy Control: Sentimental Politics and Early European Aesthetics." *Anglia* 131:1 (2013): 35-51. Print.
501. Schweighauser, Philipp. "Trauma and Utopia: Benjamin, Adorno, and Elie Wiesel's Night." *Haunted Narratives: Life Writing in an Age of Trauma* 45-81.
502. Sedlmeier, Florian. "Against Totality: Reading for Intermedial Literary Constellations." *Journal of Literary Theory* 7.1-2 (2013): 64-85. Print.
503. Sedlmeier, Florian. "The Cool Touch of Things: Libertarian Economics, Complex Simplicity, and the Emergence of the Tactile Erotic." *Is It 'Cause It's Cool? Affective Encounters with American Culture* 273-93.
504. Sedlmeier, Florian. "Cover und Transparenz: Die US-Fernsehserie *Glee*." *Coverstrategien in the Popularmusik nach 1960* 229-43.
505. Sedlmeier, Florian. "Problems of Historicizing and Practices of Reading: Ralph Ellison's Three Days before the Shooting...." *Revisiting the Sixties: Interdisciplinary Perspectives on America's Longest Decade* 217-35.
506. Seidl, Martin. "Cultural Narratology and Historical Texts: Providential Narrative in Cotton Mather's Magnalia Christi Americana." *New Approaches to Narrative: Cognition-Culture-History* 187-200.
507. Sielke, Sabine, Christian Klöckner, and Simone Knewitz. Introduction. *Beyond 9/11: Transdisciplinary Perspectives on Twenty-First Century U.S. American Culture* 13-25.
508. Sielke, Sabine. "'Joy in Repetition': Popular Culture as Process." *Detective Fiction and Popular Visual Culture*. Ed. Cecile Sandten, Gunter Süß, and Melanie Graichen. Trier: WVT, 2013. 215-29. Print.
509. Sielke, Sabine. "'Joy in Repetition': The Significance of Seriality for Memory and (Re-)Mediation." *The Memory Effect: The Remediation of Memory in Literature and Film*. Ed. Russell Kilbourn and Eleanor Ty. Waterloo: Laurier, 2013. 37-50. Print.
510. Sielke, Sabine. "Natural Sciences." *Emily Dickinson in Context*. Ed. Eliza Richards. Cambridge: Cambridge UP, 2013. 236-45. Print.
511. Sielke, Sabine. "New York, New Hollywood, Trauma: Martin Scorsese's Taxi Driver, 1976-2011." *Trauma und Film: Translationen und Inszenierungen*. Ed. Julia Barbara Köhne. Bielefeld: Transcript, 2013. 102-25. Print.
512. Sielke, Sabine. "To 'Dwell in Possibility': On the Challenges and Rewards of Teaching and Studying Emily Dickinson." *Modern American Poetry: Points of Access* 37-57.

513. Sielke, Sabine. "Why '9/11 is [not] unique,' or: Troping Trauma." *Beyond 9/11: Transdisciplinary Perspectives on Twenty-First Century U.S. American Culture* 263-87.
514. Sobral, Ana. "Performing Cosmopolitanism: Gogol Bordello and the Global Underdogs." *Music and (Be) Longing: Articulations of the Self and the Other in the Musical Realm* 28-47.
515. Sommerfeld, Stephanie. "From the Romantic to the Textual Sublime: Poesque Sublimities, Romantic Irony, and Deconstruction." *Deciphering Poe*. Ed. Alexandra Urakova. Bethlehem, PA: Lehigh UP, 2013. 75-85. Print.
516. Spahr, Clemens and Philipp Löffler. "Introduction: Conceptions of Collectivity in Contemporary American Literature." *Conceptions of Collectivity in Contemporary American Literature* 161-76.
517. Spahr, Clemens. "Erzählwelten: Die gesellschaftliche Konstruktion von Fiktionalität in Mark Millars *Kick Ass* und M. Night Shyamalans *Unbreakable*." *Medien, Erzählen, Gesellschaft*. Ed. Karl N. Renner, Dagmar Hoff, and Matthias Krings. Berlin: De Gruyter, 2013. 139-62. Print.
518. Starre, Alexander. "Normative Kanontheorien: Kontextbezogene Modelle"; "Genreliteraturen: Das Beispiel Comics." *Handbuch Kanon und Wertung: Theorien, Instanzen, Geschichte* 58-66; 345-50.
519. Starre, Alexander, and Andreas Jahn-Sudmann. "Die Experimente des 'Quality TV' - Innovation und Metamedialität in neueren amerikanischen Serien." *Transnationale Serienkultur: Theorie, Ästhetik, Narration und Rezeption neuerer Fernsehserien*. Ed. Susanne Eichner, Lothar Mikos, and Rainer Winter. Wiesbaden: Springer, 2013. 103-19. Print.
520. Starre, Alexander. "Timothy Donnelly, *The Cloud Corporation*"; "Karen Russell, *Swamplandia!*" *Kindlers Literatur Lexikon*. 3rd ed. (Online Supplement). n. pag.
521. Steffen, Therese. "Man wird nicht als Frau geboren – aber auch nicht als Mann." *Mind the Gap: Baustelle Gender*. Spec. issue of *Wespennest: Zeitschrift für brauchbare Texte und Bilder* 165 (2013). 40-43. Print.
522. Stein, Daniel. "Der Alligator und seine kulturpoetischen Funktionen in der Geschichte der USA." *Archetypen, Artefakte: Komparatistische Beiträge zur kulturellen und literarischen Repräsentation von Tieren* 91-115.
523. Stein, Daniel, and Jan-Noël Thon. Introduction. *From Comic Strips to Graphic Novels: Contributions to the Theory and History of Graphic Narrative* 1-23.
524. Stein, Daniel. "Of Transcreations and Transpacific Adaptations: Investigating Manga Versions of Spider-Man." *Transnational Perspectives on Graphic Narratives: Comics at the Crossroads* 145-61.
525. Stein, Daniel. "Superhero Comics and the Authorizing Functions of the Comic Book Paratext." *From Comic Strips to Graphic Novels: Contributions to the Theory and History of Graphic Narrative* 155-89.
526. Stein, Daniel. "Unzuverlässiges Erzählen in Comicserien." *Gesellschaft für Comicforschung*. 28 Mar. 2013. n. pag. Web.
527. Stompor, Tomasz. "Interzone Passages." *Fabrikzeitung* 296 (2013). Print.

528. Stompor, Tomasz. "Stimmen der Mimeo-Revolution: Carl Weissner und die Underground Presse — Tomasz Stompor im Interview mit Jan Herman und Jürgen Ploog, Februar 2013." *Fabrikzeitung* 289 (2013): n. pag. Print.
529. Straub, Julia. "Englischsprachiges Rezensionswesen: Geschichte und Gegenwart." *Handbuch Kanon und Wertung: Theorien, Instanzen, Geschichte* 153-59.
530. Straub, Julia. "Richard Wollheim's *Germs*: Life-Writing as Therapy, Despite Theory." *Haunted Narratives: Life Writing in an Age of Trauma* 85-100.
531. Straub, Julia. "The Stigma of the Autobiographical: Response to Aija Sakova's 'Fighting Fear with Writing': Christa Wolf's *Kindheitsmuster* and Ene Mihkelson's *The Sleep of Ahasuerus*." *Haunted Narratives: Life Writing in an Age of Trauma* 225-29.
532. Struth, Christiane. "In-Between Proust and Neuroscience: Kandel's In Search of Memory." *L'ethos, mémoire autobiographique de l'homme de science*. Ed. Beatrice Barbalato. Louvain-la-Neuve: Louvain UP, 2013. 47-57. Print.
533. Sulimma, Maria. *Die anderen Ministerpräsidenten – Geschlecht in der printmedialen Berichterstattung über Berufspolitik*. Berlin: LIT, 2013. Print.
534. Sulimma, Maria."Ein Aufschrei ohne Konsequenzen? " *Göttinger Institut für Demokratieforschung. Crosspost: Cicero Online – Magazine für politische Kultur* 3.8 (2013). Web.
535. Sulimma, Maria. "The Fanboy next Door: Whedon and his Appeal to self-professed Geeks." *In Media Res. Media Commons*. n. pag. Web.
536. Tan, Kathy-Ann. "'Creating Dangerously': Writing, Exile and Diaspora in Edwidge Danticat's and Dany Laferrière's Haitian Memoirs." *American Lives* 249-61.
537. Tan, Kathy-Ann. "Curio (us) Translocations: Site-specific Interventions in Banglatown, London." *Postcolonial Translocations: Cultural Representation and Critical Spatial Thinking* 385-405.
538. Tan, Kathy-Ann. "London Calling: The Poetics of Disruption and Social Refusal in the Works of Sean Bonney and Stephen Mooney (London under Construction)." *Contemporary Political Poetry in Britain and Ireland*. Ed. Uwe Klawitter and Claus-Ulrich Viol. Heidelberg: Winter, 2013. 229-54. Print.
539. Thiemann, Anna, Annette Kern-Stähler, and Bettina Schöne-Seifert. *Ethik in der Medizin: Literarische Texte für den neuen Querschnittsbereich GTE – Ein Studienbuch*. Münster: Mentis, 2013. Print.
540. Thiemann, Anna. "Reversing the Commodification of Life? Rebecca Skloot's Narrative Science Writing." *The Writing Cure: Literature and Medicine in Context*. 191-210.
541. Thiemann, Anna. "Shaking Patterns of Diagnosis: Siri Hustvedt and Charlotte Perkins Gilman." *Communicating Disease: Cultural Representations of American Medicine* 365-86.
542. Tischleder, Bärbel. "iDob 5.3: Wiring Wetware, or Dreaming the Medium that Holds All the Answers." *Das Medium meiner Träume: Hartmut Wink-*

ler zum 60. Geburtstag. Ed. Ralf Adelmann and Ulrike Bergermann. Berlin: Verbrecher, 2013. 271-82. Print.
543. Tischleder, Bärbel. *The Literary Life of Things: Case Studies in American Fiction*. Frankfurt/M: Campus, 2014. Print.
544. Truchlar, Leo. *Lichtmusik: Zur Formensprache zeitgenössischer Kunst*. Wien: LIT, 2013. Print.
545. Twelbeck, Kirsten. "How far could They Go? Imprisoned Nurses, Unsexed Angels, and the Transformation of True Womanhood in Civil War America." *Communicating Disease: Cultural Representations of American Medicine* 145-73.
546. Twelbeck, Kirsten. "Reconstructing Race Relations: Esther Hill Hawks' Diary and her Life Among the Freedmen." *American Lives* 173-88.
547. Usbeck, Frank. "Clash of Cultures? 'Noble Savages' in Germany and America." *Tecumseh, Keokuk, Black Hawk. Portrayals of Native Americans in Times of Treaties and Removal*. Ed. Iris Edenheiser and Astrid Nielsen. Stuttgart: Arnoldsche, 2013. 177-84. Print.
548. Usbeck, Frank. "Representing the Indian, Imagining the Volksgemeinschaft. Indianthusiasm and Nazi Propaganda in German Print Media." *Ethnoscripts* 15.1 (2013): 46-61. Print.
549. Veauthier, Ines. "Boys Will Be Boys? Subverting Traditional Power Structures in Asian-American Prose." *Linguistics and Literature Studies* 1.2 (2013): 83-87. Print.
550. Veauthier, Ines. "Invisible, inaudible, influential? Reclaiming Latino life." *Camino Real: Estudios de las Hispanidades Norteamericanas. Alcalá de Henares: Instituto Franklin – UAH* 5.8 (2013): 131-46. Print.
551. Wallinger, Hanna. "Sutton E. Griggs against Thomas Dixon's 'Vile Misrepresentations': *The Hindered Hand* and *The Leopard's Spots*." *Jim Crow, Literature, and the Legacy of Sutton E. Griggs*. Ed. Tess Chakkalakal and Kenneth W. Warren. Athens, GA: U of Georgia P, 2013. 167-85. Print.
552. Werkmeister, Till. *Domestic Nation: Der sentimentale Diskurs US-amerikanischer Romane zum elften September 2001*. Münster: LIT, 2013. Print.
553. Zacharasiewicz, Waldemar. "Canadians as Passionate Pilgrims to the Temples of European Music and Art." *Europe-Canada: Transcultural Perspectives, Perspectives transculturelles* 37- 52.
554. Zacharasiewicz, Waldemar, and Christoph Irmscher. Introduction. *Cultural Circulation: Dialogues between Canada and the American South* 11- 19.
555. Zacharasiewicz, Waldemar. "Transcending Southern Borders: Writing Home from Europe." *Unsteadily Marching On. The U.S. South in Motion*. Ed. Constante Gonzaléz Groba. València, SP: València UP, 2013, 225-34. Print.
556. Zehelein, Eva-Sabine. "'Been to Barbados' – Rum(bullion), Race, the Gaspée, and the American Revolution." *Drink in the 18th and 19th Centuries: Consumers, Cross-Currents, Conviviality*. Ed. Susanne Schmid, and Barbara Schmidt-Haberkamp. Bloomsbury, UK: Pickering and Chatto, 2013. 141-50; 216-19. Print.
557. Zehelein, Eva-Sabine. "Octavia Butlers Kindred: *neo slave narrative* als *literature of memory*." *Autobiographie: Eine interdisziplinäre Gattung zwischen klassischer Tradition und (post-)moderner Variation* 411-32.

558. Weigel, Anna. "The Rise of the New Genre 'Fictions of the Internet:' Hybridized and Medialized Reading and Writing Practices in Jeffrey Deaver's *Roadside Crosses.*" *The Cultural Dynamics of Generic Change in Contemporary Fiction: Theoretical Frameworks, Genres and Model Interpretations* 365-80.

3. History

559. Berg, Manfred. "Anatomy of a Lynching after Thirty Years. Foreword to the Updated Edition." *Anatomy of a Lynching.* Ed. James R. McGovern. Baton Rouge, LA: Louisiana State UP, 2013. IX-XXI. Print.
560. Berg, Manfred. *Geschichte der USA.* München: Oldenbourg, 2013. Print. Oldenbourg Grundriss der Geschichte 42.
561. Berg, Manfred, and Cornelius A. Van Minnen. "The U.S. South and Europe: An Introduction." *The U.S. South and Europe: Transatlantic Relations in the Nineteenth and Twentieth Centuries. New Directions in Southern History* 1-14.
562. Berg, Manfred, and Wilfried Mausbach. "Wie der Prinz in seinem Schloss?" *Frankfurter Allgemeine Zeitung* 9 Sep. 2013: 7. Print.
563. Berghoff, Hartmut. "From the Watergate Scandal to the Compliance Revolution. The Fight against Corporate Corruption in the United States and Germany, 1972-2012." *Bulletin of the German Historical Institute* 53 (2013): 7-30. Print.
564. Berghoff, Hartmut, and Thomas Kühne. *Globalizing Beauty: Consumerism and Body Aesthetics in the Twentieth Century.* New York: Palgrave, 2013. Print.
565. Berghoff, Hartmut, Uffa Jensen, Christina Lubinski, and Bernd Weisbrod. *History by Generations: Generational Dynamics in Modern History.* Göttingen: Wallstein, 2013. Print.
566. Berghoff, Hartmut, and Uwe Spiekermann. "Immigrant Entrepreneurship: German-American Business Biographies, 1720 to the Present: Zielsetzungen, Organisation und Herausforderungen Eines Forschungsprojektes Des Deutschen Historischen Instituts Washington." *Jahrbuch der historischen Forschung* (2012): 53-61. Print.
567. Berghoff, Hartmut, and Jens Beckert. "Risk and Uncertainty in Financial Markets." *Socio-Economic Review* 11.3 (2013): 497-99. Print.
568. Berghoff, Hartmut, and Andreas Fahrmeir. "Unternehmer und Migration. Einleitung." *Zeitschrift für Unternehmensgeschichte/Journal of Business History* 58.2 (2013): 141-48. Print.
569. Brammer, Frauke. "Legs d'automne. Le terrorisme des années 1970 au Canada et en Allemagne de l'Ouest." *Violences politiques. Europe et Amériques, 1960-1979.* Ed. Jean-Philippe Warren, Ivan Carel, and Robert Comeau. Montréal: Lux Éditeur, 2013. 193-220. Print.
570. Bungert, Heike. "Native Americans." *USA-Lexikon: Schlüsselbegriffe zu Politik, Wirtschaft, Gesellschaft, Kultur, Geschichte und zu den deutsch-amerikanischen Beziehungen* 763-74.

571. Clark, Thomas. "The Antebellum South and New Orleans in Tocqueville and Three German Travel Accounts." *The U. S. South and Europe: Transatlantic Relations in the Nineteenth and Twentieth Centuries. New Directions in Southern History* 33-50.
572. Dechert, André. "Von der zeitgenössischen Fiktion zur Dokumentation historischer Realität? Gender in US-amerikanischen Family Sitcoms der 1950er und frühen 1960er Jahre." *Geschlecht und Geschichte in populären Medien*. Ed. Elisabeth Cheauré, Sylvia Paletschek, and Nina Reusch. Bielefeld: Transcript, 2013. 209-31. Print.
573. Decker, Christof. "20th Century Fox. Die Eröffnungsfanfare von Alfred Newman." *Sound des Jahrhunderts. Geräusche, Töne, Stimmen 1889 bis heute*. Gerhard Paul and Ralph Schock. Bonn: BpB, 2013. 382-85. Print.
574. Decker, Christof. "Film." *USA-Lexikon: Schlüsselbegriffe zu Politik, Wirtschaft, Gesellschaft, Kultur, Geschichte und zu den deutsch-amerikanischen Beziehungen* 400-07.
575. Decker, Robert Júlio. "Immigration Restriction, Whiteness and Subjectivity in the United States, 1894-1924." *Colonialism and Beyond – Race and Migration from a Postcolonial Perspective* 33-52.
576. Decker, Robert Júlio. "The Visibility of Whiteness and Immigration Restriction in the United States, 1880-1930." *Critical Race and Whiteness Studies eJournal* 9.1 (2013): n. pag. Web.
577. Depkat, Volker. "Das Alte Reich in den Verfassungsdebatten des kolonialen Britisch Nordamerika und den USA, 1750-1788." *DTIEV-Online* 1 (2013): n. pag. Web.
578. Depkat, Volker. "Counterculture"; "Imperialism" ; "New Deal" ; "Photography"; "Reconstruction"; "Wilsonianism." *USA-Lexikon: Schlüsselbegriffe zu Politik, Wirtschaft, Gesellschaft, Kultur, Geschichte und zu den deutsch-amerikanischen Beziehungen* 287-89; 546-48; 793-95; 856-59; 930-32; 1135-36.
579. Depkat, Volker. "Freiheitsstreben und Ordnungsverlangen: Die Paradoxien der Amerikanischen Aufklärung im Lichte visueller Narrative." *Wo bleibt die Aufklärung? Aufklärerische Diskurse in der Postmoderne. Festschrift für Thomas Stamm-Kuhlmann*. Ed. Luise Güth, et al. Stuttgart: Steiner, 2013. 17-35. Print.
580. Depkat, Volker, and Jürgen Martschukat. "'Heaven Is under Our Feet.' Contextualizing Faith, Religion, and Politics in the Post-9/11 Era." *Religion and Politics in Europe and the United States: Transnational Historical Approaches* 253-65.
581. Depkat, Volker, and Jürgen Martschukat. "Introduction: Religion and Politics in Europe and the United States." *Religion and Politics in Europe and the United States: Transnational Historical Approaches* 1-11.
582. Depkat, Volker. "Karl Mays Abenteuerwelten." *"Klassiker" der internationalen Jugendliteratur: Kulturelle und epochenspezifische Diskurse aus Sicht der Fachdisziplinen*. Vol. II. Ed. Anita Schilcher and Claudia Maria Pecher. Baltmannsweiler: Schneider, 2013. 241-62. Print.

583. Depkat, Volker. "Verräter und Patriot: Die Biographik zu Benedict Arnold in den Selbstverständigungsdebatten der USA seit 1945." *Non Fiktion: Arsenal der anderen Gattungen* 8.1 (2013): 69-88. Print.
584. Diedrich, Maria I. "From American Slaves to Hessian Subjects: Silenced Black Narratives of the American Revolution." *Germany and the Black Diaspora: Points of Contact, 1250-1914* 92-111.
585. Engel, Elisabeth, and Eva Bischoff. Introduction. *Colonialism and Beyond: Race and Migration from a Postcolonial Perspective* 3–19.
586. Etges, Andreas. "Western Europe." *The Oxford Handbook of the Cold War* 158-73.
587. Etges, Andreas, and Jula Danylow. "A Hot Debate over the Cold War: The Plan for a Cold War Center at Checkpoint Charlie, Berlin." *Museums in a Global Context: National Identity, International Understanding.* Ed. Jennifer Dickey, Samir El Zhar, and Catherine M. Lewis. Washington, DC: AAM P, 2013. Print.
588. Fischer, Robert. "Historische Zeitforschung und globale Geschichtsschreibung – Krisen, Ordnungen, (Un)Gleichzeitigkeiten." *H-Soz-u-Kult* (2012): n. pag. Web.
589. Fischer, Robert. "Mobility and Morality at the Border – A Lefebvrian Spatio-Temporal Analysis in Early Twentieth-Century Ciudad Juárez and El Paso." *Space/Time Practices.* Spec. issue of *Historical Social Research* 38:3 (2013): 176-96. Print.
590. Gassert, Philipp. "'1968' als Wahrnehmungsrevolution: Eine kluge These, die umfassender untersucht werden müsste. *"1968" – Eine Wahrnehmungsrevolution? Horizont-Verschiebungen des Politischen in den 1960er und 1970 Jahren* 123-36.
591. Gassert, Philipp. "Amerika vor Gericht: Das Russell Tribunal 1966/67, die Nürnberger Prinzipien und die Politik des „Blaming and Shaming." *Toward A New Moral Order? Menschenrechspolitik und Völkerrecht seit 1945.* Ed. Norbert Frei and Annette Weinke. Göttingen: Wallstein, 2013. 149-63. Print.
592. Gassert, Philipp. "Did Transatlantic Drift Help European Integration? The Euromissiles Crisis, the Strategic Defense Initiative, and the Quest for Political Cooperation." *Europe and America in the 1980s: Old Barriers, New Openings* 154-76.
593. Gassert, Philipp. "Die Entstehung eines neuen Umweltbewusstseins im Kalten Krieg." *Das Erbe des Kalten Krieges* Ed. Bernd Greiner. Hamburg: HIS, 2013. 343-63. Print.
594. Gassert, Philipp. "Internal Challenges to the Cold War: Oppositional Movements in East and West." *Oxford Handbook on the Cold War* 433-50.
595. Gienow-Hecht, Jessica. "Protest und Dissens." *Buchners Kolleg Geschichte.* Bamberg: C. C. Buchner, 2013. 396-97. Print.
596. Gienow-Hecht, Jessica, and Mark Donfried. *Searching for a Cultural Diplomacy.* New York: Berghahn, 2013. Print.
597. Haak, Sebastian. *The Making of The Good War: Hollywood, das Pentagon und die amerikanische Deutung des Zweiten Weltkrieges, 1945-1962.* Paderborn: Schöningh, 2013. Print.

598. Hieke, Anton. "Abraham David und die Jüdische Gemeinde in Wilmington, NC." *Abraham David – Jüdische Auswanderung im Neunzehnten Jahrhundert.* 59-73.
599. Hieke, Anton. *Jewish Identity in the Reconstruction South: Ambivalence and Adaptation.* Berlin: de Gruyter, 2013. Print.
600. Hieke, Anton. "The Trans-Regional Mobility of Jewish Macon, GA, 1860-1880." *American Jewish History* 97 (2013): 21-38. Print.
601. Hochbruck, Wolfgang. *Geschichtstheater: Formen der »Living History«. Eine Typologie.* Bielefeld: transcript, 2013.
602. Hochbruck, Wolfgang. "Rescue Me: Das FDNY zehn Jahre nach 9-11." *Abschied von 9/11: Distanznahmen zur Katastrophe* 153-72.
603. Hochgeschwender, Michael. "Adventists"; "Awakenings"; "Baptists"; "Catholics"; "Christian Right"; "Church and State"; Confederate States of America"; "Congregationalists"; "Conservatism"; "Creationism"; "Episcopalianism"; "Evangelicalism"; "Fraternal Societies"; "Freemasons"; "Fundamentalism"; "Hutterites"; "Lutherans"; "Methodists"; "Muslims"; "New Age"; "Pentecostals"; "Presbyterians"; "Puritanism"; "Quakers"; "Religion"; "Shakers"; "Sororities and "Fraternities"; "Televangelists"; and "Unitarianism." *USA-Lexikon: Schlüsselbegriffe zu Politik, Wirtschaft, Gesellschaft, Kultur, Geschichte und zu den deutsch-amerikanischen Beziehungen.* n. pag.
604. Hochgeschwender, Michael. "Religious Violence in Nineteenth- and Twentieth-Century American History?" *Religion and Politics in Europe and the United States: Transnational Historical Approaches* 269-90.
605. Hochgeschwender, Michael. "Welten im Wandel: Die Stellung des römischen Katholizismus in der Geschichte der USA." *Kirche in Welt: Christentum im Zeichen kultureller Vielfalt.* Ed. Andreas Hölscher, Anja Middelbeck-Varwick, and Markus Thurau. Frankfurt/M: Lang, 2013. 127-84. Print.
606. Hochgeschwender, Michael. "Zwischen Wohlfahrtsstaat und nationaler Sicherheit: Die Geschichte der Staatsschulden in den USA." *Vom Wohl und Wehe der Staatsverschuldung: Erscheinungsformen und Sichtweisen von der Antike bis zur Gegenwart.* Ed. Thorsten Beigel and Georg Eckert. Münster: Aschendorff, 2013, 183-98. Print.
607. Honeck, Mischa. "Liberating Sojourns? African American Travelers in Mid-Nineteenth Century Germany." *Blacks and Germans, German Blacks: Germany and the Black Diaspora, 1250-1914* 153-68.
608. Jobs, Sebastian. "Shiny Happy Warfare – New York Victory Parades and the (In) Visibility of Violence." *Violence and Visibility in Modern History* 1-24.
609. Junker, Detlef, and Thomas W. Maulucci. *GIs in Germany: The Social, Economic, Cultural, and Political History of the American Military Presence.* Cambridge, MA: Cambridge UP, 2013. Print.
610. Junker, Detlef. "Schlaglichter auf die USA im 20. Und 21. Jahrhundert." *30 Rezensionen in der Frankfurter Allgemeinen Zeitung.* Heidelberg: HCA, 2013. Print.
611. Kaneti, Marina. "English as a Second Language" and "Immigrant Art and Architecture." *Encyclopedia of American Immigration.* 2nd ed. New York: M. E. Sharpe, 2013. 726-27. Print.

612. Kaneti, Marina, and H. H. Williams. "Political, Ethnic, Religious, Gender, and Sexual Orientation Persecution of Immigrants." *Encyclopedia of American Immigration*. 2nd ed. New York: M. E. Sharpe, 2013. Print.
613. Kathke, Torsten. "Power Lines: Arizona Elites, the Telegraph, and the Construction of a Regional Identity, 1870-1910." *Global Communication Electric: Business, News and Politics in the World of Telegraphy* 331-54.
614. Kreis, Reinhild. "Rüstungspolitik und Friedensbewegung: Flugblätter und Protestplakate der 1980er Jahre." *Flugblätter – Plakate – Propaganda. Die Arbeit mit appelativen Bild-Text-Dokumenten im Geschichtsunterricht* 73-84.
615. Lachenicht, Susanne. "Hurons, Iroquoians, and the French: Agents and Processes of Transculturation in Seventeenth-Century New France." *Agents of Transculturation. Border Crossers, Mediators, Go-Betweens* 51-64.
616. Lerg, Charlotte. "'We are no Teutomanics...': Cultural Diplomacy, the Study of German and the Germanic Museum at Harvard before the First World War." *Germanistik in Irland Schriftenreihe*. Konstanz: Hartung-Gorre, 2013. 43-54. Print.
617. Lerg, Charlotte. "Nationalism; National Identity; Political Correctness; Virginia; Rhode Island; South Carolina." *USA-Lexikon: Schlüsselbegriffe zu Politik, Wirtschaft, Gesellschaft, Kultur, Geschichte und zu den deutsch-amerikanischen Beziehungen*.
618. Logemann, Jan. "Remembering 'Aunt Emma': Small Retailing between Nostalgia and a Conflicted Past." *Journal of Historical Research in Marketing* 5.2 (2013): 151-71. Print.
619. Lorenz, Sophie. "'Heldin des anderen Amerika' Die DDR-Solidaritätsbewegung für Angela Davis, 1970–1973." *Zeithistorische Forschungen/Studies in Contemporary History* 10.1 (2013): 38-60. Print.
620. Lubinski, Christina, Jeffrey Fear, and Paloma Fernandez Perez. *Family Multinationals: Entrepreneurship, Governance, and Pathways to Internationalization*. Routledge: New York, 2013. Print.
621. Martschukat, Jürgen. "Eine kritische Geschichte der Gegenwart." *Werkstatt Geschichte* 61 (2013): 15-27. Print.
622. Martschukat, Jürgen. "Hinrichtungen." *Gewalt: Ein interdisziplinäres Handbuch*. 128-33.
623. Martschukat, Jürgen. *Die Ordnung des Sozialen. Väter und Familien in der amerikanischen Geschichte seit 1770*. Frankfurt/M.: Campus, 2013. Print.
624. Martschukat, Jürgen, and Silvan Niedermeier."Violence and Visibility: Historical and Theoretical Perspectives." *Violence and Visibility in Modern History* 1-23.
625. Martschukat, Jürgen. "Von Terror, Ausnahmezuständen und guter Ordnung." *Alles nur symbolisch? Bilanz und Perspektiven der Erforschung symbolischer Kommunikation*. Ed. Barbara Stollberg-Rilinger, Tim Neu, and Christina Brauner. Köln: Böhlau, 2013. 243-48. Print.
626. Mauch, Christof. "Amerikanischer Geheimdienst und französische Widerstandsbewegungen: Das Office of Strategic Services und Frankreich im Zweiten Weltkrieg." *Festschrift für Siegfried Beer* (2013): 351-80. Print.

627. Mauch, Christof. "Conservation versus Exploitation: The Double-Faced Nature of American Environmental History." *Exploring the Green Horizon: Aspects of Environmental History*. Ed. Amit Bhattacharyya, Nupur Dsgupta, and Rup Kumar Barman. Kolkata: Setu Prakashani, 2013. 58-77. Print.
628. Mauch, Christof. "Fast Food," "Food," and "Tobacco." *USA-Lexikon: Schlüsselbegriffe zu Politik, Wirtschaft, Gesellschaft, Kultur, Geschichte und zu den deutsch-amerikanischen Beziehunge* 383-85; 415-20; 1074-76.
629. Mauch, Christof, and Bernd Hermann. *From Exploitation to Sustainability*. Special Issue of Acta Nova Leopoldina. 2013. Print.
630. Mauch, Christof. Introduction. *USA-Lexikon: Schlüsselbegriffe zu Politik, Wirtschaft, Gesellschaft, Kultur, Geschichte und zu den deutsch-amerikanischen Beziehungen* 7-10.
631. Mauch, Christof, and Kate Ritson. "Introduction: Making Tracks in Environmental History." *Making Tracks: Human and Environmental*. Ed. Mauch, Christof, and Helmuth Trischler, et al. Munich: RCC Perspectives 2013. 5-6. Print.
632. Mauch, Christof. *Notes from the Greenhouse: Making the Case for Environmental History/ Ein Plädoyer für Umweltgeschichte*. München: Rachel Carson Center, 2013. Print.
633. Mauch, Christof. "Rachel Carson: Silent Spring." *Nature: Documents of Global Change*. Ed. Libby Robin, Sverker Sörlin, and Paul Warde. New Haven: Yale UP 2013. 195-203. Print.
634. Mauch, Christof. "Top Secrets und gefährliche Spiele oder Was man aus der Geschichte des amerikanischen Geheimdienstes OSS lernen kann." *Journal for Intelligence, Propaganda and Security Studies* 7 (2013): 110-22. Print.
635. Mauch, Christof. "Which World Is with Us? A Tocquevillian View on American Environmental History." *Journal of American History* 100 (2013): 124-27. Print.
636. Mausbach, Wilfried, and Manfred Berg. "Wie der Prinz in seinem Schloss?" *Frankfurter Allgemeine Zeitung* 9 Sep. 2013: 7. Print.
637. Müller-Pohl, Simone. "Working the Nation State: Submarine Cable Actors, Cable Transnationalism and the Governance of the Global Media System, 1858-1914." *The Nation State and Beyond: Governing Globalization Processes in the Nineteenth and Twentieth Century*. Ed. Isabella Löhr and Roland Wenzlhuemer. 101-26. Berlin: Springer, 2013. Print.
638. Niedermeier, Silvan. "Schmerz." *Gewalt: Ein interdisziplinäres Handbuch* 227-31.
639. Niedermeier, Silvan. "Violence, Visibility, and the Investigation of Police Torture in the American South, 1940-1955." *Violence and Visibility in Modern History* 91-111.
640. Overbeck, Anne. "'Nach Amerika' – Die Amerikaauswanderung aus dem Kreis Lippe im 19. Jahrhundert." *Wanderarbeit – Freiheit oder Zwang*. Ed. Willi Kulke. Essen: Klartext, 2013. 61-70. Print.
641. Prutsch, Ursula. "Exil." *Das Lateinamerika Handbuch*. Ed. Silke Hensel and Barbara Potthast. Bielefeld: Hammer, 2013. 100-02. Print.

642. Prutsch, Ursula. "Inter-American Affairs"; "Pearl Harbor"; "Puerto Rico." *USA-Lexikon: Schlüsselbegriffe zu Politik, Wirtschaft, Gesellschaft, Kultur, Geschichte und zu den deutsch-amerikanischen Beziehungen* 569-75; 846-47; 907-08.
643. Prutsch, Ursula, and Knud Krakau. "Isolationism"; "Monroe Doctrine"; "OAS. " *USA-Lexikon: Schlüsselbegriffe zu Politik, Wirtschaft, Gesellschaft, Kultur, Geschichte und zu den deutsch-amerikanischen Beziehungen* 586-87; 714-15; 838-40.
644. Prutsch, Ursula, and Stephan Palmié. "Caribbean Culture"; "Salsa." *USA-Lexikon: Schlüsselbegriffe zu Politik, Wirtschaft, Gesellschaft, Kultur, Geschichte und zu den deutsch-amerikanischen Beziehungen* 197-98; 964-65.
645. Prutsch, Ursula. "Von Indigenen, Europäern und Japanern: die Globalisierung Paranás im frühen 20. Jahrhundert." *Brasilien in der Welt: Region, Nation und Globalisierung*. Ed. Georg Fischer, et al. Frankfurt/M: Campus, 2013. 139-63. Print.
646. Riffel, Andreas. "The Invisible Empire – der Ku Klux Klan von 1866-1871 als Geheimgesellschaft." *Geheimgesellschaften: Kulturhistorische Sozialstudien/ Secret Societies: Comparative Studies in Culture, Society and History*. Ed. Frank Jacob. Würzburg: Königshausen & Neumann, 2013. 237-73. Print.
647. Santoro, Anthony. "Between Moral Certainty and Morally Certain: The Religious Debate over the Death Penalty in the United States." *Religion and Politics in Europe and the United States: Transnational Historical Approaches* 127-44.
648. Santoro, Anthony. *Exile and Embrace: Contemporary Religious Discourse on the Death Penalty*. Boston: Northeastern UP, 2013. Print.
649. Stieglitz, Olaf. "Bodies in Motion - Writing Sport History as a History of Modern Bodies." *Colonialism and Beyond* 20-32.
650. Stieglitz, Olaf. *Undercover: Die Kultur der Denunziation in den USA*. Frankfurt/M: Campus, 2013. Print.
651. Stievermann, Jan. "A Blackguard' Faulty Vision: Ambrose Bierce's Negative Claim for Intellectual Authority." *Intellectual Authority and Literary Culture in the US, 1790-1900* 259-88.
652. Stievermann, Jan. Introduction. *A Peculiar Mixture: German-Language Culture and Identities in Eighteenth-Century North America* 1-20.
653. Stievermann, Jan. "Defining the Limits of American Liberty: Pennsylvania's German Peace Churches during the Revolution." *A Peculiar Mixture: German-Language Culture and Identities in Eighteenth-Century North America* 207-45.
654. Stievermann, Jan. "Europe." *Emerson in Context*. Ed. Wesley T. Mott. Cambridge, MA: Cambridge UP, 2013. 31-39. Print.
655. Stievermann, Jan. "Halle Pietism and its Perception of the American Great Awakening: The Example of Johann Adam Steinmetz." *The Transatlantic World of Heinrich Melchior Mühlenberg in the Eighteenth Century* 213-46.
656. Stievermann, Jan. "Towards a Theory of the Ethnic Fantastic: A Comparison of Gloria Naylors Mama Day and Paule Marshall's Praisesong for the

Widow." *Heilige Texte: Literarisierung von Religion und Sakralisierung von Literatur im modernen Roman* 168-204.
657. Taubitz, Jan. "Making Photographs Historic: The Use of Historical Black and White Stills in NBC's Fictional Miniseries Holocaust." *Violence and Visibility in Modern History* 191-221.
658. Trautsch, Jasper M. "The Causes of the War of 1812: 200 Years of Debate." *Journal of Military History* 77.1 (2013): 273-93. Print.
659. Trautsch, Jasper M. "The History of the Canadian Governmental Representation in Germany." *Zeitschrift für Kanadastudien* 33.1 (2013): 143-69. Print.
660. Trautsch, Jasper M. "The Invention of 'the West.'" *Bulletin of the German Historical Institute Washington* 53 (2013): 89-102. Print.
661. Trautsch, Jasper M. "The Origins and Future of Liberal Democracy or the Need for Strong States." *Journal of Transatlantic Studies* 11.1 (2013): 109-16. Print.
662. Trautsch, Jasper M. "Ungenutzte Chancen: Ist eine diplomatische Lösung des Atomkonflikts mit dem Iran noch möglich?" *Neue Gesellschaft – Frankfurter Hefte* 6 (2013): 20-23. Print.
663. Von Saldern, Adelheid. *Amerikanismus: Kulturelle Abgrenzung von Europa und US Nationalismus im frühen 20. Jahrhundert*. Stuttgart: Steiner, 2013. Print.
664. Waldschmidt-Nelson, Britta. "Abolitionism"; "Christian Science/Church of Christ, Scientist." *USA-Lexikon: Schlüsselbegriffe zu Politik, Wirtschaft, Gesellschaft, Kultur, Geschichte und zu den deutsch-amerikanischen Beziehunge* 59-60; 215-17.
665. Waldschmidt-Nelson, Britta. "Barack Obama (2009-): Der erste afroamerikanische Präsdient: A Dream Come True?" *Die amerikanischen Präsidenten: 44 historische Portraits von George Washington bis Barack Obama* 439-64.
666. Waldschmidt-Nelson, Britta. "Faith and the Transatlantic Divide: The Role of Religion in America and Europe." *Geheimdienste-Diplomatie-Krieg: Das Räderwerk der Internationalen Beziehungen*. Ed. Carlos Collado Seidel. Münster: LIT, 2013. 319-36. Print.
667. Waldschmidt-Nelson, Britta. "Henry Miller – The Cattle King of California" *Immigrant Entrepreneurship: German-American Business Biographies, 1720 to the Present*. Vol. II. Ed. William J. Hausman. German Historical Institute, 2013. n. pag. Web.
668. Waldschmidt-Nelson, Britta. "'We Shall Overcome': The Impact of the African American Freedom Struggle on Race Relations and Social Protest in Germany after World War Two." *The Transatlantic Sixties: Europe and the United States in the Counterculture Decade* 66-97.
669. Wilson, Mark. "Economic Mobilization." *A Companion to Woodrow Wilson* 289-90. Print.
670. Wilson, Mark. "Economy and National Defense." *The Encyclopedia of Military Science*. Ed. G. Kurt Piehler. Los Angeles, CA: SAGE, 2013. 503-09. Print.

4. Politics, Economics, and Society

671. Abbas, Madeleine-Sophie, et al. "New Territories in Critical Whiteness Studies – Editorial." *Critical Race and Whiteness Studies E-Journal* 9.1 (2013): n. pag. Web.
672. Gerhard, Ulrike, and Andreas Putlitz. "Wissensgesellschaft und die Europäische Stadt. Ein Konzept zur wissenschaftlichen Begleitforschung im Rahmen der Internationalen Bauausstellung Heidelberg." *Wissen-schafft-Stadt. Schriftensammlung zur IBA-Vorbereitungsphase 2008-2012*. Vol. II. Ed. Heidelberg: Stadt Heidelberg, 2013. Print.
673. Gijswijt, Thomas. "Het trans-Atlantisch vrijhandelsverdrag: een economische NAVO?" *Internationale Spectator* May 2013: 2-5. Print.
674. Hahn-Santoro, Iris. "Indian Tribal Courts and the U.S. Court System." *Encyclopedia of American Indian Issues Today*. 553-61.
675. Hahn-Santoro, Iris. "The National Museum of the American Indian: Contributing to American Culture." *Encyclopedia of American Indian Issues Today* 354 -64.
676. Heinemann, Isabel. "American Family Values and Social Change: Gab es den Wertewandel in den USA?" *Gab es den Wertewandel? Neue Forschungen zum gesellschaftlich-kulturellen Wandel seit den 1960er Jahren*. Ed. Bernhard Dietz, Christopher Neumaier, and Andreas Rödder. München: Oldenbourg, 2013. 269-84. Print.
677. Heinemann, Isabel. "'Modernizing Mom'? Der Einfluss von Expertendiskursen und Werbung auf die Familienwerte in den USA des 20. Jahrhunderts." *Familientraditionen und Familienkulturen: Theoretische Konzeptionen, historische und aktuelle Analysen* 235-55.
678. Heinz, Sarah. "Not White, Not Quite: Irish American Identities in the US Census and in Ann Patchett's Novel *Run* (2007)." *Amerikastudien / American Studies* 58.1 (2013): 79-100. Print.
679. Knüpfer, Curd. "Dealing with a Nuclear Iran: Focusing on 'Known Unknowns' (Still) Makes for Poor Policy." *Atlantic Community* 12 Dec. 2013: n. pag. Web.
680. Lammert, Christian. "Congressional Support System"; "Civil religion"; "Disability Rights"; "Homelessness"; "Income Distribution"; "Social Darwinism"; "Unemployment"; "Gun Control"; "Local Government"; "New Left"; "Old Age"; "Populism"; "Poverty"; "Drugs"; "Political Parties"; "Third Parties"; "Health"; "Social Security"; "Welfare State." *USA-Lexikon: Schlüsselbegriffe zu Politik, Wirtschaft, Gesellschaft, Kultur, Geschichte und zu den deutsch-amerikanischen Beziehungen*.
681. Lammert, Christian, and Britta Grell. Introduction. *Sozialpolitik in den USA*. Wiesbaden: Springer, 2013. 7-11. Print.
682. Mayer, Margit. "First World Urban Activism: Beyond austerity urbanism and creative city politics." *City: Analysis of Urban Trends, Culture, Theory, Policy, Action* 17.1 (2013): 5-19. Print.
683. Mayer, Margit. "Fordism"; "Gentrification"; "Grassroots Democracy"; "Neighborhood." *USA-Lexikon: Schlüsselbegriffe zu Politik, Wirtschaft,*

Gesellschaft, Kultur, Geschichte und zu den deutsch-amerikanischen Beziehungen 420-22; 461-65; 784-86.
684. Mayer, Margit. "Multiscalar mobilization for the just city: New spatial politics of urban movements." *Spaces of Contention: Spatialities and Social Movements*. Ed. Walter Nicholls, Byron Miller, and Justin Beaumont. Aldershot: Ashgate, 2013. 163-96. Print.
685. Mayer, Margit. "New Lines of Division in the New Berlin," *The Berlin Reader: A Compendium on Urban Change and Activism*. Ed. Matthias Bernt, Britta Grell, and Andrej Holms. Berlin: Transcript 2013. 95-106. Print.
686. Mayer, Margit. Preface. *Squatting in Europe: Radical Spaces, Urban Struggles*. Ed. Margit Mayer. Wivenhoe: Minor Compositions, 2013. 1-9. Print.
687. Mayer, Margit. "Soziale Bewegungen in Städten – städtische soziale Bewegungen." *Stadt und Soziale Bewegungen*. Ed. Norbert Gestring, Renate Ruhne, and Jan Wehrheim. Wiesbaden: Springer, 2013. 25-42. Print.
688. Mayer, Margit. "Towards Glocal Movements? New Spatial Politics for a Just City." *Urban (In) Security: Policing in Neoliberal Times*. Ed. Volker Eick and Kendra Briken. Ottawa: Red Quill, 2013. 27-59. Print.
689. Mayer, Margit. "Urbane soziale Bewegungen in der neoliberalisierenden Stadt." *sub\urban: zeitschrift für kritische stadtforschung* 1 (2013): 67-80. Print.
690. Mayer, Margit. "Was können urbane Bewegungen, was kann die Bewegungsforschung bewirken? Replik zu den fünf Kommentaren." *sub\urban: zeitschrift für kritische stadtforschung* 1 (2013): 104-14. Print.
691. Ogden, Lucas Kent. *Uniting the States: A Commentary on the American Constitution*. Norderstedt: BoD, 2013. Print.
692. Prodöhl, Ines. "Dynamiken globaler Vernetzung: Mandschurische Sojabohnen auf dem Weltmarkt." *Zeitschrift für Agrargeschichte und Agrarsoziologie* 61.2 (2013): 75-89. Print.
693. Prodöhl, Ines. "Versatile and Cheap: A Global History of Soy in the First Half of the Twentieth Century." *Journal of Global History* 8.3 (2013): 461-82. Print.
694. Püschel, Julia. "Wage Effects of U.S. Service Offshoring by Skills and Tasks." *FIW Working Paper Series (Research Center International Economics, Austria)* 107 (2013): 1-28. Print.
695. Roesch, Claudia. "Macho Man? Repräsentationen mexikanischer Familienstrukturen durch Sozialexperten, Sozialarbeiter und Bürgerrechtsaktivisten in den USA, 1940-1980." *Das Andere denken: Repräsentationen von Migration in Westeuropa und den USA im 20. Jahrhundert*. Ed. Gabriele Metzler. Frankfurt/M: Campus, 2013. 85-116. Print.
696. Roesch, Claudia. "Umstrittene Familienkonzepte: Repräsentationen von Familienwerten US-Amerikanischer Experten und mexikanisch-amerikanischer Bürgerrechtsaktivisten im Wandel." *Familientraditionen und Familienkulturen: Theoretische Konzeptionen, historische und aktuelle Analysen* 257-80.
697. Sattler, Julia. "Detroit and the Ruhr – Two post-industrial landscapes." *New Global Studies* 7.3 (2013): 87-98. Print.

698. Thunert, Martin. "Checks and Balances"; "Consensus Politics"; "Impeachment." *USA-Lexikon: Schlüsselbegriffe zu Politik, Wirtschaft, Gesellschaft, Kultur, Geschichte und zu den deutsch-amerikanischen Beziehungen* 207-09; 270-71; 544-46.
699. Thunert, Martin. "Expert Policy Advice in Germany." *Policy Expertise in Contemporary Democracies*. Ed. Stephen Brooks, Dorota Stasiak, and Tomasz Zyro. Surrey, UK: Ashgate, 2013. 123-46. Print.
700. Thunert, Martin. "Lotsendienste für besseres Regieren? Politikberatung in Kanada." *Zeitschrift für Politikberatung/Policy Advice and Political Consulting* (ZPB) 6 (2013): 74-82. Print.
701. Thunert, Martin. "Non-University Research Institutes: Between Basic Research, Knowledge Transfer to the Public and Policy Analysis." *Policy Analysis in Germany*. Ed. Sonja Blum and Klaus Schubert. Bristol: Policy, 2013. 247-64. Print.
702. Thunert, Martin. "Understanding Canada? Zur Beendigung des Förderprogramms für Kanadastudien durch die kanadische Regierung." *Zeitschrift für Kanada-Studien* 33 (2013): 169-74. Print.
703. Trautsch, Jasper M. "The Origins and Future of Liberal Democracy or the Need for Strong States." *Journal of Transatlantic Studies* 11.1 (2013): 109-16. Print.
704. Trautsch, Jasper M. "Ungenutzte Chancen: Ist eine diplomatische Lösung des Atomkonflikts mit dem Iran noch möglich?" *Neue Gesellschaft – Frankfurter Hefte* 6 (2013): 20-23. Print.
705. Vormann, Boris, and Sonja Schillings. "The Vanishing Poor. Frontier Narratives in U.S. Gentrification and Security Debates." *Critical Planning 20* (2013): 145-65. Print.

5. Didactics

706. Finkbeiner, Claudia, Agnes Madeleine Olson, and Jennifer Friedrich. *Foreign Language Learning and Teaching in Germany: A Review of Research Literature in 2005-2010*. Cambridge UP, 2013. Print.
707. Garrett, Crister S., Catherine Sharpe, Martin Walter, and Maria Zywitz. "Introducing Service Learning to Europe and Germany: The Case of American Studies at the University of Leipzig." *Interdisciplinary Humanities* 29 (Fall 2012): 147-59. Print.
708. Hallet, Wolfgang. "Multimodale Jugendromane und autobiografisches Erzählen im Fremdsprachenunterricht." *Bildung – Kompetenz – Literalität. Fremdsprachenunterricht zwischen Standardisierung und Bildungsanspruch* n. pag.
709. Hallet, Wolfgang, and Michael K. Legutke. "Tasks Revisited: Introducing the special issue." *Tasks Revisited* 3-9.
710. Knopf, Kerstin. "Zacharias Kunuk, Atanarjuat: The Fast Runner (2001)." *Teaching Contemporary Literature and Culture: Film Part I* 47-67.
711. Knopf, Kerstin. "Chris Eyre, Smoke Signals (1998)." *Teaching Contemporary Literature and Culture: Film Part II* 611-32.

712. Ludwig, Peter H., Claudia Finkbeiner, and Markus Knierim. "Effects of the Adequacy of Learning Strategies in Self-Regulated Learning Settings. A Video-based Micro-analytical Lab Study." *Journal of Cognitive Education and Psychology* 12.3 (2013): 374-90. Print.

Index

Abbas, Madeleine-Sophie 671
Adamkiewicz, Ewa 21
Ahn, Gregor 99
Aho, Tanja 125
Adelmann, Ralf 542
Alber, Jan 278
Aleksander, Karin 469
Alexoae-Zagni, Nicoleta 415
Anton, Andreas 181
Antoni, Klaus 61, 296
Arnold, Melanie 216
Arapoglou, Eleftheria 78
Arvidsson, Alf 213
Assmann, Aleida 126-30

Bachmann, Richard 21
Baader, Meike Sophie 49
Baisheng, Zao 42
Balestrini, Nassim 131-33
Banerjee, Mita 134-37
Barbalato, Beatrice 532
Barrenechea, Antonio 62, 390
Barreto, Jose 167
Basseler, Michael 38, 138-41
Bast, Florian 21, 142, 143
Bauer, Matthias 61
Bauridl, Birgit M. 144-46
Bayman, Louis 323
Beaumont, Justin 684
Becher, Dominik 394
Beck, Günter 147
Beckert, Jens 567
Beigel, Thorsten 606
Bein, Britta 35
Benesch, Klaus 97, 148-52
Berensmeyer, Ingo 87, 153
Berg, Manfred 120, 559-62, 636
Bergermann, Ulrike 542
Berghoff, Hartmut 563-68
Bergold, Ralph 372
Bergmann, Ina 123
Bergner, Roger 213
Bernhart, Walter 158
Berning, Nora 154
Bernt, Matthias 685
Bervernage, Berber 27
Bhattacharyya, Amit 627
Bieger, Laura 65, 98, 155-58
Birke, Dorothee 94
Birkle, Carmen 30, 39, 159
Bischoff, Eva 29, 585
Blum, Sonja 701

Böger, Astrid 160, 161
Böhme, Elisabeth 21
Boesenberg, Eva 162, 163
Bogner, Ralf 228
Bonk, Jens 377
Brammer, Frauke 569
Brauner, Christina 625
Breuer, Christoph 118
Briken, Kendra 688
Brinker, Felix 164
Broeck, Sabine 165-71
Brodman, Barbara 283
Bronfen, Elisabeth 102
Brooks, Stephen 699
Brügge, Joachim 34
Buchenau, Barbara 173-75
Bungert, Heike 570
Buschendorf, Christa 15, 176-78
Butler, Martin 179, 180
Butter, Michael 181
Butter, Stella 94
Butzer, Günter 473

Caeners, Stefanie 60
Carel, Ivan 569
Caupert, Christina 182
Chakkalakal, Tess 551
Cheauré, Elisabeth 572
Christ, Michaela 56
Ciment, James 44
Clairborne, Claudius 451
Clark, Thomas 571
Claviez, Thomas 32, 183-86
Coelsch-Foisner, Sabine 436
Collado Seidel, Carlos 666
Collins, Felicity 326
Comas, Eva 365
Comeau, Robert 569
Cortés, Carlos E. 82
Crémieux, Anne 201
Cuenca, Juan 365
Czennia, Baerbel 28

Dallmann, Antje 195, 196
Danylow, Jula 587
Dassow Walls, Laura 109
Däwes, Birgit 66, 187-94
Dechert, André 572
Decker, Christof 573, 574
Decker, Robert Júlio 575, 576
Denson, Shane 116, 197-99
Depkat, Volker 95, 577-83

Detmers, Ines 200
Dickel, Simon 201
Dickey, Jennifer 587
Diedrich, Alena 19
Diedrich, Maria I. 584
Dietrich, René 202-04
Dietz, Bernhard 676
Doan, James E. 283
Domsch, Sebastian 160, 205-07
Donfried, Mark 596
Dorson, James 208, 209
Drennig, Georg 210-12
Dsgupta, Nupur 627
Dunkel, Mario 213, 214

Eckert, Georg 606
Eckstein, Lars 89, 122
Edenheiser, Iris 547
Eder, Thomas 414
Efferth, Thomas 136
Egerer, Claudia 410
Ehland, Christoph 87, 153
Eichner, Susanne 519
Eichtinger, Martin 425
Eick, Volker 688
Eisinger, Michael 60
Elsner, Daniela 51
El Zhar, Samir 587
Engel, Elisabeth 29, 585
Ernst, Christoph 93, 246, 433
Ernst, Jutta 215-17
Ertler, Klaus-Dieter 46, 342
Esch-van Kan, Anneka 218
Essi, Cedric 219
Esuruoso, Asoka 20
Etges, Andreas 586, 587
Etter, Lukas 220, 221, 462, 463

Faisst, Julia 222, 223
Farghaly, Nadine 284
Fahrmeir, Andreas 568
Fassbender, Christoph 476
Fear, Jeffrey 620
Fehrle, Johannes 224-26
Fellner, Astrid M. 70, 227, 228
Fernandez Perez, Paloma 620
Fick, Annabella 229
Fidler, Philipp 226
Finkbeiner, Claudia 706, 712
Fischer, Georg 645
Fischer, Robert 588, 589
Fisher, Rob 338
Fisher Fishkin, Shelley 71
Florescu, Catalina Florina 255
Floyd, Kevin 92
Fluck, Winfried 16, 110, 230-34

Flügge, Anna 235
Fodor, Mónika 78
Fraunholz, Eric W. 21
Frei, Norbert 591
Freitag, Kornelia 80
Freitag, Florian 236
Freudenberg, Maren 237
Friedrich, Jennifer 706
Frietsch, Ute 138
Frobenius, Maximiliane 227
Frotscher, Mirijam M. 240
Fuchs, Michael 33, 88
Furlanetto, Elena 241

Garrett, Crister S. 707
Gassert, Philipp 22, 590-94
Gau, Karl-Markus 442
Gensch, Katharina 21
Geok-Lin Lim, Shirley 71
Georgi-Findlay, Brigitte 122, 242
Gerhardt, Cornelia 227
Gerhard, Ulrike 672
Gernalzick, Nadja 113
Gersdorf, Catrin 37, 243-45
Gerund, Katharina 246, 247
Gessner, Ingrid 64, 248
Gestring, Norbert 687
Giannoulis, Elena 37
Gienow-Hecht, Jessica 595, 596
Gijswijt, Thomas 673
Gilcher-Holtey, Ingrid 1
Goebel, Walter 75, 249, 250
Goedde, Petra 86
Gohrisch, Jana 90
Götte, Petra 49
Golimowska, Karolina 251
Goltschnigg, Dietmar 371
Gonzaléz Groba, Constante 555
Graaff, Kristina 252
Grabes, Herbert 253, 254
Grabher, Gudrun 255
Graf, Hans-Dieter 9
Graichen, Melanie 242, 508
Granger, Michel 109
Greiffenstern, Alexander 68, 256, 257, 400
Greiner, Bernd 593
Grell, Britta 681, 685
Grob, Norbert 102
Grolleg-Edler, Charlotte 371
Groppe, Carola 49
Groß, Florian 258
Gruber, Patrizia 371
Grünewald, Andreas 25
Grünkemeier, Ellen 90
Grünzweig, Walter 2, 63, 477
Gudehus, Christian 56

Gurr, Jens-Martin 60, 180, 259-61, 302
Güth, Luise 579
Gygax, Franziska 262

Haas, Astrid 263-66
Habermas, Rebekka 174
Haertel, Insa 169
Hahn-Santoro, Iris 674, 675
Hallet, Wolfgang 103, 708, 709
Hampf, Michaela 57
Hamscha, Susanne 70, 267, 268
Hannah, Gabriele 9
Hansen-Schirra, Silvia 216
Haselstein, Ulla 37, 269, 270
Hassan, Zohra 175
Hausman, William J. 667
Hebel, Udo J. 115, 271
Heide, Markus 272, 273
Heil, Johanna 30, 35, 39, 274
Heinemann, Isabel 676, 677
Heinz, Sarah 678
Heinze, Carsten 76
Heinze, Rüdiger 275-78
Heissenberger, Klaus 70
Helff, Sissy 51
Henderson, Marius 279
Hennigfeld, Ursula 4, 10
Hensel, Silke 641
Hermann, Bernd 629
Herzog, Alexandra 280
Herzogenrath, Bernd 281, 282
Hieke, Anton 598-600
Hijiya-Kischnereit, Irmela 37
Hirmer, Karin 283, 284
Hochbruck, Wolfgang 53, 601, 602
Hochgeschwender, Michael 81, 603-06
Hoffmann, Julia 19
Holler, Claudia 96
Hollm, Jan 285, 286
Holms, Andrej 685
Hölscher, Andreas 605
Hölter, Achim 307
Holtz, Martin 287, 288
Holub, Maria-Theresia 88
Honeck, Mischa 55, 607
Horlacher, Stefan 92
Hornung, Alfred 11-13, 15, 42, 71, 76, 136, 146, 290-95
Horvath, Máté Vince 21
Höttges, Bärbel 296
Hühn, Peter 254

Imbert, Patrick 342
Immermann, Richard H. 86
Inderst, Rudolf 367
Innes, Christopher 77, 123

Irmscher, Christoph 36, 554
Isekenmeier, Guido 69, 297, 298
Isomaa, Saija 223

Jacob, Frank 646
Jahn-Sudmann, Andreas 197, 519
Jähnert, Gabriele 469
Jensen, Uffa 565
Jobs, Sebastian 6, 608
Juncker, Clara 111
Junker, Carsten 299-301
Junker, Detlef 609, 610
Just, Peter 367

Kabus, Andrea 372
Kaltmeier, Olaf 114, 261, 302, 303
Kamm, Jürgen 41
Kaneti, Marina 611, 612
Kanzler, Katja 304
Karner, Stefan 425
Kartheus, Wiebke 21
Kathke, Torsten 613
Keck, Michaela 305
Kelleter, Frank 306-08
Kennedy, Ross 3
Kern-Stähler, Annette 539
Khabo Koepsell, Philipp 20
Kilbourn, Russell 509
Kindellan, Michael 309
King, Lovalerie 74
Kirss, Tiina 59
Klarer, Mario 40, 310, 311
Klawitter, Uwe 538
Klepper, Martin 96, 313
Kley, Antje 314, 315
Klimke, Martin 55
Klöckner, Christian 507
Klopfer, Nadine 322
Knewitz, Simone 24, 318, 507
Knierim, Markus 712
Knopf, Kerstin 323-27, 710, 711
Knox, Melissa 328
Knüpfer, Curd 679
Koenen, Anne 142, 331, 332
Kohl, Martina 11, 146
Köhler, Angelika 329, 330
Köhne, Julia Barbara 511
Koneczniak, Grzegorz 395
Kosc, Grzesiek 111
Koubek, Jochen 101
Kovach, Elizabeth 333
Kozyrakis, Yulia 334
Krakau, Knud 643
Kramer, Jürgen 41
Kramer, Mark 425
Kreis, Reinhild 614

Kriebernegg, Ulla 5, 335-38
Kriszio, Marianne 469
Kronenbitter, Günther 22
Kühne, Thomas 564
Kuester, Martin 339-42
Kuhlmann-Smirnov, Anne 55
Kulke, Willi 640
Kumar Barman, Rup 627
Kunow, Rüdiger 108, 343-47
Kuroszczyk, Miriam 348

Lachenicht, Susanne 615
Laemmerhirt, Iris-Aya 349-51
Lakomy, Theresia 21
Lammert, Christian 98, 157, 680, 681
Landman, Jane 326
Lanzendörfer, Tim 352-54
Larson, Erica L. 21
Laschinger, Verena 355
Lawson, Russell M. 43
Leber, Manfred 228
Legutke, Michael K. 103, 709
Leikam, Susanne 64
Lembert-Heidenreich, Alexandra 262
Lemoine, Xavier 201
Lenz, Bernd 41
Lerg, Charlotte 356, 616, 617
Leuchtenmüller, Thomas 357, 358
Lewis, Catherine M. 587
Leypoldt, Günter 67, 122, 359, 360
Ley, Susanne 227
Lindner, Konstantin 372
Ljungberg, Christina 40
Löffler, Philipp 31, 361, 516
Löhr, Isabella 637
Lösch, Klaus 362
Löschnigg, Martin 46
Logemann, Jan 618
Loock, Kathleen 363, 364
Lopez-Varela, Asunción 355
Lorenz, Chris 27
Lorenz, Sophie 619
Lubinski, Christina 565, 620
Ludwig, Sämi 235, 415
Ludwig, Heinz 72
Ludwig, Peter H. 712
Lund-Andersen, Ingrid 418
Lüthe, Martin 365-67
Lutz, Hartmut 368, 369
Lyytikäinen, Pirjo 223

Macey, Deborah 107
Mackenthun, Gesa 6, 122
Mahler, Andreas 2, 158
Mahlknecht, Johannes 370
Maierhofer, Roberta 5, 335, 371, 372

Martínez-Zalce Sánchez, Graciela 100
Martschukat, Jürgen 95, 121, 580, 581, 621-25
Matter-Seibel, Sabina 373
Mauch, Christof 14, 119, 626-35
Maulucci, Thomas W. 609
Mausbach, Wilfried 562, 636
Mayer, Margit 682-90
McPherson, Annika 171
McSherry, Siofra 374
Meindel, Dieter 375
Meinel, Dietmar 376
Meiner, Carsten 204
Metz, Annekatrin 50
Metzler, Gabriele 695
Meyer, Christina 116, 199, 377-79
Meyer, Evelyn P. 380
Meyer, Sabine N. 381-86
Michael, Julia 342
Michelin, Monica 26
Michl, Susanne 137
Middeke, Martin 77, 123
Middelbeck-Varwick, Anja 605
Mikos, Lothar 519
Mildorf, Jarmila 117, 262
Miller, Byron 684
Mörtl, Heidrun 62, 390
Mohr, Hans-Ulrich 389
Monteith, Sharon 111
Moody, Shirley C. 74
Moos, Jennifer J. 70, 391
Morgan, Nina 71
Mosel, Michael 101, 392
Mott, Wesley T. 654
Müller, Kurt 73, 393-96
Müller, Markus M. 50
Müller, Monika 397
Müller, Stefanie 398, 399
Müller, Timo 185
Müller-Bahlke, Thomas 112
Müller-Pohl, Simone 57, 637
Mulvihill, Bryan 400
Munkelt, Marga 91, 401
Mussil, Stephan 108

Neu, Tim 625
Neumaier, Christopher 676
Nicolaisen, Peter 243
Nicholls, Walter 684
Niedermeier, Silvan 121, 624, 638, 639
Nielsen, Astrid 547
Nischik, Reingard M. 402
Nitzsche, Sina A. 63, 404
Nitz, Julia 403
Nünning, Ansgar 38, 85, 139, 140, 405-414, 419

Nünning, Vera 84, 99, 411
Nyman, Jopi 78

Odabas, Janna 415, 416
Ogden, Lucas Kent 691
Olson, Agnes Madeleine 706
Olson, Greta 85, 417-21
Opitz, Martin N. 21
Ortlepp, Anke 12, 422, 423
Orvell, Miles 97, 150
Ostendorf, Berndt 423-27
Ostwald, Thomas 53
Overbeck, Anne 640

Packard, Stefan 4, 10
Paletschek, Sylvia 572
Palladini, Giulia 428
Palmié, Stephan 644
Parker, Joshua 429-31
Patel, Kiran Klaus 45
Petersen, Hanne 418
Paul, Barbara 171
Paul, Gerhard 573
Paul, Heike 12, 93, 246, 362, 432, 433
Paul, Norbert 137
Paulus, Stefan 22
Pecher, Claudia Maria 582
Penke, Niels 19
Peters, Susanne 104-06
Pfeiler, Martina 434, 435
Phillips, Michael 33
Piehler, G. Kurt 670
Pinazza, Natalia 323
Pisarz-Ramirez, Gabriele 113
Plikat, Jochen 25
Poerner, Michael 216
Poole, Ralph 436-39
Popp, Susanne 52
Potthast, Barbara 641
Priewe, Marc 440, 441
Pritsch, Sylvia 171
Probst, Daniel 52
Prodöhl, Ines 692, 693
Prutsch, Ursula 442-44, 641-45
Przyrembel, Alexandra 174
Püschel, Julia 694
Puff, Simone 445, 446
Putlitz, Andreas 672

Qian, Zhaoming 79
Quendler, Christian 447

Raab, Josef 68, 257, 448
Radzilowski, John 44
Raussert, Wilfried 100, 449-51
Ravizza, Eleonora 452

Rechtsteiner, Stefanie 453
Redling, Erik 16, 454, 455
Reed, Brian M. 80
Renger, Almut-Barbara 437
Reusch, Nina 572
Richards, Eliza 510
Richardson, Brian 278
Ridvan, Askin 456
Rieser, Klaus 33
Riffel, Andreas 646
Rippl, Gabriele 7, 17, 58, 59, 457-64
Ritson, Kate 631
Robin, Libby 633
Robinson, Greg 71
Rocchi, Jean-Paul 26, 201
Rodrigues-Moura, Enrique 443
Roeber, A. Gregg 112
Roesch, Claudia 695, 696
Rohr, Susanne 465
Rödder, Andreas 676
Röder, Katrin 124, 160
Rogge, Jörg 138
Rojek, Janina 35
Rosenthal, Caroline 48, 466-68
Roth, Julia 469, 470
Roudané, Matthew C. 77, 123
Ruggenthaler, Peter 425
Ruhne, Renate 687
Rupp, Jan 99, 406
Ryan, Kathleen M. 107
Rzepa, Angieszka 47

Saal, Ilka 471
Saarikangas, Kirsi 233
Saldívar, Ramón 65, 156
Sandten, Cecile 242, 476, 508
Santoro, Anthony 647, 648
Savin, Ada 416
Sarkowsky, Katja 473-76
Sattler, Julia 477, 478, 697
Sauter, Michael 185
Schabio, Saskia 75, 249, 479
Schäfer, Heike 480
Schäfer, Heinrich 450
Schäfer, Stefanie 48, 481, 482
Scheiding, Oliver 8, 15, 81
Schemien, Alexia 266, 483
Scherr, Alexander 484
Scherr, Nadine 485
Schenkel, Elmar 394
Schilcher, Anita 582
Schillings, Sonja 705
Schirrmacher, Beate 410
Schlarb, Damien 486
Schleusener, Simon 487
Schloss, Dietmar 488

Schmid, Susanne 556
Schmidt, J. Alexander 60
Schmidt, Jochen 489-91
Schmidt, Kerstin 492
Schmidt, Silke 35
Schmidt-Haberkamp, Barbara 556
Schmitz, Markus 91
Schneck, Peter 381, 494, 495
Schnierer, Peter Paul 77, 123
Schock, Ralph 573
Scholz, Anne-Marie 497
Schöne-Seifert, Bettina 539
Schoppmeier, Sören 21
Schowalter, Lutz 50
Schubert, Klaus 701
Schubert, Stefan 498
Schultz, Dieter 499
Schultz, Ludwig 265
Schwanecke, Christine 38, 139, 405
Schwarzhaupt-Scholz, Dorothea 356
Schweighauser, Philipp 59, 458, 500, 501
Schwillus, Harald 372
Seidl, Martin 506
Sedlmeier, Florian 502-05
Seidler, Miriam 337
Seybert, Gislinde 378
Sharpe, Catherine 707
Sielke, Sabine 15, 16, 24, 318, 507-513
Sikorska, Liliana 47
Skov Nielsen, Henrik 278
Sobral, Ana 514
Sörlin, Sverker 633
Solomon, Jon 437
Sommerfeld, Stephanie 515
Spahn, Hannah 243
Spahr, Clemens 31, 361, 516, 517
Specq, François 109
Springkart, Claudius 52
Starck, Kathleen 200
Starre, Alexander 518-20
Stasiak, Dorota 699
Stauder, Thomas 378
Steffen, Therese 59, 458, 521
Stein, Daniel 54, 116, 199, 522-26
Stein, Mark 91
Stephan, Achim 495
Stieglitz, Olaf 649, 650
Stierstorfer, Klaus 104-06
Stievermann, Jan 8, 61, 651-56
Stollberg-Rilinger, Barbara 625
Stompor, Tomasz 527, 528
Straub, Julia 464, 529-31
Stroh, Silke 91
Strohmaier, Alexandra 413
Struth, Christiane 532
Sugita, Yoneyuki 351

Sulimma, Maria 533-35
Suominen-Kokkonen, Renja 223
Sutrop, Margit 59
Süß, Gunter 242, 508

Tagsold, Christian 337
Tan, Kathy-Ann 536-38
Tatsumi, Takayuki 71
Taubitz, Jan 657
Thiemann, Anna 539-41
Thon, Jan-Noël 54, 523
Thunert, Martin 698-702
Thurau, Markus 605
Trautsch, Jasper M. 658-62, 703, 704
Trischler, Helmuth 631
Truchlar, Leo 544
Twelbeck, Kirsten 545, 546
Ty, Eleanor 509

Urakova, Alexandra 515
Unseld, Melanie 171
Usbeck, Frank 547, 548

Vanderbeke, Dirk 104-06, 160
Van Minnen, Cornelis A. 120, 561
Vargas, Juan Carlos 449
Veauthier, Ines 549, 550
Veel, Kristin 204
Vierbrock, Britta 51
Villaverde, José M. 418
Viol, Claus-Ulrich 538
Völkl, Yvonne 46
Völz, Johannes 65, 156
Volkmann, Laurenz 104-06
Von Hülsen-Esch, Andrea 337
Von Saldern, Adelheid 663
Vormann, Boris 705

Wåghäll Nivre, Elisabeth 410
Waldschmidt-Nelson, Britta 111, 664-68
Waligorska, Magdalena 83
Wallinger, Hanna 551
Walter, Martin 707
Walter, Sven 495
Wangerin, Wolfgang 118
Warde, Paul 633
Warren, Jean-Philippe 569
Warren, Kenneth W. 551
Wehrheim, Jan 687
Weigel, Anna 558
Weisbrod, Bernd 565
Weisbrode, Kenneth 45
Wellenreuther, Hermann 112
Welzer, Harald 56
Wenzlhuemer, Roland 637
Werkmeister, Till 552

Werning, Stefan 101
Weyel, Birgit 61
White, Tyrone T., Jr. 21
Wobring, Michael 52
Weber, Wolfgang E. J. 22
Weinke, Annette 591
Wenk, Silke 171
Wieland, Katharina 25
Wiemann, Dirk 89
Williams, H. H. 612
Wilson, Mark 669, 670
Winko, Simone 58

Winter, Rainer 519
Wischer, Ilse 124, 160
Wolf, Werner 2, 158

Zacharasiewicz, Waldemar 36, 553-55
Zapf, Hubert 16, 473
Zehelein, Eva-Sabine 556, 557
Zilles, Klaus 365
Zirker, Angelika 61
Zymner, Rüdiger 307
Zyro, Tomasz 699
Zywitz, Maria 707

American Studies – A Monograph Series

Universitätsverlag
WINTER
Heidelberg

Volume 239
NEUENFELDT, SUSANN
Schauspiele des Sehens
Die Figur der Flaneurin,
Voyeurin und Stalkerin im
U.S.-amerikanischen Essay
2015. 294 Seiten, 26 Abbildungen.
Geb. € 45,–
ISBN 978-3-8253-6184-6

Volume 252
KURZ, KATJA
Narrating Contested Lives
The Aesthetics of Life Writing
in Human Rights Campaigns
2015. x, 271 Seiten, 2 Abbildungen.
Geb. € 48,–
ISBN 978-3-8253-6349-9

Volume 253
KLEY, ANTJE
PAUL, HEIKE (Eds.)
Rural America
2015. VII, 510 Seiten, 59 Abbildungen.
Geb. € 70,–
ISBN 978-3-8253-6383-3

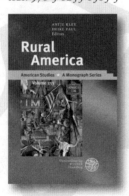

Volume 254
HIRSCHFELDER, NICOLE
Oppression as Process
The Case of Bayard Rustin
2014. IV, 309 Seiten.
Geb. € 39,–
ISBN 978-3-8253-6390-1

Volume 256
SCHMIDT, CHRISTIAN
Postblack Aesthetics
The Freedom to Be Black in
Contemporary African American Fiction
2015. ca. 384 Seiten.
Geb. ca. € 45,–
ISBN 978-3-8253-6380-2

Volume 257
KINDINGER, EVANGELIA
Homebound: Diaspora Spaces and Selves in Greek American Return Narratives
2015. 223 Seiten. (American Studies
Geb. € 40,–
ISBN 978-3-8253-6421-2

D-69051 Heidelberg · Postfach 10 61 40 · Tel. (49) 62 21/77 02 60 · Fax (49) 62 21/77 02 69
Mehr Information unter www.winter-verlag.de · E-mail: info@winter-verlag.de

Contributors

BALBIER, Dr. Uta; Institute of North American Studies, King's College London; Strand, London, WC2R 2LS, UK (uta.balbier@kcl.ac.uk)

BASSELER, Dr. habil. Michael; Gießener Graduiertenzentrum Kulturwissenschaften (GGK) / International Graduate Centre for the Study of Culture (GCSC), Justus-Liebig Universität Gießen; Alter Steinbacher Weg 38, 35394 Gießen (michael.basseler@gcsc.uni-giessen.de)

BUTTER, Prof. Dr. Michael; Englisches Seminar, Abteilung für Amerikanistik, Eberhard Karls Universität Tübingen; Wilhelmstraße 50, 72074 Tübingen (michael.butter@uni-tuebingen.de)

CAMASTRA, Dr. Nicole J.; Department of English, University of Georgia; 254 Park Hall, Athens, GA 30602, USA (njc@uga.edu)

CAPRIOARA, Laura, M. A. (ecaprioa@students.uni-mainz.de)

DÄWES, Prof. Dr. Birgit; Department of English and American Studies, University of Vienna; Spitalgasse 2-4, 1090 Vienna, Austria (birgit.daewes@univie.ac.at)

FABINY, Professor Dr. Tibor; Institute of English Studies, Károli Gáspár University of the Reformed Church in Hungary; Budapest, Reviczky u.4., H-1088 Hungary (fabiny_tibor@gmail.com)

HANKINS, Prof. Dr. Barry; History, Baylor University; Waco, Texas 76798 USA (barry_hankins@baylor.edu)

KRABBENDAM, Dr. Hans; Roosevelt Study Center; Abdij 8, 4331 BK Middelburg, the Netherlands (jl.krabbendam@zeeland.nl)

KLEPPER, Prof. Dr. Martin; Institut für Anglistik und Amerikanistik, Humboldt Universität zu Berlin; Unter den Linden 6, 10099 Berlin (martin.klepper@staff.hu-berlin.de)

MEINIG, Dr. Sigrun; DFG-Projekt Literature at Work, Institut für England- und Amerikastudien, Goethe-Universität Frankfurt; Grüneburgplatz 1, 60323 Frankfurt am Main (sigrun.meinig@web.de)

PLANK, Prof. Dr. Geoffrey; American Studies, University of East Anglia; Norwich Research Park, Norwich, NR4 7TJ, UK (g.plank@uea.ac.uk)

PROHL, Prof. Dr. Inken; Institut für Religionswissenschaft, Universität Heidelberg; Akademiestraße 4-8, 69117 Heidelberg (inken.prhol@zegk.uni-heidelberg.de)

SANTORO, Dr. Anthony; Department of History, Sogang University; J921 Jeong Hasang Hall; 35 Baekbeom-ro, Mapo-Gu; Seoul 121-742, Korea (asantoro@sogang.ac.kr)

SCHLARB, Damien B.; Ph.D. Candidate Georgia State University Atlanta; Jakob Welder Weg 18, 55128 Mainz (schlarbd@uni-mainz.de)

SCHMIDT, Dr. Klaus H.; Arbeitsbereich Amerikanistik, Johannes Gutenberg-Universität Mainz, Fachbereich Translations-, Sprach- und Kulturwissenschaft; An der Hochschule 2, 76711 Germersheim (schmikla@uni-mainz.de)

SCHWEIGHAUSER, Prof. Dr. Philipp Schweighauser, Associate Professor and Head of American and General Literatures; University of Basel, Department of English; Nadelberg 6, 4051 Basel, Switzerland (ph.schweighauser@unibas.ch)

SILLIMAN, Daniel, M. A.; Heidelberg Center for American Studies, Universität Heidelberg; Hauptstraße 120, 69117 Heidelberg (dsilliman@hca.uni-heidelberg.de)

VOELZ, Dr. Johannes; Institut für England- und Amerikastudien, Goethe-Universität Frankfurt; Grüneburgplatz 1, 60323 Frankfurt am Main (voelz@em.uni-frankfurt.de)

STIEVERMANN, Prof. Dr. Jan; Heidelberg Center for American Studies, Universität Heidelberg; Hauptstraße 120, 69117 Heidelberg (jstievermann@hca.uni-heidelberg.de)